Editor: Konstantinos Fylatos
Authors: Despoina Tsounaka & Panagiotis Ioannidis

© Fylatos Publishing
e-mail: contact@fylatos.com
web: www.fylatos.com

ISBN: 978-960-658-283-7

Despoina Tsounaka & Panagiotis Ioannidis

Become
INSEPARABLE, UNSHAKABLE, and UNSTOPPABLE
in your romantic relationship

Volume I

Fylatos Publishing
MMXXIV

Disclaimer

This book doesn't provide any kind of medical advice or advice about mental and emotional health. The purpose of this book is to inspire the readers to make their own decisions for their romantic relationship and life. Anything written in the book, as well as the Togetherness-Fulfillment™ Method and all the models created by the authors, is the authors' personal opinions and views based on their personal life and not scientific research, evidence, or advice. People mentioned in the book and the acknowledgments are purely mentioned because they have been inspiring figures to the authors. The authors do not claim that these people share the authors' opinions. In case the readers apply the contents of the book, the authors have no responsibility for the results.

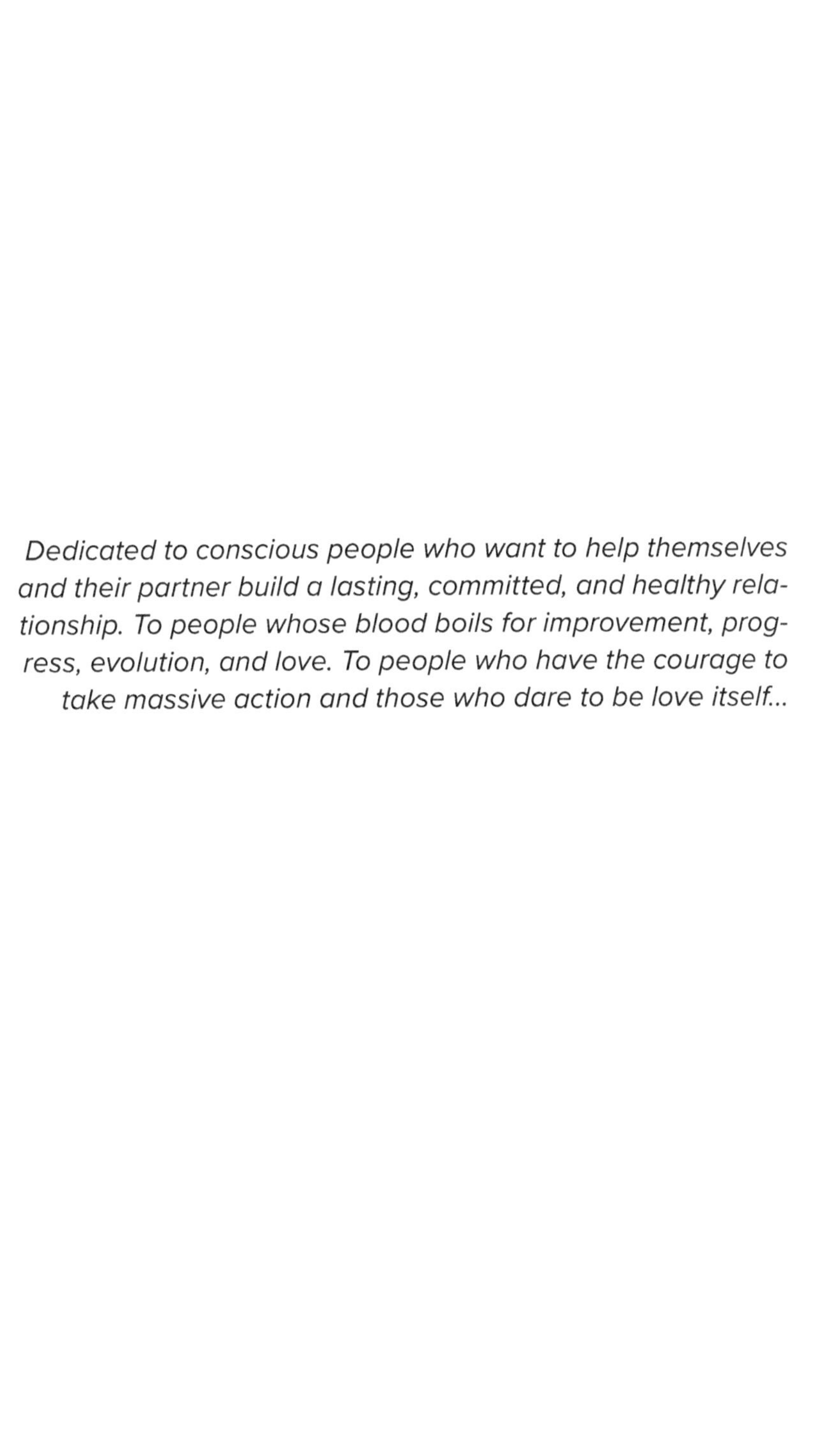

Dedicated to conscious people who want to help themselves and their partner build a lasting, committed, and healthy relationship. To people whose blood boils for improvement, progress, evolution, and love. To people who have the courage to take massive action and those who dare to be love itself...

We thank our teachers, Kain Ramsay, Joeel and Natalie Rivera, and Peggy Guglielmino for all the knowledge and lessons they have taught us, and through them, we have improved ourselves and our relationship to a great extent. Thank you to all the people in our family environment who have supported us over the years...

Contents

About the authors

Despoina Tsounaka and Panagiotis Ioannidis are deeply passionate about helping couples improve their romantic relationships and empowering people to lead meaningful lives. From the beginning of their relationship in 2014 and through the difficulties they faced and overcame together, they wanted to inspire other people to overcome their difficulties effectively and experience peace and fulfillment by uncovering the full potential of the unity in their romantic relationship.

Through their relationship, they went through a spiritual transformation and united as one. They realized that what they experience together surpasses what modern society describes as love and a healthy relationship, and thus wanted to share this experience with the world. So, they coined the terms *"Togetherness-Fulfillment"* (meaning the highest spiritual state a couple can experience and embody and the absolute unity between the partners) and *"Fulfilled Reflecting Self"* (the one and only life partner), terms that describe the greatest expression of love and the complete spiritual nakedness between the romantic partners who become one and the same. They also created the Togetherness-Fulfillment™ Method, a complete practical system and philosophy of helping couples become inseparable, unshakable, and unstoppable.

Besides their passion for helping couples strengthen their relationships, Despoina and Panagiotis have extensive work experience in complex clinical healthcare and rehabilitation, the mental health field helping people with personality disorders and various mental health conditions to become independent and effectively manage their emotions, and people with suicidal ideations helping them find meaning in their lives, have a smile on their face, and enjoy life with their loved ones. They also have experience in team leadership, teaching, coaching, and mentoring in the healthcare sector and the niche of romantic relationships which is their specialization area.

Furthermore, they started their life coaching journey in 2019. Since then, they have obtained dozens of certificates and diplomas in Life, Relationship and Couples Coaching, Marriage Mentoring, Couples Therapy, Relationship Counselling, Relationship Science, Relationship Goal Setting, Relationship Psychology, Hypnotherapy, Neuro-Linguistic Programming, Cognitive Behavioral Therapy, Family Therapy, Psychology, Mindfulness, Communication, Leadership, Motivational Interviewing, Behavior Change, Health and Wellbeing Coaching, Philosophy and Sexuality, as well as School Age Education, studying at leading educational institutions and accrediting bodies.

They are the founders of "thatlovecouple.com — couples coaching and mentoring", where they help couples improve their relationships and promote self-improvement by challenging people to act daily to evolve and live the life they deserve.

Through their books and thatlovecouple.com, they analyze the practical philosophy of Togetherness-Fulfillment and share their work on love and togetherness to help as many couples as possible experience fulfillment in their relationship.

Foreword

When we met, we were both very young and immature. We didn't know who we were or what we wanted to do with our lives. We were living in a blur. But in that blur, one thing was clear to us from the beginning; we wanted to be together all the time and experience every aspect of life together. We were completely ignorant of many things in life, but our love was the one and only constant and value that we would never, under any circumstances, negotiate for any other person or any reason. We may have sometimes looked for fulfillment in external things, but we always realized that fulfillment was within ourselves and in our relationship with each other. Love and unity have always been our guiding principles in life.

Therefore, this book is called "Together" because it explores the power of romantic and companionate unity as a miracle of existence, leading only to miracles and evolution. Since the beginning of our relationship, we have always wanted to be together, however impossible it may have seemed at times due to the distance in the first year of our relationship, age, financial difficulties, and family issues. Nothing and no one ever stopped us. We did not compromise with other people's "wants" or with anything less than our pure unity. We wanted to live together, experience everything together, grow up together, take risks together, make mistakes together, fail together, learn together, succeed together, work together, learn about the world together, grow old together, and do it all together, walking hand in hand on the path of endless progress. We achieved this early in our lives through unstoppable work both as individuals and as a couple, introspection, dedication, commitment, honesty, integrity, discipline, passion, forgiveness, gratitude, love, and being mentally, emotionally, and spiritually naked between us. We have found our "what", "why" and "how". The "what" is together. The "why" is together. The "how" is together.

So, united now, we overcome every difficulty together and achieve every goal together. We are fearless. That is what we want to inspire through this book and its second volume, and that is the legacy of love and truth that we are building: that couples together can achieve anything. Nothing is impossible. If your love is the number one priority in your life, you will more easily face any obstacle that comes before you. If your love is true, you will never leave each other, you will never give up no matter what, and you will always be together. Choose "together", push away the ego, and fly high.

Introduction

The writing of this book began when we started living together in 2015. As young people with love, passion, and a will to grow, but also with mistakes, weaknesses, and flaws, we faced many difficulties and exhibited many negative and unhealthy behaviors when we started living together. Of course, we exhibited these types of behaviors before that, but all our negative elements increased when we moved in together.

Whenever we faced a difficulty, a challenge, a problem, or simply argued and took it out on each other out of ignorance and weakness, we would talk for hours to understand ourselves and each other. We would ask ourselves what we could do individually and together to improve. From the beginning of our relationship, we had each other as the number one priority in every situation, and so we did not want to continue to clash, especially without knowing the reason.

So, we observed ourselves, our behavior, thoughts, and emotions, and we discussed these for hours.

After each conversation, we wrote down the lessons we learned, the knowledge we gained, and what we realized we needed to do to improve and change each negative situation and behavior. In this way, we got to know ourselves and each other better, clarifying who we are, our priorities, and our life and relationship purpose.

At the same time, we constantly read articles and books on psychology and self-improvement to gain relevant knowledge and apply it to our life. Of what we learned, we kept only that which, after personal testing, produced positive results in our life. This way, we developed our relationship at a rapid pace. We were willing and determined to get to know ourselves and each other in the best and most meaningful way possible. After two years of continuous work on strengthening our relationship, in 2017, we decided to use all the material we had written through our experiences to write a unique book on creating unshakable romantic relationships.

In addition, writing the book increased our passion for learning and progress, and we trained in various disciplines, such as life coaching, in 2019, to further elevate our relationship, and to be better able to help other people improve theirs. Through our studies and training, combined with personal experience and progress in our relationship, and after much internal work, we have created our own system for creating unshakable romantic relationships, which we call *"The Togetherness-Fulfillment Method"*, a method that helps couples be inseparable, unshakable, and unstoppable.

The Togetherness-Fulfillment™ Method and Philosophy

The Togetherness-Fulfillment Method and Philosophy were created through a journey of four years of unstoppable love, difficulties and problems, inner pain, frustration, and even despair, through joys and sorrows, but above all —we stress again— with true and unconditional love. As we evolve and grow together, so will we evolve and develop this method...

Togetherness-Fulfillment is a term we coined, inextricably linked to unconditional acceptance and unconditional love. We created this term because there is simply no term that clearly expresses the total unity between two people, united on every level and driven by true love. Along with the Togetherness-Fulfillment term, we have also coined the term Fulfilled Reflecting Self.

The definition we have given to Togetherness-Fulfillment is the following:

Togetherness-Fulfillment is the highest spiritual state and evolutionary course of our existence, in which we unite with our Fulfilled Reflecting Self wholly and on every level (spiritual, mental, psychological/emotional, and physical/sexual), being completely spiritually naked in front of each other, with awareness, and experiencing true and unconditional love, with constant individual and couple work and improvement.

The definition we have given to the Fulfilled Reflecting Self is the following:

The Fulfilled Reflecting Self is our one and only life partner with whom we unite as one on every level (spiritual, mental, psychological/emotional, and physical/sexual), where in our relationship we are both individually fulfilled and free from inferior needs and become each other's reflection.

Throughout the book, we develop the Togetherness-Fulfillment Method and Philosophy and in the final chapter, we delve into the concept and definition of Togetherness-Fulfillment and how to achieve it. Everything we discuss in the two volumes and the whole Togetherness-Fulfillment Method is something we have experienced, created, applied, changed, and consolidated over the years. It is our own personal practical philosophy, beliefs, opinions, and knowledge of how to live as a couple. We do not mention anything that we have not first experienced ourselves and know very well in practice.

This book and the Togetherness-Fulfillment Method are therefore developed in the following way:

1 - Understanding of self and partner.
    a) Each partner begins to develop their self-awareness individually.
    b) The partners develop their awareness of each other together.

This is achieved through a series of models that help develop one's self-awareness, created by us which we named Self-Awareness Cultivating Models.

2 - Couples recognize the importance of the dynamics of each other's feminine and masculine elements and identify and correct problematic behaviors in their relationship.

3 - Couples build a solid foundation of trust by further deepening self-awareness and awareness. They cultivate responsibility and maturity with the help of other models of understanding human existence.

4 - Couples discover Togetherness-Fulfillment which, once it has begun, never ends and is a process, a spiritual state, and a way of life of continuous evolution and progress for the couple. Couples further understand the dynamics of their feminine and masculine elements.

5 - Having got to know themselves and their partner in-depth, together they set specific goals for their life and relationship and have all the tools and resources they need to achieve them in the shortest possible time (this step is discussed in the second volume).

You see, before we discuss true love and Togetherness-Fulfillment, we will explore many other important topics. We do this because to experience true love and achieve Togetherness-Fulfillment, we need to do a lot of individual and couple work and introspection.

The Togetherness-Fulfillment Method is therefore developed in two volumes of books. In the first volume, we deal more with the profound understanding of all the above concepts practically, and in the second volume with even more precise practical steps that a couple can follow to strengthen their relationship and achieve their goals. These are two books that require a lot of reading and practice on the part of the reader. The books are aimed at couples, but they can also be of great benefit to people who are not yet in a relationship and want to find their life partner.

We are sure that they will help you to develop your relationship on every level, whether you are facing many difficulties or not, if you are looking for the essence within yourself and are a person of action. We are very excited to share all this wealth of experience and insight with you.

Get ready to explore your relationship with yourself and your partner in depth. You will embark on a journey of self-discovery and ceaseless work and couple unity that will lead you to the truth of yourself and the life and relationship you truly want and deserve. The Togetherness-Fulfillment Method, as developed in the books of the series, will help you to work miracles in your relationship with your partner, not because we tell you so, but because we have structured it in such a way that you, the reader, are invited to take total responsibility for yourself, your actions, the results of your life, and to take massive action for self-improvement every day. Therefore, anyone who follows the method, answers all the questions, and works through all the exercises in Volume Two is sure to achieve tremendous results.

It is important to add here that we, as authors, are experts only in our own life and relationship and not in all relationships in general. What we write in this book is our truth, knowledge, and understanding of romantic relationships, and we aim to help as many couples as possible. You, on the other hand, are the only expert in your relationship, and only you really know within yourself what the truth is. You have all the inner strength you need to create the relationship you want, and through the tools we offer, you have the opportunity to discover this strength and transform yourself. That's why we don't promise magic solutions, we don't tell you how to live with your partner, but we ask you to take full responsibility for yourself and to work deeply with the tools we share with you to find the answers to your existence on your own and as a couple. So, if you do this, if you understand and apply what you read in these two volumes, you will become the captain of your life, and together with your partner you will steer the ship of your relationship and reach very high levels of togetherness and fulfillment...

1

Getting to know and understand
yourself and your partner

Humans are multidimensional beings. We function in so many ways, which are interrelated in even more different ways. That's why it is difficult to identify and understand them all. This is the reason there are so many disciplines within psychology and many other sciences and practices that deal with human existence, such as life coaching, neuro-linguistic programming, mindfulness, neuroscience, sociology, and many others. No single discipline can completely explain exactly who we are and why we behave the way we do. In fact, all sciences and philosophy, struggle to explain the mystery of human existence. This is because not only do we all function in countless ways, but each of us responds in a very different and unique way to all these ways of thinking, behaving, and being that we all share.

That is why we, as authors, combine the best of what we have learned from all the disciplines we have studied with our personal experiences to gain a deeper understanding of ourselves. In this way, we have created a series of models for understanding the self, studying some of our teachers, and judging by our personal experiences and our own successes and failures. These models are ways of visually representing the processes that take place within us and help us to clarify the ways in which we operate internally (on a spiritual, mental, and emotional level) and externally (in our behavior and relationships with other people). It is our own way of understanding ourselves and does not claim to be the absolute truth, nor is it scientifically proven. However, we believe it will be of great benefit to you.

In this first chapter, the Togetherness-Fulfillment Method begins and analyses the subject of self-awareness because if we do not know and understand ourselves in depth and truth, we will not be able to know and understand any other person. Unless we first build a strong and healthy relationship with ourselves, we will not be able to build a strong and healthy relationship with our life partner.

So, the necessary first step for a couple on the path of continuous improvement, but also for any person not yet in a relationship or marriage, is self-awareness, which is of course a never-ending process. Only then one will be able to know their life partner in a meaningful way and live a peaceful, healthy, and fulfilling life together.

Therefore, in this chapter, we will develop the relationship we have as human beings with ourselves, and through this, you will be able to know and understand your life partner better. This means that as you develop your self-awareness, the true knowledge of yourself, you will also develop your awareness of your partner, the true knowledge of your partner.

Each of the Self-Awareness Cultivating Models, which we will develop below, helps us to understand:
   a) ourselves,
   b) our partner,
   c) the similarities with our partner,
   d) the different elements with our partner,
   e) how we can unite in the relationship with our partner, utilizing both our similarities and our differences,
   f) how we can unite in the relationship with our partner, enhancing our positive elements and addressing our negative elements.

We should point out that in many parts of the book, and especially at the end of each topic, we ask some introspection questions. These questions are designed to help you evaluate yourself and your relationship in depth, and thus to give constructive criticism of yourself and your relationship, always with the aim of self-improvement and not of self-condemnation.

By answering these questions, you can get to know yourself much better and find the areas where you need to improve, as well as identify various dysfunctions in your relationship and correct them by building a healthy collaboration with your partner. We suggest that you write the answers where it is convenient for you, and not just think of them. Writing down the answers is very helpful in retaining them and understanding them better.

So, these questions are the whole point. Finding the answers within you is the essential work you need to do because these answers cannot be given to you by us or anyone else.

1.1 — The Unlimited Aware Self Model

The first model of understanding the self that we are going to explore is deeply inspired by the teachings of Kain Ramsay, who, we believe, is one of the greatest instructors of our time in the world of personal growth. His teachings (in life coaching), which we recommend you try, have inspired us to improve our life on tremendous levels, and to create the following three models that you will see next. This model is one of the most important, and we call it the "Unlimited Aware Self Model". It is designed to help us characterize ourselves and our life partner in a more meaningful way and realize that the way we describe and define ourselves can be either limiting and negative or unlimited and positive. This choice that we make about how we define ourselves will have a massive impact on the way we behave.

The Unlimited Aware Self Model

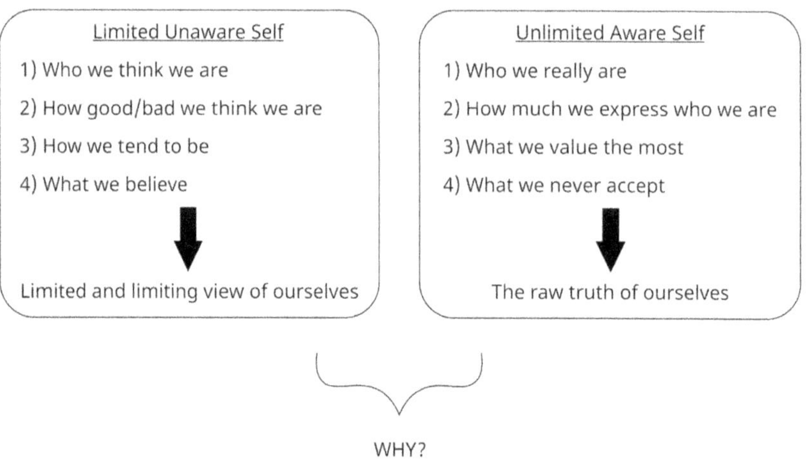

As we can see in the model above, there are two aspects of how we can see ourselves: the Limited Unaware Self and the Unlimited Aware Self. Unfortunately, some people operate, make decisions, and act in life based on their Limited Unaware Self. This is because they never learned how to characterize themselves in a more meaningful way and how to tap into the unlimited potential of their existence. If we want to live a fulfilled and peaceful life with our partner, it is critical that we stop operating based on the Limited Unaware Self and bring out our Unlimited Aware Self. But how can this be done? By clearly understanding these two aspects of ourselves.

1.1.1 — The Limited Unaware Self

First, we will look at the Limited Unaware Self. The Limited Unaware Self is a limiting perspective we can have for ourselves. It is more related to what we do, our perceptions, behaviors, and actions.

So, let's analyze the elements of the Limited Unaware Self:

1) Who we think we are
The first element of the Limited Unaware Self is "who we think we are". The mistake that some people make is to characterize and judge themselves based on labels that they either put on themselves or other people put on them.
These labels are usually:
a) Their social roles (mother, father, brother, sister, husband, boyfriend, girlfriend, colleague, etc.).
b) Their profession and various other activities (musician, dancer, cyclist, programmer, manager, businessman, etc.).
c) Their political and religious views (Christian, Muslim, atheist, right-wing, left-wing, democrat, nationalist, etc.).
d) Sexual preferences and gender (heterosexual, homosexual, asexual, female, male, etc.).
e) Dietary habits (meat eater, vegetarian, vegan, etc.).
f) Origin, nationality, and skin color (Greek, American, white, black, etc.).

2) How "good" or "bad" we think we are

At the same time, they judge positively or negatively whether and how "good" or "bad" they are based on the above labels. That is, whether they are good or bad parents, siblings, co-workers, musicians, businessmen, Christians, atheists, heterosexuals, homosexuals, vegetarians, liberals, or whatever else they think they are.

The problem with these two types of characterizations is that they are not about who we really are, but about what we do. The confusion also comes from our use of language because we tend to say, "I am a mother", "I am a musician", "I am a Christian", "I am a vegetarian", and so on, thinking that we are these labels. But these are just things that we do.

Let's look at some examples to make this clearer. A mother helps a child to grow up and provides food, care, warmth, etc. A musician composes or performs music. A Christian prays and takes part in the sacraments. A vegetarian eats certain foods. A heterosexual and a homosexual have relationships and sexual intercourse with certain people of the opposite or same sex. All of these are actions, not who we are. They are external things that have nothing to do with our essence and existence, and so there is no reason to judge ourselves by them.

Of course, it is important to always do our best to perform our roles, but we do not have to live by these roles or any other labels. This is essential because if we think we are the roles we have and the things we do, we can be led to great disappointment.

For example, let's say that a person who plays the guitar wants to become one of the best guitarists and thus spends most of their time trying to be considered a great guitarist. If they have an accident and can never play the guitar again, they will most likely find themselves in a state of despair and misery because, in their eyes, they have lost themselves and their reason for being. The limiting perception they have of themselves as a "guitarist" no longer exists. On the other hand, if they characterize themselves not by their ability to play the guitar, but in a more meaningful and without limitations way (which we explore later), then they will not reach a state of despair if they can never play the guitar again. They will feel bad, but it won't be the end of the world, and they will be able to continue their life and development with greater ease.

This example can be applied to anything else about the things we do or our social roles. So, we challenge you to take the same look into yourself, the things you do, and the roles you play, and you will see for yourself that they all limit your potential and trap you in a one-sided and small view of yourself.

3) How we tend to be

The third element of the Limited Unaware Self is our limiting characteristics. These characteristics are the inclination, preference, and choice of self-expression. They are not who we are, but how we tend to be. They are a guideline that pushes us into certain ways of expressing and behaving. So, we can direct and largely change these characteristics, and they are not fixed or unchanging.

The main ways that people tend to describe themselves based on limiting characteristics are introvert and extrovert. Introverts have a natural tendency to keep to themselves, to be careful about what they say and whom they associate with, to be observant and selective, not to open up easily to other people, and to look for the essence in a conversation and a person rather than the surface. Extroverts naturally open up to many people, even if they are not intimately involved, express their opinions without hesitation, and try to connect with everyone, even superficially.

We are all more inclined to one or the other direction, and neither of them is all positive or all negative. However, both can lead to different emotional states and behaviors that can easily cause disruption or conflict in our relationships with other people.

Thus, more limiting characteristics emerge, such as: anxious, shy, nervous, reserved, abrupt, emotional, jealous, enthusiastic, excited, fearful, reckless, critical, submissive, dominant, harsh, perfectionist, hesitant, etc. All of these are not a reflection of who we are, but of how we tend to be.

The problem with judging ourselves by these limiting characteristics is that we automatically lock ourselves into such narrow and specific patterns of behavior and expression. Thus, we tell ourselves that we "must" behave in "this" way because we are "this" characteristic, or that because we are "this" characteristic, it is only normal to behave similarly. This is destructive.

For example, if someone thinks and characterizes themselves as introverted, shy, and anxious, they will behave in a similar way, which is not good for their life. This means that in a relationship with their partner, they may shut down, hide things because they are ashamed, and often stress about what to say and how to say it, and they will consider their behavior normal. Eventually, this will damage the relationship.

On the other hand, if someone describes themselves as extroverted, dominant, and irritable, they may not think about how to talk to their partner, may speak impulsively without logic, may not respect their partner's difference, may judge them negatively without a second thought, and may consider this way of expressing and behaving as normal. Again, all this will create conflict in the relationship.

Especially in a relationship where both partners operate primarily based on their limiting characteristics and each has a very different inclination, they will either clash frequently or lose their passion and interest over time.

Therefore, although we all have limiting characteristics, it is not the best way to characterize ourselves or who we really are. These characteristics are a set of ways of behaving and expressing ourselves, and only when we discover a more meaningful way to define ourselves can we change these limiting characteristics and use them in a healthy way that will help the progress of our relationship and not harm it.

4) What we believe

The fourth element of the Limited Unaware Self is our beliefs. Beliefs are ideas that are deeply rooted in us and appear to be proven truths. They are conclusions that we have drawn from our experiences and believe to be the exclusive reality. Our beliefs usually act as blinders, blocking our minds and causing us to see life in a one-sided and limited way. But this is something we can change. We can create better beliefs that help us in life.

Beliefs can be social dictates, prejudices, and rules that we have set for ourselves or rules that other people (usually parents, teachers, and people who played a big role in our upbringing) taught us when we were children. These are not just opinions and views, but much deeper elements that dramatically determine how we see ourselves, life, the world, and other people.

So, based on the beliefs we have, we determine:

1. What we "should" and "should not" do (e.g., "I should respect my elders", "I should not tell the truth if I know it might upset someone else").

2. What we can and cannot do (e.g., "I can be rich", "I cannot be rich").

3. What is "good" and "right" and what is "bad" and "wrong" in life (e.g., "It is good to look happy when you are with other people", "It is bad to have too much money because too much money only comes from exploitation").

4. What results we expect today judging from our past results (e.g., "I failed my exams in the past, so I will fail today", "Because I broke up with a woman in the past, I will never be able to find my life partner").

5. How much we are stuck in the past or future and how much we live in the present (e.g., "Things used to be better, but now the world is broken", "When I start my own business, I will be happy").

6. Whether people are "good" or "bad" (e.g., "All men are bad", "All women are inferior").

7. Who we think we are based on what we do and the roles we have (e.g., "I'm a good musician", "I'm a bad sister", as explained above).

8. What we believe about the existence and creation of humans and the world (e.g., "We come from monkeys and anyone who believes otherwise is a fool", "We were created by the universe and anyone who believes in a religion is wrong").

As you can see, these kinds of beliefs are not mere opinions, such as "I like the color blue" or "the Argentina national football team is the best football team", but strong "beliefs", which can be:

    a) either limiting

    b) or helpful.

They can also be associated with
   a) either the truth
   b) or our false perception of reality.

Beliefs are significant because what we believe greatly affects our daily lives and our relationships. This is because typically, we act based on what we believe.

So, if you believe that you are worthy and capable of achieving great things, you are likely to achieve them. On the other hand, if you believe that you are not worthy and capable of achieving great things, you are likely to fail. So, beliefs can lead us to success or failure in life and our relationships.

But just because we believe something doesn't mean it's true, and this is necessary to understand. For example, we may believe that we are not worthy, but this may be a lie, and we may be capable of achieving our goals, but because of this belief, we do not dare to do what we want. Or we may believe that we are great and powerful, and this may not be the case, thus it can lead to arrogance, which can damage the relationship with our partner. So, we need to find truth, balance, and realism and not be blindly driven by what we believe.

Our beliefs can also easily lead us into conflict with other people, especially with our partner. This is because, most of the time, beliefs act as blinders and do not allow us to see the truth or hear a perspective different from our own. This is why some people exhibit racist and sexist behaviors, others end up arguing about which diet is best, which political ideology is the "right" one, couples argue about who is right and who is wrong, or someone ends up even killing in the name of their religion because they simply believe it is the right thing to do.

In short, our beliefs often prevent us from accepting diversity. Therefore, it is crucial that we free ourselves from our limiting beliefs and not make decisions in life based on them, because they are not the best judges and, in fact, they frequently lead us to despicable acts or actions that we later regret.

Of course, when our beliefs are positive and not very much in tune with reality, they can often be useful. For example, we may believe that we can build a life and relationship with an abundance of material and spiritual goods, even though we are now experiencing financial difficulties and tension in our relationship. This belief can lead us to take actions that will help us create the life we want. We may look for new jobs, learn ways to earn more money, improve our communication skills, and do anything else that will help us build the life and relationship we want. So, positive beliefs, even if they are not true in the present moment, can help us move forward and strengthen our relationship.

Being truly self-aware of our beliefs and their value and also about any other element, negative or positive, of ourselves is something that requires constant introspection and honesty. It is important to be able to identify what we believe, why we believe that, and what value this belief adds to our life and romantic relationship because otherwise, we may end up living a life with no clear direction.

Many people end up becoming a combination of what they have come to believe, and they think they know themselves, but in reality, all they really do is go wherever the wind blows, making choices and decisions by following beliefs that have no value and no truth. For example, they can get married because they have this belief that marriage is a beautiful fairytale-like way of life. Because they follow this false belief, they get disappointed and even feel that their whole world is crushed when they see that, in reality, being married and having a meaningful romantic relationship requires immense individual and couple work and improvement as well as spiritual unity. So, they give up and end their relationship. Others end up having children because they believe that children are the way to build a beautiful family and a way to improve their romantic relationship and marriage. But then they face the reality that raising children is one of the most important responsibilities and that using them as a way to improve their romantic relationship isn't working because the romantic relationship needs immense individual and couple work and improvement by itself.

In conclusion, now that you have seen all four elements of the Limited Unaware Self, you can understand why each of them is a limiting, restrictive, confining, and often damaging and untrue way of characterizing ourselves and our partner. Meaning and true freedom lie in other aspects of existence, which we explore below.

Time for introspection

- Do you operate based on your Limited Unaware Self?
- Do you judge yourself by what you do, how well you do what you do, and how many material possessions you have?
- Do you know who you are deep down inside?
- Do you judge yourself based on your limiting personality characteristics and how you tend to behave?
- Do you know what your limiting beliefs are? If so, what are they, and where do they benefit you? If not, do you want to identify them and change them? How can you do that?
- Ask yourself about each of your beliefs, and whether they serve you in your life and relationship. If they do not serve you, then what is the reason for believing in them?
- Ask yourself if and how much it benefits you to judge yourself and your partner based on all the elements of your Limited Unaware Self.
- What will you do to change any imprisoning and limiting ways of seeing yourself and your partner?

1.1.2 — The Unlimited Aware Self

So far, we have developed the limiting perspective we can have for ourselves, such as what we do, what we believe, and how we tend to be. But is this really all that defines us? If we take all that away, who are we? Can you answer this question? Who are you without labels, social roles, limiting characteristics, and beliefs? And who is your partner really?

1) Who we really are
Who we really are is the first and foremost element of the Unlimited Aware Self. It is a meaningful way to describe and define ourselves, a choice we can make to break away from limitations and embrace our unlimited nature.

Who we really are consists of:
a) qualities
b) positive states of being

QUALITIES	STATES OF BEING
Mature	Love
Responsible	Health
Strong	Fulfillment
Worthy	Togetherness-Fulfillment
Capable	Progress
Courageous	Evolution
Decisive	Gratitude
Dedicated	Forgiveness
Intelligent	Peace
Trustworthy	Balance
Inventive	Freedom
Sincere	Wealth
Authentic	Abundance

Peaceful	Success
Compassionate	Unity
Creative	Spirituality
Passionate	Kindness
Optimistic	Help
Patient	Strength
Persistent	Support
Reliable	Selflessness
Pure	Respect
Humble	Appreciation
Loving	Harmony

As you can see from these two lists, who we are has no boundaries and limitations, no limiting labels, and false perceptions, but unlimited potential. It is made up entirely of positive qualities and different states of being that we embody.

All of us, without exception, are responsible, mature, strong, worthy, honest, and all the other qualities from the first list. It's just that some of us practice them and express them more, while others bury them deep inside.

This is mainly due to ignorance, which is reinforced by our limiting beliefs and the false perception we have of ourselves, as we explained in the Limited Unaware Self. So, when we behave immaturely or irresponsibly, it does not mean that we are immature and irresponsible people, but that we are mature and responsible people who have had difficulty expressing our maturity and responsibility and have done something immature. If we lie at some point, it does not mean that we are liars, but that we are honest people who have lied because of some weakness. If at some point we feel fear for our future, it does not mean that we are pessimists, but that we are optimistic people who simply felt fear at a particular moment.

This is because none of us is perfect and never will be. No matter how much we work on our personal and relationship development, we will always have plenty of room for improvement. So, we are responsible, strong, optimistic, creative, honest, etc., but we are not perfect and flawless. We can always become more responsible, patient, and all the other qualities on the first list, no matter how much we improve.

We all make mistakes and have weaknesses.

Our mistakes and weaknesses are our teachers, helping us to express who we are in the most authentic and complete way, based on constant evolution.

It is therefore important to understand that we are not our actions

Our actions are a result of the development of our self-awareness. If we don't develop our self-awareness and the limited and negative elements of ourselves take control, then our actions will be negative. If we constantly develop our self-awareness and the unlimited and positive elements are nurtured and take control, then our actions will be positive.

Every time we engage in a negative behavior, we have the chance to stop it or change and improve it, because deep inside we are all the qualities we have listed above.

Ask yourself if you can be more responsible, mature, determined, passionate, bold, peaceful, capable, and whatever other qualities you are. You certainly can, the question is whether you want to.

So, based on the above, if you describe yourself as honest, which is more likely, lying or telling the truth? If you describe yourself as a liar, which is more likely, telling the truth or lying more easily? *We see that when we describe ourselves based on our qualities, this can be a guide to positive actions.* If we know and say that we are all the qualities on the first list, we are much more likely to act accordingly. Whenever we see ourselves being led into immaturity, dishonesty, fear, pessimism, indecisiveness, etc., our qualities will remind us of our true unlimited potential, and it will be much easier to behave in a positive way that helps us and our relationship.

Furthermore, apart from our qualities, we are —or can become— the expression and embodiment of great life forces such as love, health, abundance, gratitude, forgiveness, etc. When we say embodiment of these forces, we mean their full expression through everything we do in life. They are states of our being and the most powerful way to view and characterize ourselves because they lead us to be the expression of what is best in us.

We can all cultivate love in our romantic relationship, live with absolute gratitude for everything we have in life, be healthy, and live abundantly. By recognizing that we can be love itself, we understand that it is easier to express love in our life and to treat our partner in the most beautiful way possible. When we recognize that we are health itself, it stands to reason that we do what is necessary to be healthy, such as exercise, a balanced diet, meditation, etc. The same applies to every other state of being on the second list.

So, who we are is an expanded way of seeing and characterizing ourselves, helping us not to judge ourselves negatively and not to be driven to self-destruction.

Of course, we also need balance to avoid reaching levels of arrogance. It is important to be humble. It's essential to recognize all the positive aspects of ourselves and align with them, rather than condemning ourselves for moments of weakness. At the same time, however, we should accept that we make mistakes and have flaws that require improvement. Rather than characterizing ourselves by our mistakes, we choose to characterize ourselves by our qualities, and in doing so, we correct and reduce our mistakes more easily. This way, we focus on essence and progress rather than weakness and self-condemnation.

When you begin to behave in terms of your qualities and positive states of being that you can embody and see their vastness, you can turn these into powerful helpful beliefs that will replace old limiting beliefs and be a light of progress in your life and romantic relationship. This is because they will be beliefs that are not only helpful but also true.

So, now you can see that we have a choice. A choice to define who we are based on our qualities and positive states of being and a choice to define who we are based on our roles, limiting characteristics, and limiting beliefs. This choice will play a massive role in how we behave and the quality of our romantic relationship and every other social relationship we have.

2) How much we express who we really are

The second element of the Unlimited Aware Self is how much we express and experience who we really are. That is, how responsible, mature, strong, creative, honest, determined, giving, humble, etc. are we? And correspondingly, how much do we experience life with love, health, abundance, gratitude, forgiveness, evolution, balance, unity, etc.? These are two questions we challenge you to ask yourself.

In fact, after answering these questions for each of the elements on the two lists of who we are, ask yourself how much you are willing to improve in each of these areas. We assure you that you will discover a great deal about yourself and thus begin a path of self-improvement and a deeper understanding of your partner. Finally, add to these two lists any other elements you feel are missing that relate to the truth about yourself.

So, we see that who we are and how much we express who we are is something very practical. It is a way of life, a way of being. So, for example, saying to ourselves that we are strong as a quality, or that we are the embodiment of strength as a positive state of being, means that we don't give up when situations are difficult, we don't allow our negative elements to take control or behave in a negative and immature way to our life partner. It means that we don't please people, but we always speak our truth, we don't follow blindly what we have been taught by our parents and society but we live based on our unlimited potential. We say no when and where we want to say no to. The same applies to any other quality and positive state of being and the entirety of our Unlimited Aware Self and any other positive element of our existence, such as some of the other Self-Awareness Cultivating Models and the positive elements in Chapters Three and Four.

3) What we value the most

Having explored, who we really are, it is now time to look at the third element of the Unlimited Aware Self, which is our values.

Values are whatever is most valuable to us. They are some of our driving forces in life and largely determine our actions and how we experience our relationships with other people and therefore with our life partner. Our values are very much connected to who we really are. We all have the same values within us, we just prioritize them differently depending on where we are in life and our experiences.

It is important to clarify our values. By doing this we can, individually and as a couple, only say "yes" and "no" where we really want to say "yes" and "no" because we will be very clear about what is of great value to us.

By clarifying your values, you will be able to understand each other much better and find a common path in life.

Some of the most important values are:

1. Love
2. Health
3. Fulfillment
4. Togetherness-Fulfillment (to be explored later)
5. Truth
6. Authenticity
7. Time
8. Serenity
9. Freedom
10. Connection
11. Unity
12. Progress
13. Change
14. Faith
15. Recognition
16. Approval
17. Security
18. Risk
19. Comfort
20. Help
21. Contribution
22. Power
23. Success
24. Fun

Now that you have seen some fundamental values that we all carry within us, ask yourself which ones are most important to you. Some values work together on the same level. For example, love, fulfillment, and progress always go together, as we will explain in the final chapter. However, some values will always be "sacrificed" because other values have a higher priority.

So, do you sacrifice your progress for security?
This means that you sacrifice your personal and relationship development because you know that to improve, you have to face the truth about yourself and thus get out of the false security you have built in your life.

Do you sacrifice your health for success?
This means that you sacrifice your physical and mental health to appear successful in the eyes of others. This way you work hard and burn out.

Do you sacrifice authenticity and truth for approval?
This means that you don't express your truth because you are afraid of not being accepted by other people and not being considered important.

Do you sacrifice your time for connection?
This means you sacrifice your precious time with people you don't fit in with because you are afraid of being alone.

Do you sacrifice change for comfort?
This means you choose to stay stagnant because you are afraid to step out of your comfort zone.

Do you sacrifice peace for strength?
This means that you sacrifice your inner peace and serenity to appear strong in the world. You experience daily stress in order to climb the ladder of material "success".

Do you sacrifice help for power?

This means that you sacrifice helping others to gain more power and prestige for yourself.

You see how values work and how if we give priority to one, we are bound to put another in the background. This is why we need to work on our values to live the life we really want.

How we use and prioritize our values can have a positive or negative effect on our lives

If we don't put love and fulfillment first, how can we expect to have a healthy and balanced relationship with our life partner? If we don't value progress and change, how can we expect to improve? If we put connection with others first and our authenticity second, how can we expect to have meaningful and honest relationships with others? If we don't believe in ourselves, how do we expect to achieve our goals?

Based on the above, ask yourself these questions, both individually and as a couple. Give clear answers so that you can build a life together and not have a relationship that follows two different paths because of different values. As a couple, it is important that you share the same values and priorities.

Once you have clarified your values, you may find that, over time, your priorities change

The things that motivate us change depending on where we are in life, and this is normal. So, when you have built a secure and comfortable life and relationship, you will no longer be totally motivated by that because you have achieved it, and you can make room for the value of taking risks to move forward by trying new things.

But when you really get to a level where you have a clear picture of who you are, then your values can become stable; you will only make small changes to your list of priorities. This will happen because you simply know yourself and your life partner very well. This doesn't mean that you will remain stagnant. It means that as you develop your awareness you will evolve with greater certainty, and that is a huge achievement in your life and romantic relationship.

4) What we never accept

Once we have clarified our values, the next step towards the Unlimited Aware Self is to clarify what we never accept, our "non-negotiable nos". The "non-negotiable nos" are anything we won't tolerate in our life and relationship for any reason. They are actions and behaviors that we don't want to accept from our partner and actions and behaviors that we don't accept from ourselves and commit to never doing. They can include obvious and necessary things, such as never using physical violence against our partner. This is a "non-negotiable no" that is required in every relationship, without exception. Unfortunately, some couples don't follow it. Other "non-negotiable nos" can be very personal, depending on the uniqueness of each person and couple.

Just as we have worked on what is most valuable to us and our relationship, it is equally important to find within ourselves what we do not want to accept in our life. For example, we, as a couple, have dramatically reduced the tension between us simply by being crystal clear about what we don't accept. We're very aware of what we both don't accept, and we behave in a respective way, which prevents anger and tension. We don't expect our partner to read our minds and find out what we don't accept, but we make it honestly clear.

Find the "non-negotiable nos" in your life. We assure you that they will clarify your relationship significantly, and you will solve various kinds of difficulties and conflicts.

So, these are the four elements of the Unlimited Aware Self. Now that you know exactly which is the Limited Unaware Self and which is the Unlimited Aware Self, you can begin the path of continuous development of self-awareness, and this way get to know your partner in depth and accept their diversity and truth.

Now you can see that whether we operate more based on our Limited Unaware Self, or our Unlimited Aware Self, is entirely our choice and our responsibility. Every day, we choose who we are and how we behave.

The only improvement we can make is choosing to live by who we really are – our qualities and positive states of being we can embody. This is achieved by committing ourselves to be better than we were the day before and to be better tomorrow than we are today.

Whether we choose to characterize ourselves and our partner by what we do, our roles, behaviors, beliefs, and mistakes, or by our qualities and values, we are entirely responsible. How we judge ourselves and our partner determines the degree of health and progress we experience in our life and relationship.

The Unlimited Aware Self Model has a big "WHY" (see p. 26) at its base to remind us to ask "why" every time we make decisions, take actions, and believe something to be true. We should ask: why do I think this is a true belief? Why am I behaving this way? Why am I wrong? Why didn't I speak respectfully to my partner? Why is "this" value important to me and my partner? Why do I choose to operate based on my Limited Unaware Self and not my Unlimited Aware Self? The "why" will always help us find the truth and get rid of the rubbish and anything that doesn't serve us in our life.

Time for introspection

- Do you operate with your Unlimited Aware Self?
- Do you know who you really are?
- Do you embody the states of being that we have explored above? How do you embody them?
- Do you see yourself and your partner with the expanded truth of the Unlimited Aware Self or with the limited perception of the Limited Unaware Self?
- Do you have clear values in your life and relationship with your partner?
- Do you have the same values and priorities in your life and relationship with your partner?
- Have you made clear as a couple what you do not accept under any circumstances in your life and relationship?
- Do you wonder "why" every time you do something in your life, whether it is positive or negative? Do you answer with brutal honesty or based on your limiting beliefs?

- Is it beneficial for you to operate based on your Limited Unaware Self or your Unlimited Aware Self?
- How are you going to describe and define yourself and your partner from now on?

1.2 — The Balanced Aware Self Model

The second model we will explore we call the "Balanced Aware Self Model", and it helps us to be balanced in our behavior and our relationships with other people.

The Balanced Aware Self Model

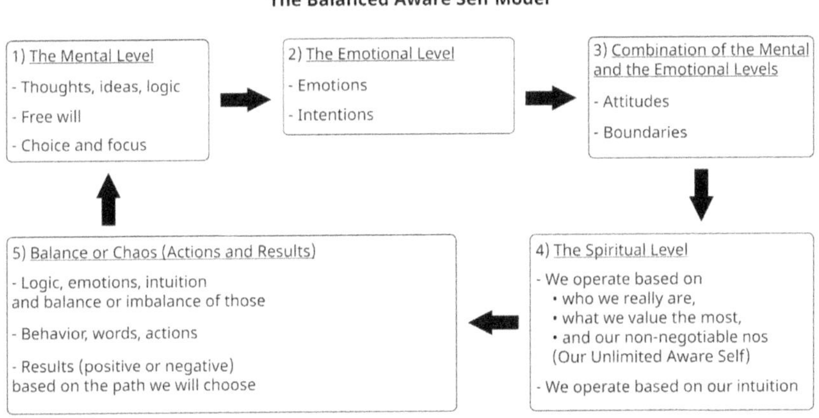

As we can see in the model above, we have three levels at which we operate: the mental, the emotional, and the spiritual.

Very simply we can say that the mental level is about our thoughts, our choice to focus on them, ideas, and logic. The emotional level is about our emotions and intentions. The spiritual level is about our Unlimited Aware Self (as we explored in the previous model), our intuition, and the healthiest ways we can operate. We also have a stage where the mental and emotional levels are combined, and this includes our attitudes and the boundaries we set for ourselves. Each of these levels interacts with each other and leads us to specific actions and behaviors. To live a balanced life and build a balanced romantic relationship, it is necessary to understand how these three levels are connected and how they can affect us positively or negatively.

1) The Mental Level

The mental level, as we said above, is related to our thoughts. *It is important to understand that we cannot control all our thoughts.* Most thoughts come to us through our senses or because of a memory.

For instance, we hear a song and think of a concert we went to years ago, smell food and think of a lovely dinner with our partner, or see an attractive person and think of going out with them. These thoughts are impossible to control since they emerge from a sense or memory. So, when you think of something negative, or even something hideous and perhaps extreme, don't beat yourself up because it may simply have come up automatically for some reason.

But our power lies in our free will. Although thoughts often come to us through our senses and memories, we can also consciously think of positive or negative things. This means that we can bring a positive or negative thought into our mind without any sensation or memory intervening. For instance, when cooking, we may daydream about our bright future, a promotion at work, or a gift for our lover because we choose to. The same can happen with a negative thought, of course. In short, because we have free will, we can think whatever we want, regardless of our senses and memories.

Free will also allows us to do something else very important; our free will allows us to choose our focus. As we said above, we can consciously think about many things, but usually, our thoughts come to us automatically. So, we cannot control the thoughts that automatically come to our minds, but we can choose which ones to focus on and which ones to reject or overlook. If a pessimistic thought comes into our mind, we have the choice to focus on it or ignore it. The same goes for optimistic and positive thoughts. We have no control over if or when many of them come into our minds, but we can decide to focus on them or simply observe them without judgment and let them go. The same applies to the thoughts we consciously bring to mind. We can continue to focus on them if they are positive, or we can ignore them if they are negative and detrimental to our mental health.

Any thought that we focus on can be more easily repeated in the future. This means that the more we focus on a thought, the more likely it is to come back to mind and become a strong idea, perhaps even an obsession. In fact, many times the idea created by constantly focusing on a thought can become deeply ingrained in us and thus become a limiting or helpful belief, depending on whether the idea is negative or positive. For instance, if a person focuses on the idea that they are worthless (because they failed examinations, made blunders at work, etc.), they may believe they are unworthy. If they hold on to this idea, over time it will likely become a limiting belief that will cause many difficulties in their life.

Therefore, it is necessary to:
a) not blame ourselves for any negative thoughts, as we do not have complete control over them, and
b) exercise our power of focus because this is the only power we have over our thoughts, whether we consciously think them, or they come automatically.

Logic, which also exists at the mental level, can help us to select and focus our thoughts appropriately. Of course, logic is not always a healthy way of choosing, as some may believe, because it is a one-sided and limiting way. It is only one perspective and not the whole picture. In fact, logic can often lead us into misunderstandings because it can be influenced by the false and limiting reality that our limiting beliefs have built up. So, we need to evaluate our logic and not act on it alone.

2) The Emotional Level

If we concentrate on one thought for a long time or think about it many times, we can move from the mental level to the emotional level without realizing it. Each thought we focus on evokes corresponding emotions. If we focus on a thought related to the future success of a goal, we will feel joy and excitement;

if we focus on a thought associated with failure, we will feel sadness or disappointment.

It is important to understand that our emotions come and go. They are not permanent states that should define us, nor are we what we feel.

So, we are not happy, sad, angry, frustrated, etc., as we tend to say, for example, "I am happy". Instead, we only feel joy, sadness, anger, etc., at certain times, and whatever we feel is impermanent. That's why we are not our emotions. When we free ourselves from the limiting belief that we are whatever we feel, we will be free from the emotional chaos in which we can easily become imprisoned.

The emotions that arise from our reinforced thoughts influence our intentions. Our intentions are most often linked to one or more emotions. For this reason, no one actually has bad intentions, they are simply acting emotionally and immaturely because they have had negative stimuli in life and have not yet learned the necessary lessons. So, we usually have an intention to do or say something positive or negative because we feel certain emotions.

When we manage to recognize and control our emotions in a healthy way and understand why we have the intentions we have before we do or say something, we can also successfully recognize and understand the emotions and intentions of other people, especially our life partner, with whom we are closely connected.

3) Our Attitudes and Boundaries

Depending on the level of emotional charge and the intentions involved, each person will adopt a particular attitude. This is where the boundaries that we set for ourselves come in, which will also greatly influence our attitude.

The boundaries that we set for ourselves are simply the voices of reason telling us to put the brakes on the emotions, which take on great dimensions when we focus on them.

Boundaries come from the mental level and are related to logic. Basically, our logic asks us to ignore our emotions and adopt a rational attitude. So, the mental and emotional levels are in a state of confusion. These are the moments when we feel that something is "right" and because we feel it, we automatically believe it is true, but at the same time, we think logically, which is contrary to what we feel.

For example, a couple is arguing, and one partner feels anger (emotional level), which controls their behavior, but at the same time, they think (mental level) that their behavior is not healthy and that it is good to set some boundaries to themselves to prevent acting emotionally and immaturely and making things worse. This is the confusion between these two levels and how much the boundaries we set for ourselves will determine our attitude.

4) The Spiritual Level – Intuition

There is another element in this confusion. This element is intuition, which belongs to the spiritual level and can also influence our attitude. *Intuition is the sense of knowing that something is right or wrong.* It is a "voice" beyond reason and emotion. It is not about what we think is right, nor is it about what we feel is right; it is about what we know deep down inside to be right.

So, in the previous example, intuition can "tell" the partner that their anger is justified because they have been wronged (i.e., intuition takes the side of the emotions), or it can reinforce logic by showing that their emotions are irrational because they are wrong. The ideal state, however, is when these three elements (logic, emotion, and intuition) are in balance. This means that the partner should judge the situation and themselves based on the combination of all three elements to find the truth.

So, if the partner had balanced all the levels, they might come to the following conclusion: They behaved immaturely by reacting so emotionally, even though they were right to some extent. However, they did not consider their partner's perspective because they were overwhelmed by their emotions. The solution is to calm down, apologize, and discuss it again calmly with their partner, not being influenced on just one level, but judging from all three levels and their partner's perspective; that is to be understood and respected as a unique and equal perspective.

This is the spiritual level, and we operate more easily on this level when we operate based on our qualities and positive states of being, such as love. The spiritual level leads to respect, understanding, and realism and is about operating based on our Unlimited Aware Self. The spiritual level helps us make the best decisions and get out of the confusion that is caused by the mental and emotional levels. When we operate on our spiritual level, we do not judge situations one-sidedly. We view everything that happens within us with maturity, and balance based on who we really are, not with labels, limiting beliefs, cold logic, or emotional outbursts.

5) Our Actions and Results

Whether the mental, emotional, or spiritual level prevails in us, we will do certain actions. *The level of maturity of the actions will be judged by our choice.* If we choose logic, we may act in a very superficial way without much concern for our partner. If we choose emotions, we are very likely to react in a completely immature way and lash out. However, if we choose the spiritual level, we will behave in a more mature and balanced way.

Behaviors based on logic and emotion are immature reactions because they are automatic and inconsiderate, whereas behaviors based on the spiritual level are balanced and mature reactions because they are conscious and controlled by us.

Our every action and behavior will have a corresponding result in our life and relationship. The result can be positive or negative and depends entirely on the whole process as explained above.

So, to summarize, when thoughts come into our minds they are often out of our control, but we have the power to choose where to focus because of our free will. If we hold on to a thought for a long time, it can become an idea that can grow and become a belief, either limiting or helpful. Our logic can also help us determine which thoughts we will focus on. Depending on where we focus, we will feel corresponding emotions, which will influence our intentions. Again, depending on our limitations as humans, and how aware we are of our emotions and our intentions, we will form a particular attitude, and that attitude will be reinforced by either logic —due to the boundaries we set for ourselves—, emotion, intuition, or a balance of all three. Our mental and emotional levels can be in confusion, and our spiritual level, which is about our Unlimited Aware Self, can help us make the best decisions and get out of this confusion. Whether we choose our mental, emotional, or spiritual level, we will say certain words and act in certain ways which will have negative or positive results in our life. Depending on these results, new thoughts and emotions will come, and depending on the level of self-awareness we have developed so far, our mental, emotional, and spiritual levels will be either in chaos or in balance.

For a balanced life and relationship with our partner, we should first be in inner balance. We should not be guided by our emotions, nor act only based on cold logic, and certainly not do everything we do only based on our intuition, because our intuition can sometimes be wrong and take the side of our logic or emotions. The balance between logic, emotion, and intuition, as well as our Unlimited Aware Self, will lead us to know what is best for us. So, it is important to listen to our logic, emotions, and intuition, but the best way to make the healthiest decisions will always be to operate based on our spiritual level and our Unlimited Aware Self and this is a way of life.

Use this model to improve your behaviors and build inner balance and peace.

Time for introspection

- Have you noticed how much control you give to your thoughts, especially the negative ones?
- Do you usually focus on your positive or negative thoughts?
- How easily can you overlook your negative thoughts and focus on the positive and beneficial ones?
- Do you judge yourself and your partner negatively because of your negative thoughts?
- Can you easily control your emotions or are they controlling you?
- Do you allow your emotions to damage your relationship with your partner?
- Have you thought of your intentions, boundaries, attitude, and the interaction between them? Do you usually adopt a mature or immature attitude?
- Do you listen to the voice of your intuition? When making decisions, do you judge based on logic, emotions, intuition, or the balance of these?
- How often do you operate on your spiritual level?
- Is there chaos or balance within you? If there is chaos, what do you need to do to change it? If there is balance, what do you need to do to maintain it?
- Is there chaos or balance in the relationship with your partner? If there is chaos, what do you need to do to change it? If there is balance, what do you need to do to maintain it?

1.3 — The Evolved Aware Self Model

The next model we call the "Evolved Aware Self Model"; it helps us to operate on a spiritual level and based on the truth of ourselves to achieve whatever we want in life. It is the model for success in life in general and a relationship in particular.

The Evolved Aware Self Model

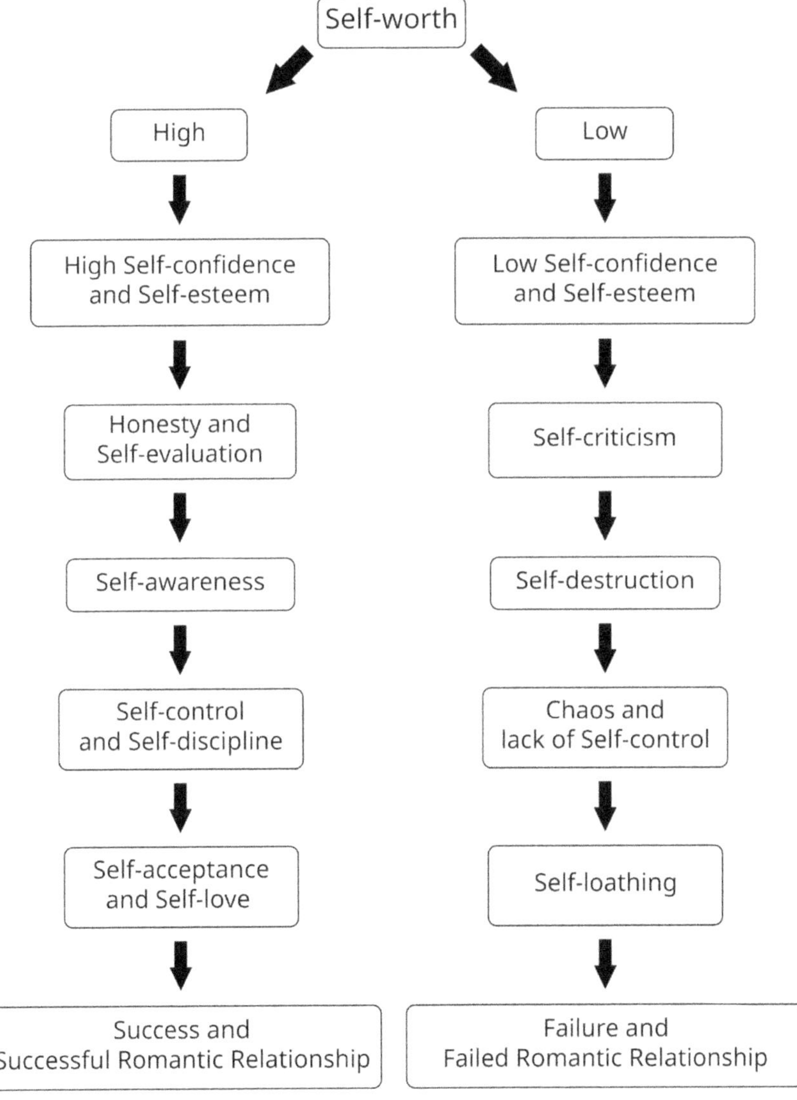

1) Self-worth

As we can see in the model above, it all starts with our self-worth. Self-worth is the great or small value we place on ourselves. If we characterize ourselves by what we do, how well we do it, and our beliefs, i.e., based on the Limited Unaware Self, then we are likely to "place" very little value on ourselves and judge ourselves in a very limiting way. If, on the other hand, we characterize ourselves based on who we really are and the entirety of our Unlimited Aware Self, then we are likely to value ourselves much more.

2) Self-confidence and Self-esteem

How much we value ourselves determines our self-confidence and self-esteem. Self-confidence is the belief we have about ourselves. It is what we believe about ourselves today, about what we are good at and what we are not good at. This means that our self-confidence is mainly about what we believe about our abilities and how capable we are of carrying out certain tasks, e.g., whether we are very confident in our work or very confident in playing football. That is, whether we think we are good at our job and whether we think we are good at playing football. The more we practice at something, whether it is our job, football, music, or anything else, the more our self-confidence increases.

On the other hand, self-esteem is how much we appreciate ourselves. It is more about our inner world and whether we appreciate ourselves, not for our abilities and what we do well or not, but for who we really are. That is, whether we appreciate ourselves for being honest and strong or we think we are liars and weak.

If we have high self-worth, meaning, if we recognize ourselves as a worthy person, then our self-confidence and self-esteem will be high and will continue to grow. Thus, we will see every failure and difficulty in our lives as opportunities for improvement and challenges to overcome, confirming that we are worthy people. In this way, self-worth is linked to our self-confidence and self-esteem. If we have low self-worth and do not think we are a worthy person, then our self-confidence and self-esteem will also be low. We will see every failure and difficulty in our lives as another reason to affirm that we are unworthy. How we see ourselves now will very much determine our choices in our life and romantic relationship.

3) Self-evaluation and Self-criticism

Depending on our self-confidence and self-esteem, we will either be honest or question ourselves. We are honest when we have high self-confidence and self-esteem. We understand that we are imperfect and make mistakes, but we also recognize our positive aspects, which are many. We seek, find, and acknowledge the whole truth about ourselves. We, therefore, engage in constructive self-criticism with a view to self-improvement, and we reach levels of balanced self-admiration and deep trust in ourselves.

On the contrary, when we have low self-confidence and self-esteem, we end up with self-doubt. Because we focus on our weaknesses and mistakes, or even a false image of ourselves, and do not believe that we are worthy and capable people, we question everything we do. Here, self-criticism is entirely negative and not constructive. The result is self-sabotage, where we keep making excuses and promoting constant procrastination. This is how we stagnate or, even worse, go downhill.

4) Self-awareness and Self-destruction

Constructive self-criticism helps us on our journey of self-awareness. By continually evaluating our positive and negative elements, our mistakes, and successes, we come to a more profound understanding of ourselves and thus the journey of self-awareness takes an even more beautiful course.

On the other hand, negative self-criticism and fixation on our mistakes eventually lead to self-destruction, first internally and then externally, in our relationship with our partner and other people.

5) Self-control

The journey of self-awareness helps us to gain self-control through self-discipline. Healthy self-control is the healthy way in which we control our emotions and operate on a spiritual level, as we explored in the previous model. Healthy self-control has nothing to do with suppressing our emotions or putting on a mask to please people.

Suppressing our emotions is not healthy. If we suppress our emotions, we will need to lash out at some point. This is what leads a father, who has problems at work but doesn't express them for fear of being fired, to take it out on his wife and children when he comes home.

To avoid suppressing our emotions or taking them out on other people, we can practice healthy self-control. In short, we should practice the Balanced Aware Self Model and learn to focus on what we want rather than what we don't want.

When we practice healthy self-control, we will continue to feel various unpleasant emotions, but to a tiny degree and with very little frequency. So, if we are on the path of self-awareness we can develop healthy self-control, whereas if we are on the path of self-destruction we will live in chaos.

6) Self-acceptance and Self-love vs. Self-loathing

If we have cultivated healthy self-control, we will be led to self-acceptance and self-love. But if our self-control is low, we will be led to self-loathing. This is because, through self-control and self-awareness, we come closer to ourselves and are in a state of spiritual balance. We respect ourselves and know that we are capable and worthy of dealing with whatever happens in a mature and healthy way. This is the ground on which our self-acceptance and self-love grow and strengthen. It is the level at which we become love itself, as we explained in the first model of the Unlimited Aware Self.

Of course, if we follow the path of low self-worth, which leads to low self-control, outbursts, and self-destruction, then we can reach self-loathing. We can end up hating ourselves, which is the worst stage someone can reach because it leads to very dark and extreme behaviors.

7) Success and Failure

Finally, if we love ourselves, then we can love our life partner, leading to a successful relationship and life. If we do not love ourselves, we will end up with failures in all areas of our lives. Success and failure are of course unique to each person and are a reflection of our future selves. So, based on the self-worth and image we have of ourselves today, we will build a corresponding image of our future self, which will be associated with either success or failure.

The whole path above does not only work in the way we have described, and there are many ways in which the concepts we have developed relate to each other. This model describes the most common path that we see, from the present image of ourselves to the future image which will express either love or dislike of ourselves. Work through this entire process of self-awareness, recognize your worth, evaluate yourself honestly, and commit to continuous self-improvement, above all with self-love. This will make it easier for you to achieve what you want. A couple with both partners in alignment with their true worth and self-love can work wonders.

Time for introspection

- Do you consider yourself worthy? If so, why? If not, why?
- Do you consider your partner worthy? If so, why? If not, why?
- Do you have high or low self-confidence and self-esteem?
- Do you evaluate yourself and your relationship with your partner honestly and respectfully, or do you question yourself and your relationship?
- Are you on a path of developing your self-awareness or a path of self-destruction?
- Are you developing your healthy self-control? If so, how exactly do you do it? If not, why don't you?
- Do you accept yourself with all your flaws? If so, why? If not, why?
- Do you accept your partner with all their flaws? If so, why? If not, why?
- If your answers to the above questions tend towards a negative view of yourself and your relationship with your partner, what do you need to do to change this view?

1.4 — The Existential Aware Self Model

We call this model the "Existential Aware Self Model" and it is related to discovering the purpose of our existence.

As we have seen so far, each person makes decisions in their life and romantic relationship based on:

1) Who they are and the level of development of their self-awareness.
2) What they value the most.
3) Their beliefs about themselves and society.
4) Their ability to manage their emotions in a healthy way.
5) The overall balance between their mental, emotional, and spiritual levels.
6) Self-worth and self-love.

But the different ways in which we perceive ourselves, our life partner, and the world, how we operate, behave, and act do not end here. We are very much motivated by the purpose for which we exist. So, how do we find this purpose?

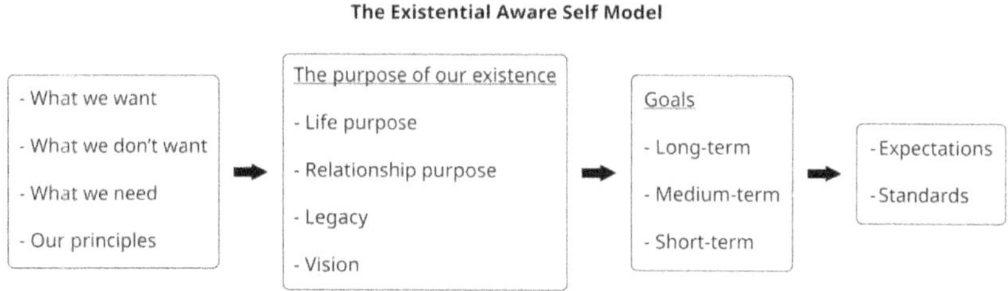

1) In order to find the purpose of our existence, it is beneficial to first understand and clarify some more truths about ourselves

a) What we want

As we can see in the model above, we all have different "things we want" and "things we don't want" in our life and romantic relationship. What we want can be effortlessly clarified if we clarify our values (explored in the first model) and prioritize them.

For example, if the value of progress is very high, we might want to get some training in psychology or read a book on personal and relationship development. If the value of success is high, we might want to get a promotion at work. If the value of security is high, we might want to buy a house that provides us with comfort. If the value of risk is high, we might want to start our own business. In this way, we can be clear about what we want.

As for what we don't want, we can easily clarify this by having already clarified what we want, but also by our "non-negotiable nos" (the Unlimited Aware Self Model). Be careful, though, the "non-negotiable nos" are things we can't tolerate for any reason. Whereas what we don't want defines things we simply don't like and can tolerate and accept in certain circumstances. For example, a "non-negotiable no" means that, as a couple, we will not accept speaking abusively to each other, whereas something that we don't want might be that one partner doesn't want to party in nightclubs while the other does. In the first case, things are serious and absolute. In the second case, there is no serious problem.

Clarifying as a couple what each of you wants and doesn't want in life can help you avoid conflicts and misunderstandings and change your relationship for the better.

b) What we need

But apart from what we want and what we don't want, there is also what we need and what we don't need. So, we may want to spend all day binge-watching TV series, perhaps because the value of comfort is too high, but we may not need it because it is not beneficial to us. Similarly, we may not want to understand ourselves in depth, perhaps because the value of progress is low, but we need to do so to improve our life and relationship. So, we see that it is important to balance what we want and don't want with what we need and don't need to make healthy choices. If we don't balance them, we risk being driven by completely meaningless "wants" or getting caught up in things we mistakenly believe we need.

What we really need can be found by knowing and clarifying our needs. Needs, like values, are driving forces in life, but they can often lead us to negative outcomes if we do not understand them.

We have fundamental and quality needs. Fundamental needs are mainly related to our survival, such as the need for water and food, and the need for shelter and warmth. But these also include the need for sexual intercourse, but also the need for recognition, acceptance, and socialization, in which we try to fill inner emotional voids rather than connect with another human being meaningfully.

In the quality needs, we find the need for improvement, change, and progress as well as the essential and deep connection with other people and especially with our life partner. This is also where we understand the connection between needs and our values.

It is therefore clear that we all have to meet the basic needs for food, water, and shelter to focus on our progress and evolution. It is also vital that we do not succumb to the need for acceptance and approval. We can be strong and mature human beings who are grounded in who we are and therefore do not need the acceptance and approval of anyone else. Only then we will seek meaningful connections with other people and our life partner. The reason for connecting is not to gain approval and validation from someone else, but to experience shared progress and evolution.

This is how mature adults operate. With children, however, it is critical that we do our best to meet their needs for warmth, acceptance, and validation. If these are not adequately met in their early years, they are likely to exhibit various dysfunctional behaviors with their partner when they grow up. We explore this in Chapter Two.

c) Our principles

Having clarified our "wants" and needs, we can define our principles. Principles are a set of statements that we consider to be beneficial and useful for our life and relationship. Based on them, we adopt an attitude to life. Each person and each couple have different principles. Some of them might be the following:

1 - Our love always comes first.

2 - We enjoy life and do not complain.

3 - No one is a victim in life in general and in our relationship in particular.

4 - We are masters of ourselves, and only we are in control of our minds.

5 - Life is beautiful and difficulties are opportunities for improvement.

Our principles can play a major role in shaping our life and romantic relationship.

2) How the above connect to the purpose of our existence

So, we've noted that what we want and don't want, our needs, and our principles are crucial to the choices we make every day. But how do they relate to the purpose of our existence? They are closely related because they can help us discover it.

We believe that the purpose of our existence consists of four levels:

Our life purpose, our relationship purpose, our legacy, and our vision.

a) Life purpose

Life purpose is obviously of paramount importance. Unfortunately, some people have no idea what their life purpose is. However, without a life purpose, we don't have a clear path and destination, meaning, self-awareness, awareness, and control over our lives. Our life purpose, as a couple, for example, is to be together, healthy and loving, experience Togetherness-Fulfillment (to be discussed in the last chapter), and be true to ourselves. It is for this purpose that we build all our goals and do everything we do in life. Thus, all our behavior and actions are guided by our love, health, Togetherness-Fulfillment, and truth, and this obviously helps us greatly in our life and relationship.

The life purpose of a couple must be mutual; otherwise, the partners will not move towards the same direction in life. If the couple doesn't share the same life purpose, they will end up being nothing more than housemates, in a meaningless relationship or marriage. Our life purpose very much defines what we do, and where we want to go in life. So, it's crucial that you define your purpose as a couple so that you can grow together.

b) Relationship purpose

The relationship purpose is as critical as the life purpose. Have you ever asked yourself why you are in a relationship with your partner? Are you in a relationship to fill inner emotional voids? Are you in a relationship to just have a "good time" and not be alone? Are you in a relationship because your family told you so? Are you in a relationship because your partner is wealthy? Are you in a relationship because you're in love? Are you in a relationship because you deeply love each other? Why are you together? Think about these questions and carry on reading later.

The purpose of a romantic relationship is always Togetherness-Fulfillment, which we explore in the final chapter. In short, however, we can say that the purpose of a romantic relationship and marriage is progress and love. Through the relationship and unity with our life partner, we learn wonderful lessons in life, we develop our self-awareness constantly, we cultivate our respect and understanding, we learn to love ourselves, and so we love our partner, and we are on a path of continuous evolution. All of this happens with such intensity and power that we cannot experience it in any other human relationship except the romantic one. So, find within yourself the truth of why you are in a relationship with your partner, and don't stay on the surface. Dare to dive deep and find the essence.

c) Legacy

Once we have clarified our life and relationship purpose, we can discover the third level of the purpose of our existence, which is our legacy. Legacy is what we leave behind in the world after we die; it is our way of contributing to the betterment of humanity; it is our footprint to make the world a better place. This book, for example, is part of our legacy that will continue to exist and help people after we are gone.

d) Vision

The fourth level of the purpose of our existence is our vision. Our vision is simply how we want to be remembered by other people now and after our death. Do we want to be remembered as irritable, uncaring, fearful, or not remembered at all? Or do we want to be remembered as strong and compassionate people? In our case, our vision is to be remembered as a loving couple who helped other people and couples in every way possible.

So, these are the four levels of the purpose of our existence.

In short, the purpose of our existence as a couple is to be together, healthy, loving, and experiencing Togetherness-Fulfillment, driven by our continuous progress, and doing our best to help other couples grow and experience true love through the legacy we create.

The purpose of your existence can be defined with absolute certainty, after much personal and couple work, and based on all the Self-Awareness Cultivating Models we have explored so far in this chapter. Now you can understand even better how our "wants", needs and principles are linked to the purpose of our existence.

3) Goal setting

When we are sure of the purpose of our existence, we can set our goals in our life and relationship. If we set goals without knowing the purpose of our existence, then it is most likely those goals will have no substance. We will probably not achieve them because we will not be powerfully motivated to pursue them. So, the purpose always comes first and the individual goals second. Goals can be long-term, medium-term, or short-term and are inextricably linked to our purpose and our ambitions and desires. Each goal requires an action plan and commitment to ensure its success. Goal setting is covered in detail in Volume 2.

4) Expectations and Standards

Depending on our purpose and goals, we will have certain expectations or standards. Expectations are the results we expect, assume, and imagine we will get. They are usually unrealistic and have to do with what we expect from other people and situations rather than from ourselves. It is a dysfunctional way of thinking that is typically not based on reality. In fact, we often take for granted what we expect to happen.

For example, one expectation might be that we expect our partner to buy us a present because we bought them a present a few days ago. Another expectation might be that we will get a promotion because we have performed better at work this month. Another expectation might be that our partner will greet us with hugs and kisses when we come home from work. As you can see, expectations are about what we imagine other people will do, without any evidence or control that they will act accordingly.

Standards, on the other hand, are the conditions we set for what we will and will not accept in life. Standards are very much linked to our principles, values, and "non-negotiable nos" and are a quality way of thinking and more realistic than expectations.

One standard may be that we do not want to associate with people who do not respect and value us. Another standard might be that we don't accept not doing our best to achieve our goals. Another standard is that we value our time very highly and make the best use of it, refusing to waste it. Here we see that standards are about what we do and what we expect from ourselves, not from another person.

Standards help us live a high-quality life, but we may sometimes fail to live up to our high standards because we are simply not perfect. This helps us to create a balance between achieving our difficult goals and accepting the truth that not everything will go exactly as we plan. It's a beautiful and mature combination of realism and freedom, and it helps us to have higher success rates in our goals.

Expectations and standards can be linked in different ways:
a) The healthy and mature way

Here we have high standards in our life and relationship, but low or even zero expectations. We have high standards because we recognize our worth and therefore accept nothing less than what we deserve. We take action to achieve what we want without taking anything for granted or expecting anything from others.

b) The reckless and excessive way

Here we have high standards and high expectations. Usually, at this level, we think we know everything, we act arrogantly, and we set exaggerated and unrealistic goals that are very difficult to achieve. Many people even become obsessed with being considered "successful" in the eyes of others.

c) The irresponsible way

Here we have low standards and high expectations, expecting a lot from others but not from ourselves. We typically put the responsibility on other people and just expect positive things to happen to us without doing anything to make them happen. We also set small goals or have no goals or purpose in life because we live meaninglessly and without responsibility.

d) The weak way

Here we have low standards and low expectations. We become victims, constantly putting off what we know is useful to do. We have absolutely no meaning in life and therefore expect nothing from life and ourselves. So, we take no action and no responsibility. It's a state of self-pity.

Have you ever asked yourself which of the above stages you are in? If not, ask yourself now. The attitude we develop towards our expectations and standards can lead us to great success in life, or failure and misery. As far as our relationship with our life partner is concerned, all we need to do is ask ourselves if we accept not to be on the first, healthy, and mature path, and choose one of the other three.

In this model, we have noted that what we want and don't want, along with our needs and principles, can help us define the purpose of our existence, which consists of our life purpose, relationship purpose, legacy, and vision. It is significant that we define these together with our life partner and based on our truth.

When we find our purpose, we can then set appropriate goals, the success of which is largely determined by our relationship with our expectations and standards.

Time for introspection

- Have you and your partner been clear about what you want and don't want in your life and relationship?
- Have you and your partner been clear about your needs in life and relationship?
- Have you and your partner been clear about your principles in life and relationship?
- Do you know what your life purpose is?
- Do you know what the relationship purpose with your partner is?
- Do you know what is the legacy you want to leave to the world?
- Do you know what your vision for the future is?
- Do you set clear goals that reflect the purpose of your existence?
- If the answer to the above questions is "yes", ask yourself if you are sure about them.
- If the answer to the above questions is "no", ask yourself why and find out what you need to do to clarify the above.
- Do you have high or low expectations in your life and relationship with your partner?
- Do you have high or low standards in your life and relationship with your partner?

1.5 — The Reactive Unaware Self Model

We call this model the "Reactive Unaware Self Model" and it helps us to understand the main negative ways in which we operate so that we can control them and avoid damaging the relationship with our partner. It also helps us to better understand some of the elements we have already developed. It has much in common with the Limited Unaware Self of the first model.

This model has to do with our survival and protection and is driven by the selfish, manipulative, and possessive part of us. This part of us is insecure and driven by fear and anxiety and therefore causes us more fear, anxiety, and insecurity. It constantly tries to protect itself from other people and situations and always seeks to get what it wants from other people. The result is the creation of meaningless, superficial, and problematic relationships or the destruction of our relationships. So, let's look at the elements.

The Reactive Unaware Self Model

The selfish, manipulative, and possessive part of us

1) Our Fundamental and Inferior Needs

2) Our Limiting Beliefs

3) The inner immature child

4) Our Fears

↓

Emotional and Immature Reactions

- Defensive

- Aggressive

↓

The purpose of these reactions is our survival and protection

↓

The solution

- Our Unlimited Aware Self

- Our Balanced Aware Self

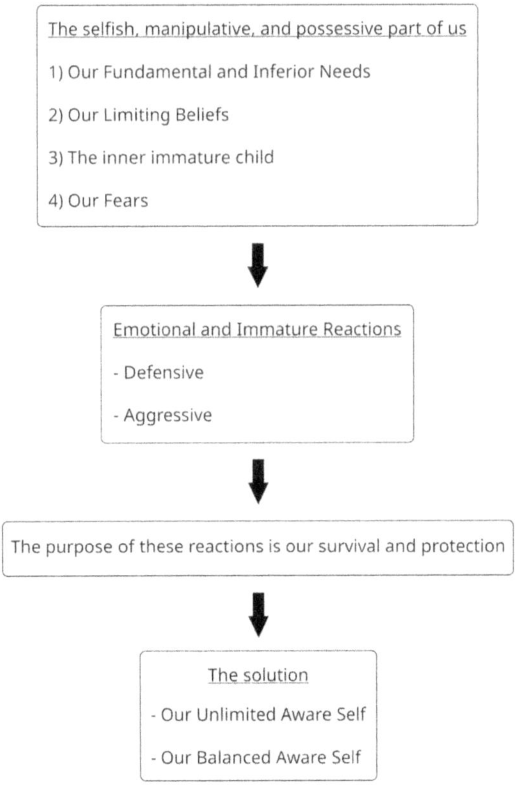

1. Our Fundamental and Inferior Needs

As we can see in the model above, the first element of the selfish, manipulative, and possessive part of ourselves is our fundamental and inferior needs. As we explained in the previous model, we all have some needs that motivate us. If we do not get the very basic needs of food, water, and shelter, you can understand that it is reasonable to act in negative, even violent ways towards other people to survive. This is because our lives literally depend on food, water, and shelter. So, if we don't have enough of these, we can be driven to extreme behavior. At this level, we function more materially than spiritually. We operate on animal instincts of survival and maintenance rather than instincts of progress and evolution.

In addition to the needs for food, water, and shelter, there are more survival needs. These are the needs for acceptance and socialization. Some people may think that these are higher-level needs, but they are not.

Human beings are, by their very nature, creatures who conduct all of their actions through the lens of interpersonal relationships. We all seek connection with other people because we are not here to live in isolation. Humanity has evolved and continues to evolve because people work together for a better future. Parents work to provide for their children, couples are together to progress and improve, and friends maintain relationships to have fun and support each other. Whatever we do, we do it not just for ourselves, but for someone else too.

And you might ask, what's wrong with that? Of course, there is nothing wrong with that. The problem arises when the connection we seek in others does not come from who we are and what we value the most but from inferior needs for acceptance. These needs lead us to choose to connect with others only because we fear rejection and loneliness. These needs are selfish because we want to build relationships to fill the emptiness and insecurity within ourselves. The motivation here is purely about meeting needs, not about love, progress, or meaningful connection. This is why you see people who have many friends but are empty inside. Their relationships are about covering up insecurities. So, these friendships can be lost at the slightest opportunity if they no longer satisfy these selfish needs.

Another example is that some couples are together to feel that someone accepts them. So, they have relationships with anyone, fall in love fleetingly and superficially, and fight over the smallest things. They take it out on each other when they face the slightest difficulty and end up not being able to manage anything in the relationship because of ignorance. They either compromise or break up. If they compromise, they end up living different lives, having different friends, different interests, different values, different purposes, and different goals, just staying in the same house. If they break up, they will find another partner and break up again, and so on. This happens because the purpose of the relationship is not love. These people are in relationships to satisfy the need for acceptance because of insecurity and immaturity, and so the romantic relationship becomes a simple relationship like any other, except that in this case there is also sexual intercourse.

Someone who is mature and secure in who they are never has to satisfy needs for acceptance and insecurity. That is because they know very well who they are and what they want, and are motivated in their relationship with their life partner by love and progress. What they are looking for in the relationship is not acceptance but fulfillment and then Togetherness-Fulfillment, which we will explain in detail in the last chapter. So, the problem is not socialization and acceptance, but the reason we are motivated to socialize and experience acceptance. Do we do it out of insecurity, or do we do it because we are completely sure of our truth and want to progress with other people?

You see if we are motivated by the need for acceptance out of insecurity, we will never be able to create a balanced, healthy, and fulfilling relationship with our partner. Instead, if we are motivated by love and truth, we will be able to unite with our partner on every level of our existence. Ask yourself if the relationships you have (romantic, friendship, family, etc.) are driven by insecurity or by meaningful connection.

2. Our Limiting Beliefs

In addition to the fundamental needs and the needs arising from insecurity and ignorance, as we said in the Unlimited Aware Self Model, we have various limiting beliefs which are the second element of the selfish, manipulative, and possessive part of ourselves.

One limiting belief might be that men are superior and women are inferior. Another is that we should always be with a romantic partner, even if there is no love because that is what society has taught us. Another is that our way of thinking is the only correct way of thinking and perceiving things. You see, these beliefs will damage the relationship. Obviously, sexism doesn't need to be analyzed. A relationship in which one partner is sexist is unhealthy and cannot flourish. A relationship in which the partners have no idea why they are together cannot easily progress and have meaning. A relationship in which one partner believes that they are right in every situation will lead to endless conflict and cannot grow.

So, our limiting beliefs are a giant obstacle to creating a meaningful, lasting, and loving romantic relationship.

What are your limiting beliefs that create tension in your daily life and relationship with your partner, and which would be beneficial to change immediately? What can you do to change these limiting beliefs? Which helpful beliefs and principles (Existential Aware Self Model, see p. 61) can you adopt to help you form better behaviors and habits?

3. The inner immature child

The third element of the selfish, manipulative, and possessive part of ourselves is the immature child within us. As children, we had needs for acceptance and validation that were not fully met. This was because our parents were imperfect people who were simply doing the best they could, and as immature children, this was not enough for us. Children's minds have a limited understanding of maturity issues because they are still in the process of learning the basic elements of life. So, if a child does not get what it wants or needs, it will cry, shout, get angry, etc. These are unconscious ways of manipulating and drawing attention to themselves to get what they want.

The immature child continues to exist within us and because of ignorance of ourselves, it automatically comes out when we are adults, and we don't get what we want. So, in a couple, if one partner wants to go on holiday to a certain place and the other partner doesn't, if the first partner is not a mature adult, they are likely to react immaturely and emotionally, get angry, and shout, bringing out the immature child in them. That is, they will react to their partner the way they reacted to their parents when they were a child and didn't get what they wanted.

Unfortunately, some couples operate mostly on the emotional level of the immature child. They are physically adults but mentally little children, demanding attention and not taking "no" for an answer. It is important to understand that no relationship can be healthy if one or both partners think and behave like immature children. This issue will be discussed further in the next chapter, which looks at the main negative behaviors between a couple.

Ask yourself when and how often you act manipulative and possessively like an immature child in your relationship with your life partner.

4. Our Fears

The fourth and final element of the selfish, manipulative, and possessive part of ourselves is our fears. Fear is linked to both our inferior needs and insecurities, our limiting beliefs, and our immature and childish side. It is not only an emotion but also a defense and survival mechanism. Fear warns us about fire, flood, automobile horns as we cross the road, and falling from a certain height, which can damage or kill us. It is a way of preventing us from risking our lives and protecting us from hardship and difficulties. This fear is a survival mechanism, dating back to the times when humans had to face very extreme situations, such as extreme weather events or even becoming food for predators. These fears are still with us today.

In modern life, the situations we face are rarely dangerous, or at least not as dangerous as they used to be. So, we often automatically fear situations, either imaginary or real, that are not dangerous at all, and they cause us to focus on our fear and increase it. For example, we may become fearful and anxious about asking someone we like out on a date, speaking in front of a large audience, asking for a raise at work, going to a job interview, expressing ourselves authentically and speaking our mind or about what someone else might think of us.

All of this may sound ridiculous, but unfortunately, the selfish part of ourselves sees it as a danger and creates difficulties in some people's lives. This happens because this part of ourselves is set up to protect us, and so it wants to "protect" us from these theoretical dangers and other people. For example, if our partner says something we don't agree with, a fight may arise over the disagreement. Then the selfish part of us comes forward to protect and defend us. This can lead to even more conflict. Therefore, it is important to consciously take control of ourselves and understand what real dangers are, such as a fire, earthquake, etc., and what is not, such as a disagreement with our partner or another person's thoughts and opinions. In this way, when tensions arise, we will know how we and our partner operate, and we will be able to control ourselves or help our partner more easily.

5. Emotional and Immature Reactions

We can see that some of the above elements of the selfish part of ourselves, or the combination of all of them, can cause issues in our relationship. This is because our needs, beliefs, and fears are deeply ingrained in us and automatically explode.

So, we react emotionally and immaturely to various stimuli, to our partner's words, to the body language we see, or because some lower needs of acceptance have not been met, or because of our imagination and what is happening exclusively in our mind.

The automatic response can be either defensive or aggressive. But both responses are essentially defensive. When we react defensively, we may say: "But it's not my fault", "how can you talk to me like that?", "I behave better than you", "don't blame me", "but what have I done?", "I can't see what the problem is", and so on. If we react aggressively, we may say: "It's your fault", "you're useless", "you're not doing enough", "you're not good enough", "do as I say", etc.

All these reactions are immature and without thought or awareness (see p. 50 about immature reactions in the Balanced Aware Self Model). Often these reactions are also revengeful, even if we don't realize it. We react automatically to get back at something our partner (or even another person) has done in the past, and we want to let out whatever has been held inside us. This is one of the main issues we see many couples face in their relationship. In fact, depending on the level of immaturity and total lack of self-control, even physical violence can be triggered, and this is serious.

Unfortunately, our mind identifies and focuses much more easily on the negative elements or what it perceives to be negative, which is why we typically argue with our partner easily and quickly. We can only improve these reactions when we become aware that we are behaving this way, why we are reacting this way, and decide and commit not to act based on the selfish part of ourselves again.

The solution is to cultivate and develop balanced and mature responses, as mentioned in the Balanced Aware Self Model, and to always be aware and in control of everything we do. This means that we need to train our minds to focus on the positive and be grateful until gratitude becomes a habit. We can do this by practicing the Unlimited Aware Self Model and the Balanced Aware Self Model.

We have noted that our selfish, manipulative, and possessive part expresses itself effortlessly and automatically because it is ingrained in us and is designed for our survival and protection. Often, however, it does not serve us but harms us because it is based on false things and misconceptions, causing difficulties in our relationship with our partner. So, it is crucial to work carefully and intensely on all the elements of our Reactive Unaware Self and understand and accept them as an integral part of our being. Then we will be able to manage them healthily and not create unnecessary tensions in our life and romantic relationship.

Time for introspection

- How often do you operate with your Reactive Unaware Self?
- How do you behave when your Reactive Unaware Self takes control? What does your partner do when they see you behaving this way? Do they react immaturely, or do they help you?
- How does your partner behave when their Reactive Unaware Self takes control? What do you do when you see your partner behaving this way? Do you react immaturely, or do you help them?
- How often are you negatively affected by your fundamental needs?
- How often are you negatively impacted by your limiting beliefs?
- How often are you negatively influenced by the immature child inside you?
- How often are you negatively impacted by your fears and insecurity?
- How often do you behave defensively towards your partner?
- How often do you behave aggressively to your partner?
- Can you quickly come back to behaving based on your Unlimited Aware Self when your Reactive Unaware Self takes control?
- What will you do to stop operating with your Reactive Unaware Self?

1.6 — The Feminine and Masculine Aware Self Model

The next model is what we call the "Feminine and Masculine Aware Self Model". It helps us to understand the dynamics of the feminine and masculine elements in a couple. The feminine and masculine elements are the driving forces in the relationship. The dynamics are how the feminine and masculine elements in each partner smoothly connect or clash. So, let's discuss more about them.

People usually have problems in their relationship when they think they don't understand their partner. So, they either fight with each other or end up compromising and have a superficial relationship with no deep connection. Many also talk about the secrets to understanding women and men. But the truth is that both men and women operate in exactly the same way. That is, we all operate in all the ways that we have discussed so far in this chapter, regardless of our gender or sexual preference. Of course, there are biological and hormonal differences between men and women, which to some extent affect our mental and emotional nature, and so we are a little different. But spiritually, in terms of our qualities and positive states of being we can embody, we all function in the same way. So, there are no secrets to understanding men or women. What we need to understand very well are the feminine and masculine elements that we all have within us, without exception.

All human beings, whether we are men or women, have both feminine and masculine elements. A man has feminine elements in addition to masculine elements, and a woman has masculine elements in addition to feminine elements. The difference between all of us is the degree to which we have these elements and how and how much we express them. If we understand and accept this, it will be the key to the success of our relationship with our life partner.

The feminine and masculine elements can be:
- qualities
- emotions
- behaviors

We have divided these elements into feminine and masculine based on how we understand them, and how they are expressed in our own relationship. We also considered our observations of other people and their dynamics. So, it doesn't mean that everything is exactly as we present it, and of course, we have no intention of reinforcing any kind of stereotype. Clearly, we do this to better understand what goes on in relationships and to dispel various stereotypes that do enormous damage to the lives of many couples. Let's see what the most important feminine and masculine elements are:

FEMININE ELEMENTS	MASCULINE ELEMENTS
Tranquility	Power
Peace	Anger
Caresses, hugs	Imposing
Kindness	Dominance, Arrogance
Laughter	Tension
Joy	Seriousness
Fear	Courage
Grief	Solving problems
Victim	Hero
Shame	Dynamism
Crying	Fighting Spirit
Excitement	Maturity
Sentimentalism	Responsibility
Insecurity	Security
Manipulation	Assurance
Warmth	Stability
Creativity	Inventiveness
Passivity	Energetic
Existence (Being)	Act (Doing)

These two lists can, of course, include many more elements, but we use the very basic ones here. You can add other feminine and masculine elements that you see in yourself and your partner. Note that some elements could be on the other side of the list, depending on someone's interpretation. We also need to remember that all the elements on each list can have both positive and negative connotations, depending on how we express them and how we use them. Some tend more towards the positive and others towards the negative, and we suggest that you explore them in depth. From these lists, you can see that a man does not only have the elements from the masculine list and a woman does not only have the elements from the feminine list. We all have a mixture of all these elements, expressed in different proportions and uniquely.

So, male readers can say, if they wish, that they never laugh, they never smile, they never get happy, they never get scared, they never get excited, or they never get embarrassed. They can also say that they don't want peace and quiet in life, or that they've never been manipulative. In the same way, women can say that they don't get angry, that they don't feel brave, or that they aren't mature and stable at all. Anyone who denies that they have both masculine and feminine elements is either insecure, a hypocrite, or simply ignorant of themselves.

In fact, many men are afraid (feminine element) to admit that they have feelings, that they cry, or that they want to be hugged, lest their masculinity be compromised. This is clear insecurity, which is a feminine element. So, we see that even if we don't want to express the elements that are opposite to our gender, they will still come out in some way because they are just an integral part of who we are, how we tend to be, and how we experience the world.

On the other hand, it is common for men to be more masculine and women to be more feminine. But there are men who are more feminine and women who are more masculine, and that is normal. Meaning, a man may be very calm or enthusiastic and a woman may be very dynamic and imposing. For example, a homosexual person may have more elements of the opposite sex, and this may seem strange to other people who are driven to racist and homophobic attitudes, again because of ignorance or limiting beliefs (fear of what they don't understand). But same-sex attraction is natural because we are attracted to a person's essence, who they are. We are also attracted to the richness of the dynamics between the feminine and masculine elements of the other person and how they combine with our own.

Therefore, in essence, there are not many substantial differences between men and women, only a few, and for a man and a woman to understand the opposite sex better, two things are necessary:

1 — To understand all the Self-Awareness Cultivating Models in Chapter One because the elements of these models exist in all people without exception. This requires a great deal of inner exploration and work on oneself.

2 — To understand that they have both feminine and masculine elements within them, just in different proportions. This is what makes us all unique. The balance of our feminine and masculine elements is the key to developing our relationship with our partner, whether they are of the opposite or the same sex.

How can the feminine and masculine elements be expressed in a relationship?

1. Both partners are expressing only masculine elements at the same time

This way, they are more likely to be either very energetic and productive (positive combination of common masculine elements) or to clash and argue (negative combination of common masculine elements).

2. Both partners are expressing only feminine elements at the same time

This way, they can be either balanced and peaceful (positive combination of common feminine elements) or bored and passive (negative combination of common feminine elements).

3. One partner is expressing masculine elements and the other feminine elements

This way, they can either find a balance between them or help each other to be in a state of peace (e.g., if they are in a state of anger) and prevent conflict. Both of which lead only to positive results.

So, we should be very careful how we combine these elements, as they will either greatly help or harm our relationship.

Now you can understand yourself and your partner even better and discover many reasons you may be in conflict. Most importantly, you can accept and embrace both your feminine and masculine elements and be harmonizing with all these. This way, you will be able to accept and embrace every aspect of your life partner and love them for who they really are. Accept your differences and use your feminine and masculine elements with freedom, without shame, and for the benefit of your relationship.

The dynamics of the feminine and masculine elements do not end here, and there are other ways in which we can unite with our life partner. In the final chapter on Togetherness-Fulfillment, we explore this topic in more detail.

Time for introspection

- What feminine elements do you notice in yourself?
- What masculine elements do you notice in yourself?
- What feminine elements do you notice in your partner?
- What masculine elements do you notice in your partner?
- Are you ashamed of your feminine and masculine elements, or are you comfortable with them? Do you accept or reject them? If you reject them, why do you do so?
- Are you ashamed of your partner's feminine and masculine elements, or are you comfortable with them? Do you accept or reject them? If you reject them, why do you do so?
- How are the feminine and masculine elements in you and your partner related? Are they in balance or do they clash? If they are in balance, what do you do to achieve this balance? If they are in conflict, why is that? What do you need to do to prevent them from clashing?

1.7 — The Sexual Aware Self Model

We call this model the "Sexual Aware Self Model" and it helps us to understand how healthy the sexual relationship we have with our partner is, which depends very much on how meaningful our relationship with ourselves is.

Sexuality is a part of ourselves. It is closely linked to human society and culture as well as to procreation and the continuation of the human species. There are many views on sexuality, but what we need to understand is the two main ways in which it can be expressed. For us, sexuality can be a lower or a higher expression of ourselves.

We are therefore made up of the Lower Sexual Self and the Higher Sexual Self.

The Lower Sexual Self has the following elements:

a) We are mainly guided by infatuation and not by love (the differences between infatuation and love will be discussed in the last chapter).

b) We demand frequent sexual intercourse from our partner because this is the main or only reason for our relationship. We seek quantity of intercourse, not quality.

c) We are not meaningfully connected in our sexual and love life. We only want physical intercourse and do not know what it is like to be spiritually united with our partner. We seek only our own physical satisfaction.

d) Our partner is no longer sexually attractive to us, and sex becomes a "must".

e) We think sexually about other people or even desire other people sexually.

f) We think about cheating on our partner.

The lowest form in which the Lower Sexual Self is expressed is to cheat on one's partner or to separate and divorce.

The Higher Sexual Self has the following elements:

a) We are guided by true love and at the same time we continue to be in love.

b) We do not demand anything from our partner because we love them. Sex is not just a physical need for us, but a physical and spiritual way of uniting with our partner.

c) We unite completely with our partner. We are not motivated by temporary physical pleasure, but by pure unity, which ultimately gives us much more pleasure.

d) Our partner is sexually attracted to us, and we do not judge intercourse by frequency but by quality. Similarly, we do not judge our relationship by sex, but by all the ways we and our partner operate, behave, connect, and unite. Sex is an honest "want" for both partners.

e) We do not desire another person sexually. But if we think about another person sexually because we can't always control what thoughts come into our minds, we simply ignore them and are completely honest with our partner, who understands us.

f) We want to live together with our partner every moment of our life, and we even know that we will live together all our life. Our partner is our number one priority, and we experience Togetherness-Fulfillment.

The highest form in which the Higher Sexual Self is expressed is to feel, know, and experience life as one spirit, one mind, one soul, and one body, as a couple. This is the highest level we can reach with our life partner, and we discuss it in the final chapter about Togetherness-Fulfillment.

As we can see, sexual instincts are often inferior needs for the purpose of temporary pleasure. So, it is not the end of the world to sometimes have sexual thoughts about other people. They may simply be triggered by a stimulus or a memory. We know that we have no control over this (see p. 46 Balanced Aware Self Model), but we do have control over whether we focus on and nurture these thoughts. Thus, we must be conscious of why we thought them and decide if they are just fleeting notions or needs from a troubled and unfulfilling relationship with our partner.

Our thoughts, desires, needs, and values in relation to our sexuality can show us the truth of whether we are operating with our Lower or Higher Sexual Self. In this way, we can understand if we truly love our partner or if we are in a relationship of compromise, operating within our Lower Sexual Self. By understanding and accepting our sexuality and our lower instincts, we can grow and rise to its higher nature, which is the ultimate unity with our life partner. Only then can we experience fulfillment as a couple.

When you reach levels of fulfillment with your partner and are not motivated by the transient physical orgasm, you will experience a spiritual orgasm, which naturally leads to an even greater physical orgasm. This is because you are not having sex just to feel "good" and to satisfy an animalistic physical need, but to connect and bond even more with each other. So, the pleasure is even greater and more real because you are not only physically naked but spiritually naked as well. You are showing each other your absolute truth, and indeed you are experiencing your truth together. You are united on every level and with a true awareness of who you are and what you want from your life and relationship.

Reflect on the following questions to see if your partner is the person with whom you will be completely spiritually naked, expressing your absolute truth, or just one of the many sexual partners with whom you compromise.

Time for introspection

- Do you operate with your Lower or your Higher Sexual Self?
- What is the reason for the sexual relationship with your partner?
- What is sex for you?
- Are you and your partner united spiritually or do you have sexual intercourse only to satisfy each other or worse just one of you to be satisfied by the other one or simply to satisfy yourself alone?
- Do you sexually desire only your partner, or other people too?
- Are you aware of your sexual thoughts? Do you think about other people sexually? If so, why do you do it? Do you focus on these thoughts? If so, why?
- Is your partner the only person you want to be with sexually? If yes, how can you connect in a more meaningful way? If not, why is that?
- What discussion do you need to have with your partner about sex and your sexual relationship?
- What will you do to strengthen the sexual relationship with your partner?

1.8 — The Fulfilled Reflecting Self Model

This is the last model in this chapter, and we call it the Fulfilled Reflecting Self Model. This model helps us understand one of the most important ways in which we can come closer and unite with our life partner. It is the model of the couple's unity.

Through all the Self-Awareness Cultivating Models you have learned a lot about yourself, but also about your partner. All the previous models are mainly about understanding how each of us works individually. So, you can understand very well how you operate individually, but also how your partner operates individually, and find ways in which you can connect and unite together. The Fulfilled Reflecting Self Model explores, even more, the unity of a couple and the ways we operate.

The Fulfilled Reflecting Self Model

Partner A		Partner B
Unlimited Aware Self ➡	Fulfilled Reflecting Self	⬅ Unlimited Aware Self
Balanced Aware Self ➡		⬅ Balanced Aware Self
Evolved Aware Self ➡	True Unconditional Love	⬅ Evolved Aware Self
Existential Aware Self ➡	Total Unity	⬅ Existential Aware Self
Reactive Unaware Self ➡	Togetherness-Fulfillment	⬅ Reactive Unaware Self
Feminine/Masculine Aware Self ➡		⬅ Feminine/Masculine Aware Self
Sexual Aware Self ➡		⬅ Sexual Aware Self

Who is the Fulfilled Reflecting Self?

As we can see in the model above, it is a combination of all the previous models and is about the connection to our life partner.

But who is our Fulfilled Reflecting Self? The Fulfilled Reflecting Self is a term we have coined because there is no equivalent term that adequately covers and describes the human being with whom we can fully unite.

The definition of the Fulfilled Reflecting Self that we have given is:

The Fulfilled Reflecting Self is our one and only life partner with whom we unite as one on every level (spiritual, mental, psychological/emotional, and physical/sexual), where in our relationship we are both individually fulfilled and free from inferior needs and become each other's reflection.

The Fulfilled Reflecting Self is not just any sexual and romantic partner. It is the person who is meant to be with us for the rest of our life. They are the sexual romantic partner with whom we experience every aspect of life together. The person with whom we are now one and the same.

They are truly a reflection of ourselves.

They are the reflection of the same values, "wants" and purpose of existence as we are for them; they are the reflection of the same and opposite elements of our Feminine and Masculine Aware Self as we are the reflection of theirs; they are the reflection of all the ways in which we operate, and we are the reflection of all the ways in which they operate. Through this reflection, we can better understand both ourselves and our life partner and correct our mistakes faster. It is the person with whom we are individually fulfilled, and together we reach even higher levels of unity and Togetherness-Fulfillment (to be discussed in the final chapter).

We know that for some people, the idea of the Fulfilled Reflecting Self sounds crazy and alien. This is because, unfortunately, those people have very superficial experiences when it comes to romantic relationships and marriage. People can be in a relationship or marriage because of various reasons: society or their family told them to, they were needy and insecure, for financial gain, an infatuation that ended in compromise, or for some other superficial reason. So, they have never experienced unity and true love with their partner to know what it means to be united with their partner and to love each other.

In fact, some people are in a marriage for many years without having the slightest idea why they are married and have children, so they live like two strangers in the same house. Such limiting beliefs and experiences have led people to believe that it is impossible to have an unshakable relationship of unconditional love where both partners literally become one spirit, one mind, one soul, and one body. Unfortunately, all they know is to settle for a relationship or marriage because they simply want to have someone with them out of weakness and fear of being alone and responsible for themselves.

In short, some people have learned that relationships and marriage are a way of validating their worth. Others have learned that relationships and marriage are situations in which they can express their possessiveness and feel good about themselves because they think they own their partner, and then they own the children they will have. Others have learned that relationships and marriage are the rules they must follow because society has taught them that they must marry, have children, work hard, and live to please other people. Others, unfortunately, have learned that marriage is a problem as well as a "must". The standards of marriage they saw from their parents were not healthy. These people's parents had a dead marriage of compromise. So, as children, they learned that marriage is a compromise full of issues and conflict, and as a result, they built a similar dead marriage for themselves.

However, the romantic relationship and marriage have absolutely nothing to do with all the limiting beliefs above. There is a great deal of essence to your romantic relationship and marriage, and you can experience it as we experience it. You can live a meaningful, beautiful, and progressive life with your partner specifically your Fulfilled Reflecting Self. We suggest that you stop perceiving your relationship with your partner in a limiting way and see it as a pathway to progress with unlimited possibilities, if, of course, you don't already.

In essence, then, our Fulfilled Reflecting Self is:

The person with whom we will unite after a lot of individual work as well as couple work; it is the person with whom we feel that special attraction and intense love from the very beginning. But the connection does not end with this attraction. It needs constant work and improvement. It is the person to whom we want to devote and will devote all our time and essence; it is the person with whom we will be completely spiritually naked, as we said in the previous model; it is the person with whom we share the same values and purpose of existence; it is the person who is always the number one priority in our life; it is the person with whom we have experienced true love and have gone through many challenges, difficulties, and hardships and yet, regardless of them, we have continued to be together out of love and conscious choice; it is the person with whom we have wonderful times together, even when we just look at each other without doing anything else; it is the person with whom we not only don't get bored but want to spend even more time together.

This unity with our Fulfilled Reflecting Self feels like magic, but it is realism and something you can experience if you have not already. It is difficult as it requires courage, dedication, commitment, maturity, strength, and constant evolution with complete spiritual nakedness. A relationship with our Fulfilled Reflecting Self is something that we can all create and experience, but few people achieve. This is because few people are determined within themselves to live a peaceful life of true love, as this requires tremendous inner and couple work. Being in a relationship with our Fulfilled Reflecting Self requires us to constantly admit our mistakes, correct and change our bad habits, change our limiting beliefs, and be completely spiritually naked in front of our partner, to whom we are open books with absolutely no secrets or lies. We accept our life partner with all their faults and weaknesses and embrace and love their diversity. Together with our Fulfilled Reflecting Self, we become better and more aware people every day.

The relationship with the Fulfilled Reflecting Self is the path of truth, and the truth is difficult and painful for some people, which is why only a few couples experience such a high-level relationship or marriage. All of this is priceless and cannot be properly described in words, for it is truly a miracle of life that we can experience only with one person.

Uniting the individual work on the Self-Awareness Cultivating Models

Now that you understand who the Fulfilled Reflecting Self is, you can more easily understand your connection and unity with them. All the models of this chapter are combined to create the Fulfilled Reflecting Self Model. If each partner works a lot on all these models, they will be able to clearly understand themselves. They will know their positive elements and their flaws. They will know the positive and negative ways in which they operate, and thus learn to behave in a much more mature and conscious way. By applying all this daily, each partner will gradually become a much more responsible and stronger person and will even be able to understand their partner in depth. Since they develop their self-awareness and can recognize their own positive and negative elements, they can identify these in their partner too, and thus appreciate them more and respect their uniqueness.

So, knowing all this, and after all this inner work, partners can develop their relationship to a high level. They now escape from their low survival and acceptance needs, they are not influenced by their limiting beliefs, nor guided by insecurity or fleeting emotions, and operate from their qualities and positive states of being they can embody, their values, their "non-negotiable nos" and their Higher Sexual Self. They know the purpose of their relationship and marriage, which is progress and love (Togetherness-Fulfillment), and operate on that basis.

As you work hard on yourself and your relationship, you will, for the first time, experience a deep unity, and the more you are united, the more you will be free from lower needs, and motivated by your love.

You can now identify and remove your limiting beliefs, understand your survival instincts, and no longer reinforce them but control them healthily. You can also have a clear picture of who you are and what you want in life. With all these models given to you, you can make tremendous changes in your life and relationship together.

As you can see in the model (see p. 83), the work that you do individually on all these models and the work that your Fulfilled Reflecting Self does on the same models unite, and so you unite as a couple. As each of you develops your self-awareness individually, you can develop the awareness that you have of your life partner, your Fulfilled Reflecting Self. If you are the light and inspiration for each other, then together, as one, you can become the light and inspiration for others.

Of course, the idea of the Fulfilled Reflecting Self will be better understood if you write down the answers to the questions we ask in each section of the book and discuss them in depth with your partner. Doing the practical exercises in Volume Two will also be necessary. That's because the idea of the Fulfilled Reflecting Self is not something theoretical, but something completely practical that we experience every day.

So, this is the Fulfilled Reflecting Self Model and the unity of the two partners after individual work on self-awareness. The Feminine and Masculine Aware Self Model, Sexual Aware Self Model, and Fulfilled Reflecting Self Model give you a glimpse of Togetherness-Fulfillment, which we shall discuss in the last chapter. But throughout the rest of the book, you will be able to get an even clearer and more complete picture of the Fulfilled Reflecting Self.

Time for introspection

- Are you in a relationship with your Fulfilled Reflecting Self or with a random romantic partner? If you are in a relationship with a random romantic partner, why are you? What is the meaning of this relationship if it is not a relationship with your Fulfilled Reflecting Self?
- If you are in a relationship with your Fulfilled Reflecting Self, how can you be sure that this person is your Fulfilled Reflecting Self?
- Can you clearly write down on a piece of paper all the ways in which you connect with your Fulfilled Reflecting Self? How do you experience this unity in your daily life?
- What do you need to do daily to further unite with your Fulfilled Reflecting Self? What positive elements do you have to

develop? How are you going to develop these? What negative elements do you need to improve? How are you going to improve these?

1.9 — Summary

Now that we have explored all the models in this chapter, you can understand very well how and why you think, feel, behave, act, and operate the way you do. You can reflect and work on all these aspects of yourself to develop your self-awareness, and then be able to fully understand your partner so that you can unite and experience true love and Togetherness-Fulfillment.

The self is therefore the set of ways in which we operate (positively or negatively) as human beings and includes all the elements we have explained in each of the models in this chapter. In short, the self is our very existence. But do not confuse self with who we really are. Who we are (our qualities and positive states of being we can embody) is only a part of the self and one of the most important and qualitative ways in which we can function and live. It is our choice to operate based on these qualities and not based on every limiting element of ourselves.

So, let's look again at each of the elements of ourselves to understand them better. We classify them into totally positive and helping elements, totally negative and limiting elements, and elements that can be either positive or negative depending on our level of understanding and awareness.

TOTALLY POSITIVE ELEMENTS	TOTALLY NEGATIVE ELEMENTS	EITHER POSITIVE OR NEGATIVE ELEMENTS
Who we are (qualities and positive states of being we can embody)	False perception of who we are i.e. what we do and our roles	Limiting characteristics
Helpful beliefs	Limiting beliefs	Mental level
Values	Self-doubt	Emotional level
"Non-negotiable nos"	Self-sabotage	Choice of focus

Spiritual level	Self-destruction	Boundaries
Balance	Self-loathing	Attitude
Honesty	Expectations	Logic
Constructive self-evaluation	Inner immature child	Intuition
Balanced self-admiration	Fears	Behaviors
Self-awareness	Insecurity (needing/ seeking acceptance and validation)	Acts
Self-discipline	Defense	Self-worth
Self-control	Attack	Self-confidence
Balanced and mature reactions	Automatic and immature reactions	Self-esteem
Self-acceptance	Lower Sexual Self	What we want and what we don't want
Self-love		Needs
Principles		Goals
Purpose of our existence		Priorities
Standards		Feminine elements
Higher Sexual Self		Masculine elements

So, these are the main ways in which we operate as human beings. Of course, there are more ways, but we have explored what we believe is crucial to the development of our self-awareness and of the relationship with our Fulfilled Reflecting Self. In Volume Two we mention some other ways too.

But why each of the three lists above contains the elements it does, we will not go into, leaving it for you to reflect on. Ask yourself why some elements are beneficial, some are harmful, and some can be either beneficial or harmful depending on how we use them.

We challenge you once again to work a lot on all these concepts before moving on to the next chapter. Everything we discuss in this book is very much about our own perspective as a couple, and it is important that you find your own questions and answers about all these matters. There is not always one "right" answer to a question, especially when it comes to human existence. Therefore, the inner search and discovery of the truth about ourselves is something that we need to do on our own and with our life partner, using various tools and knowledge that we acquire throughout our lives. Let us keep our horizons open so that we can evolve even more as we acquire and apply new knowledge.

Use consciously what you have learned so far and to your advantage to improve yourself, your life, and your relationship. Own yourself and cultivate total control over your actions and behaviors.

In the next chapter, we look at the key negative behaviors that some couples exhibit, which once you recognize and accept, you will be able to correct and not repeat them using what you have learned in Chapter One.

2

Common negative behaviors and situations
in a couple

This chapter discusses the very basic negative behaviors between a couple and the negative situations we can get into in our life and relationship. It will challenge you in many ways and help you to recognize many of the errors and flaws in your behavior and to begin to act in a more mature and conscious way. You will see even more how elements of your Limited Unaware Self, Reactive Unaware Self, and Lower Sexual Self are expressed, and discover how to stop acting in such negative ways.

We, as a couple, have experienced all the behaviors we analyze in this chapter more or less, too often or even with tragic intensity in our relationship, and some of them are still present today. We say this as it is natural for these behaviors to happen because of our imperfect nature and because no matter how much we work on ourselves and our relationship, we will still need more individual and couple work. So don't panic and assume that there is no hope for your relationship. If there is true love, everything will be resolved.

By looking at the behaviors in our relationship, we can understand ourselves and our partner even better. To be clear, when we talk about your relationship with your partner, we are talking about your relationship with your Fulfilled Reflecting Self, the person you love and know you want to spend your whole life with. We are talking about the person who, even if you are not sure about your relationship yet, because you just started this relationship (which is reasonable), you want to try to make it work as it may be your lifelong relationship.

We are not talking about casual relationships with every single person you have sex with. We make this clear because, unfortunately, some couples we have met think that because they have sex with someone and spend some time having fun together, it is a serious relationship. So, any reference we make to a romantic relationship is only about the one in which we develop our awareness and love our partner. If we don't know ourselves that deeply yet, haven't developed the necessary self-control, and don't know the appropriate ways to behave, simply means that we just need to work together.

Furthermore, before we start analyzing behaviors, it is useful to say that problems in life have to do with health problems, serious financial problems, self-destructive tendencies, physical abuse, and all kinds of violence. Anything else that we face, such as a verbal conflict with our partner or a difference of opinion, is simply a difficulty or a challenge to help us improve. So, with this in mind, ask yourself how important and how big the "problems" are in your life and relationship. This perspective will help you not to exaggerate what you are experiencing and to see the truth about the size and severity of a situation and behavior; because often we tend to magnify whatever we are experiencing in our minds, resulting in us "torturing" ourselves over small things.

This is important to understand, as many of the "problems" we experience in life are related to another person. That is, we may have "problems" with family, "problems" with friends and colleagues, or "problems" with our life partner. Therefore, to avoid damaging our relationship with our partner and our other social relationships, it is crucial that we judge each situation based on the truth, not on what we believe to be true; to treat each situation with the seriousness it deserves and not to exaggerate or become the prey of other people, but to be in a state of maturity and balance.

One last thing, which is equally essential to have as a primary requirement in our relationship, is to treat our partner in the best way possible. That is, to treat them as we would like them to treat us, but also based on their uniqueness and healthy "wants". Respect their diversity and don't do things that we would not want our partner to do to us. This means being the pure, authentic, and honest reflection of each other (see pp. 83-84 Fulfilled Reflecting Self Model). For example, if we feel like yelling at our partner, speaking badly, or behaving in any other negative way, let's think very seriously about the following:

1 - If my partner treated me like this, would I like it?
2 - Would I treat a stranger or someone who is not closely related to me in the same negative way as my partner?
3 - If I love my partner, why do I treat them like this?
4 - Do I take my partner for granted and as a person with whom I feel so familiar that I end up taking it out on them because I "can't" do it to others?

5 - Is there a better and more dignified way to behave towards my partner?

6 - Am I the one who should behave better?

7 - Does my negative behavior stem from defensive instincts and immaturity?

8 - Since my negative behavior is not in line with who I am (responsible, mature, strong, compassionate, etc.) then why do I choose to behave in this harmful way?

9 - I don't like my partner to treat me negatively, and I wouldn't dare treat people I know or strangers in an extreme way, so why should I do it to my partner, who is the most important person in my life?

10 - What do I need to change to improve each negative behavior?

These questions are very useful, but also necessary, to ask yourself every day. Also, as you read this chapter, for each behavior or situation we discuss, ask yourself if you are behaving in that way and then ask these ten questions. This way, you can confront yourself and recognize many of your mistakes. It is a method of introspection and taking responsibility. If both of you ask these questions and answer them honestly, you will be able to make big changes in the negative behaviors in your relationship.

2.1 — The relationship is not the number one priority

The main issue in a romantic relationship, and especially in a marriage, is not some negative behavior, but the fact that the relationship is not the number one priority in life. So, before you look at your negative behaviors, you need to clarify if and how you prioritize your relationship. If it is just another shallow social relationship for you, then don't expect to ever experience true love and fulfillment. This goes without saying, but unfortunately, many couples do not consider this because they have not clarified who they are, their values and priorities, and their life and relationship purpose. The relationship with our life partner is the most intimate and meaningful relationship we can have in life (we discuss this in detail in the final chapter). Our life partner is the person who will unite with us on every level, and the only person with whom we will create a life together, and eventually have children, out of pure love. We experience this miracle of life with only one person. A healthy relationship with this person is our number one priority.

Of course, we're not talking about unconscious choices. Many people have children with anyone for various reasons, such as unwanted pregnancies, one-night stands, etc. In this book, we are only talking about people who want to take their relationship further, to get to know themselves and their partner better, and to learn ways of overcoming various difficulties. Of course, some people who have made unconscious actions and mistakes in the past, such as having children with someone they met drunk one night in a bar, can become conscious and make healthier choices in the future. The past does not determine whether and how much we take control of our lives and whether and how much we grow spiritually today. What matters is what we choose to do now and how committed we are to our personal and couple development. We believe that you, our readers, are conscious people, and so we speak to you with the appropriate maturity and honesty, as well as the appropriate respect.

So, if our relationship with our partner is not the number one priority in our life, how can we expect to have a healthy and balanced loving relationship? For example, if our number one priority is our career, how can we expect our relationship to flourish if we only see our partner at weekends or late at night when we are exhausted? If having a good time and going out for drinks with superficial friends comes before our relationship with our partner, how can we expect to grow together instead of growing apart and stagnating? If we are not engaging in any activities with our partner and being productive and creative together, how do we expect to maintain healthy passion in the relationship? If we don't spend quality time with our partner and choose to sit on the couch and watch TV, how do we expect not to drive the relationship into a "dead" state of compromise?

Having children doesn't mean that your romantic relationship has to take a back seat

Even if you are in a marriage where you have children, if your relationship with your partner is not the number one priority, you will not be able to grow. Raising children is, if not the greatest responsibility, certainly one of the greatest responsibilities we can take on as human beings. Therefore, it is crucial that children be born out of true love and a conscious choice by the couple, not out of a "must" such as "we have to get married and have children because the years are passing by", nor out of an immature mistake or carelessness. This is important because if pure love is not the reason, it is likely that the children will be brought up superficially and inadequately.

Parents are crucial in setting a healthy example of love, mutual support, and unity for children. But if they don't put their relationship first, how can their children learn what love is? If parents don't stay in love, don't support each other, don't spend time together, and have a superficial relationship, how will children get a healthy and balanced picture of a romantic relationship? If partners set their relationship aside, they are also doing their children a disservice because they will learn that marriage is a superficial, unloving, and even problematic thing. The children will likely have a similar superficial marriage in the future and not experience true love in their lives.

It is also important that the parents do not downgrade their relationship when the children are born. While it is necessary to do the best they can for their children, if they "forget" each other as the children grow up, they are likely to become unhealthy role models for them.

So, by that, we don't mean to neglect their children, but being so close and loving as a couple that together they can be the best parents for their children and express both romantic and parental love in the best possible way.

In fact, if the parents have worsened their relationship over the years, they will have a "dead" relationship and feel like strangers when their children grow up, leave home, and start their own lives. This will cause a lot of frustration for the couple, and it's a sad thing to happen after so many years of marriage.

It is healthy to grow closer to your partner over the years rather than drift apart, as some married couples do.

This is why it is important to keep the relationship as the number one priority. That's when partners can give their children all the care and attention needed to become mature, strong, independent people when they grow up, and it's time to go off and have a life with their partner.

We can see how significant it is for the couple to put their relationship first, both for their own development and for the proper upbringing of their children, when they decide to take on such a big responsibility. This will become even clearer when we look at behaviors that are related to the past later in this chapter.

So, reflect on everything we have explored above to find out what the truth is for you. Work carefully and honestly with all the models from Chapter One, especially the Existential Aware Self Model, which aims to discover the purpose of our existence and therefore our relationship purpose. Find out individually, and then together with your partner, what your relationship purpose is, and determine its course together, without leaving it to its luck.

Being clear about our relationship purpose and making it a number one priority are two of the most important requirements for the success of a relationship, as we will see in more detail in the next chapter. If these conditions do not form a solid foundation of our relationship, then we will not be able to develop it further.

Time for introspection

- Is your romantic relationship the number one priority in your life? If so, why, and where does this benefit you? If not, why? Is your relationship with your partner a superficial or meaningful relationship?
- Do you put other people before yourself, your partner, and your relationship with each other? If so, why do you do this? Where does it benefit you?
- What do you need to do to make sure that your relationship with your partner is always the number one priority in your life?

- What do you need to do to make your relationship with your partner flourish?

2.2 — Criticism, blame, belittling, and ridicule

Now that we have laid a solid ground for reflection on the foundations of a relationship and its priorities, we can look at the main negative behaviors and situations we may experience in our relationship.

Let's start with negative criticism and blame

Have you ever judged your partner negatively? Have you ever blamed your partner? The answer to both questions is probably yes. Unfortunately, criticizing and blaming are two of the most common behaviors in relationships. We can often criticize our partner constructively to help them improve. This is healthy if it is done with respect, understanding, and the intention to help our partner. In this way, criticism takes on the connotation of evaluation, aimed at progress and further unification of the couple. At other times, we may even identify a negative behavior in our partner and politely communicate our observations. Thus, we can discuss whether we were right and, if so, respectfully ask them to change it and help them to do so. These are important things that couples should do, and both partners should help each other to correct negative behaviors through a conversation of understanding and love.

Unfortunately, however, we do not always behave in such a balanced and honest way and resort to criticism or blame. This is because our minds automatically focus more easily on negative elements, as we explained in the first chapter, in the section about the Reactive Unaware Self Model. Criticism and blame are behaviors that involve not taking responsibility for our actions and not admitting our mistakes or negative behavior.

In short, we blame our partner for our own negative traits. We may judge our partner to be insecure because we are insecure and don't like it, or we may judge our partner to be rude when we are rude. We may accuse our partner of being angry because we are angry, or of being anxious at the slightest thing when we are the ones who are anxious. Not only that, but we may be responsible for something bad that has happened, but we deny it and blame our partner. In other words, whatever negative thing we do that we don't want to admit, we blame our partner, so we feel better. For this reason, many people tend to blame their partner for various difficulties they have in their relationship or for the slightest thing that happens, but never themselves. They don't take responsibility for themselves, their emotions, and their actions.

Of course, we may blame our partner for negative behavior or a mistake that is real and not related to our inability to admit our mistakes. But again, this is not a mature way of coping. It is better to speak kindly to our partner and make our observation respectfully, not only because we love them and don't want to treat them badly, but also because if we go against them and judge them, they are likely to reinforce their already negative behavior as a form of defense. So, it is clear that judging and blaming our partner is not a balanced way to behave.

Belittling and ridicule

At other times, criticizing our partner may result in ridicule or belittling. We can end up making fun of them; not in the form of innocent teasing, as when we can even tease ourselves, but in an attempt to, unconsciously or even consciously, lead them into the same negative emotional state we are in.

So, we can say "You can't achieve anything because you are incompetent and stupid" or "Whatever you have achieved you have done by luck because you are stupid". This happens because we feel bad about ourselves. So, we want to belittle our partner to feel good ourselves. That is, because we have "placed" low self-worth in ourselves (see pp. 53-54 Evolved Aware Self Model), we want our partner to have low self-worth too so that we think we are not the only one who is "incompetent" or some other label. The aim is to elevate ourselves in our own eyes by degrading our partner, whom we are likely to envy.

A common example of belittling is about how much money they make. That is, someone who is not financially comfortable mocks a rich person by saying that they got their money through exploitation. They do this to belittle someone they envy because this person has achieved something they have not. This behavior is also found in the context of a romantic relationship, where if one partner has a lucrative career whereas the other does not, the latter may judge them by saying that they did not make that money by merit. This happens because of jealousy. But the healthy thing to do in a relationship is to admire and help each other, and to be genuinely happy about your partner's successes. It's even better if partners can set common goals and achieve them together.

You obviously understand how dysfunctional it is to be jealous and belittle our partner and that this needs to be changed immediately. It is important to emphasize that although our partner may want to mock and belittle us, it is probably because they don't know a better way to express the inner difficulties they are experiencing. That is, it doesn't mean that they don't love us, but that they don't know how to express their love because they haven't clarified who they are and haven't worked enough on themselves. So, they judge on the best information they have which is unfortunately limited and restrictive. This is why they need understanding and, of course, help from us.

It is also essential to understand that no human being, including our Fulfilled Reflecting Self, can "lift" or "lower" us. That is, no one has the power to increase or decrease our quality and truth. So, whether our partner praises and admires us or mocks and insults us, they cannot influence us unless we allow them to. If we know who we really are and are sure and firm about it, no one can influence us in any way in life. This is our inner strength, and we will explain more in the next chapter when we discuss responsibility and its relationship to emotions and insults.

Now you know that if your partner judges, blames, or mocks you, they have no power to influence you. So, you, as a more mature and empowered person, can help them to correct the negative ways they express themselves, or your partner can help you if you are being judgmental.

Time for introspection

- Think about when and how often you judge, blame, and belittle your partner. Think about the reasons why you behave this way so that you can get to the root of the problem.
- Think about and find alternative ways of expressing yourself in a more respectful way, without blaming your partner. What exactly do you need to change about each of these behaviors?
- Answer the ten questions from the beginning of this chapter again, this time specifically about criticizing, blaming, belittling, and ridiculing.

2.3 — Manipulation, control, possessiveness, and demands

Another dysfunctional behavior that we can show in our relationship is manipulation. Manipulation is a behavior in which one partner wants to lead the relationship by trying to secretly influence and direct their partner's decisions. The partner who engages in manipulative behavior often does so based on expectations and limiting beliefs they have built up about how the relationship and their partner's behavior "should" be. Manipulation can easily destroy a relationship if the partners, or at least one of them, are not aware that it is happening and do not know how to deal with it. Manipulation is also linked to other negative behaviors, such as possessiveness, which we analyze later on.

We can behave manipulatively either unconsciously or consciously. In either case, we must stop this behavior, or we will damage our relationship.

Manipulation is usually expressed in the following ways:

a) Manipulation is frequently intended for the purpose of domination

As mentioned above, the manipulative partner wants to have the "upper hand" in the relationship or wants to feel that they have the "upper hand" in the relationship. Because they are insecure and have a strong need for acceptance (as described in the Reactive Unaware Self Model), they want to satisfy this need and "boost" their self-worth by taking control of the relationship.

They want their partner to be submissive and to do whatever serves their needs and selfish "wants". To achieve this, they play the role of the victim so that they can "turn" their partner into a "real victim" who is unaware of this insidious behavior. This means that the manipulative partner will use guilt, remorse, and threats to make themselves appear to be the victim in the relationship, thus exploiting their partner's emotions. They behave immaturely as if they were a child to get what they want. They may say, "You made me feel bad because you didn't pick me up from work yesterday when you said you would" (use of guilt), or "If you don't pick me up from work tomorrow, we'll have a problem" (use of threat). As you can see, the use of language itself is completely manipulative.

But as we explained in the case of belittling behavior, no one can influence us if we don't allow them to. So, guilt and threats can have no effect if we are strong and unshakable. But if we are not, then we may end up in a state of emotional chaos with our partner, where we constantly feel bad about everything we do (the manipulative partner achieves their goal), or we will get into major conflict with our partner because we do not accept this behavior (the manipulative partner does not achieve their goal). Of course, in both scenarios, the result is damage to the relationship or even separation.

b) In addition to controlling the relationship through guilt and threats, manipulation can also take the form of possessiveness

That is, one partner wants to feel that they "own" the other. This stems from insecurity and a need for acceptance, as in the case of dominance. The partner who expresses possessiveness desperately wishes to feel that someone accepts them and "gives" them value. So, they attach themselves to their partner in such a way that they intend to be "their own". This means that they want to be in control of their partner's actions again to feel good about themselves.

Because of this possessiveness, the partner is forbidden to have friends or close relationships with other people or to do anything without the partner's approval. If they do not satisfy the possessive partner's selfish "wants", they should feel bad about themselves. For example, they might tell their partner that it is unacceptable for them not to invite them out for coffee with their friends and that they didn't prioritize their relationship.

In a balanced relationship, it is healthy for partners to have mutual friends and literally do everything together. But this is healthy if it is done out of love and not out of coercion or oppression. If one partner wants to do something on their own, they are free to do so. For this reason, we must be clear with our partner about what we want and don't want, why we do what we do (see p. 58 Existential Aware Self Model), and that we both consciously put our relationship first.

So, we can clarify that we want to do everything in the relationship together, but it is important that it is a shared "want" of the couple's connection and not out of the insecurity of one partner.

You can see here how essential it is to place a high value on ourselves, based on who we really are so that we do not have to try and "take" value from something external, such as a situation or a person, i.e., our partner. When we know our true value and the value of our partner, only then can we create a common path in life with shared "wants" and without the need to control each other.

c) Another way in which manipulation can be expressed is through complaining

To get what we want, we often tend to complain. We complain that our partner does not do enough for us, does not behave the way we want, or does not give us what we want. We complain to "force" our partner to do what we want because we have this belief that a romantic relationship is about giving and especially receiving, and thus we desperately want to get what we expect to stop feeling insecure and meet our inferior needs.

So, after complaining, we end up making demands. We demand that our partner behaves the way we want them to. The demands may be followed by threats, and by denying responsibility. For example, we may threaten to fight or break up with our partner if they do not meet our demands. We may also demand our partner to stop behaving in a certain negative way while, at the same time, we behave in the exact same way ourselves.

The healthy way is to ask our partner politely what we want and decide together what is best to do. Making demands of our partner means that we are not accepting them completely and that we are relying on false expectations based on our own distorted version of what our partner should and should not do. So, instead of having unrealistic expectations of our partner's behavior and trying to control them, it is healthy to set strong standards together for how our relationship should go. These standards are a way of preventing any manipulative behavior that we might show, and of stopping any such behavior.

So, a relationship that involves manipulation, possessiveness, and demands cannot be healthy. Manipulation can be obvious, but also not easily noticed. The point is that manipulative behavior can be exhibited in tiny things in our daily lives, with little frequency, and we may not even notice it. This means that we may have a wonderful relationship with our partner, but without realizing it, we may sometimes behave in a manipulative way.

To deal more effectively with this kind of behavior in your relationship, work wisely on the models of the Evolved Aware Self, Existential Aware Self, and Reactive Unaware Self in Chapter One. Look closely at your partner's behavior and your own to see if one or both of you behave manipulatively as described above. This is the first step in dealing with such behavioral patterns.

It takes strength to pinpoint these cases because a manipulative person will not easily admit their mistakes and their manipulative behavior. For this reason, looking within ourselves, understanding how we operate, and developing our self-awareness are the best ways to change for the better and improve our behavior. No behavior management technique will help us if we do not first get to know ourselves and our partner in depth.

Time for introspection

- Do you behave in a manipulative way towards your partner? If so, how often and in what ways? Why do you behave this way?
- Do you try to control your partner? If so, why?
- Do you want to feel that you own your partner? If so, why?
- Do you make selfish demands on your partner and relationship, or do you understand your differences and make decisions together?
- Answer the ten questions from the beginning of the chapter again, this time specifically about manipulation, control, possessiveness, and demands.

2.4 — Expected and learned habitual behaviors

The next types of behavior are related to what we are used to seeing our partner do. That is because we have often seen our partner behave in a certain way, we expect them to continue in the same pattern. We assume that because something has happened many times in the past, it will happen again in the future. This is one way we learn. We connect information, events, and experiences in a way that makes sense to us and in this way, we come to conclusions in our imagination. We are often right, and our conclusion is related to the truth, but other times we misunderstand and completely misinterpret the situation. This happens because we make predictions based on the expectations we have built up. As we have explained many times, this is not a mature way of operating because it is not based on the truth (see p. 64 Existential Aware Self Model).

In the relationship with our partner, if we see that they frequently repeat a behavior, we may conclude that they will always behave in this way. So, we build up an expectation. For example, we may notice that our partner frequently reacts with fear when we tell them to move to another country. If we see that our partner expresses fear in many of our conversations about this topic, we may, after a while, come to the conclusion that our partner is afraid of moving. So, we may believe that every time we talk about it, our partner will feel fear. This expectation leads us to behave in a certain way ourselves, such as becoming aggressive when we discuss the subject. The point is, however, that it is by no means a given that the partner will always express fear in this discussion, or even that they are afraid of moving in general. This is our own conclusion, which may or may not be true. Therefore, when we talk to our partner about moving again, we may use an aggressive tone from the beginning of the conversation simply because we believe that our partner will react with fear. So, we will be aggressive, even though the partner may not react as we expect.

This happens because we react to our expectations and not to reality. We react to what we expect to happen and not to what really happens.

This pattern is what we call "expected and learned habitual behaviors", and healthily dealing with them has helped us immensely in our relationship. Expected habitual behavior is the behavior we expect from our partner, and learned habitual behavior is the behavior we create in response to our partner's expected habitual behavior. So, in the example above, the expected habitual behavior is a fear response, and the learned habitual behavior is aggression. That is, because we expect our partner to react with fear, we learn by habit to react aggressively as a method of responding to this expectation. In this case, we tend to blame our partner for always behaving in a certain way just because we have seen them behaving this way on some occasions.

We can analyze any expected and learned habitual behavior in the following way:

- One partner (the accused) often behaves in a certain way.
- The other partner (the accuser) notices this behavior after a while.
- The accused partner continues to behave in the same way occasionally.
- The accuser expects their partner to exhibit the usual behavior.
- The accused partner repeats the usual behavior (expected habitual behavior).
- The accuser creates a behavior as a "response" to the accused partner's behavior.
- The accuser continues to behave in the same way (learned habitual behavior) whether the accused partner behaves in the expected way or not.

All this simple process happens unconsciously at first, because of our limiting beliefs. Then it becomes conscious, but again automatic, because that is how we are used to reacting. So, using the previous example, we might say to our partner, "You always act out of fear and don't want to look at things differently and consider moving", while our partner denies it because it is not true.

The expectations we have created completely cloud our minds and cannot see things clearly. It is we who misunderstand the situation because we are acting based on our expectations. So, what is completely destructive to our relationship in such a situation is the blinders we "wear" when we create a learned habitual behavior because of the expected habitual behavior we often observe. Because we believe so strongly that our partner will behave in the expected way, we are already behaving in our learned way, and we don't give our partner the space and opportunity to do something different. We are already creating tension even without our partner behaving the way we expect.

So, based on our example, we become aggressive even before our partner expresses fear. Thus, all we achieve is a fight with our partner without any realistic trigger. We create conflict because we imagine, assume, and expect our partner to behave in a way we don't like.

Learned habitual behaviors can also be created because we associate experiences we have had with other people (relatives, friends, colleagues, etc.) with the behavior of our partner. For example, we may have had many negative experiences in the past with our previous partners, whether men or women, and have created the limiting belief that all men or women are untrustworthy. So, in our current relationship with our partner, we may have great difficulty trusting them, even if they are a person who expresses themselves authentically and cares deeply for us. Especially if we notice expressions, body language, or anything else that reminds us of past experiences and other people, we will unconsciously make the connection that our partner is untrustworthy because they are "the same" as all our previous partners.

But the truth is that the partner is not aware of these experiences and cannot imagine why we do not trust them. So, they are likely to be confused. We will expect the partner to act in ways that we do not trust (expected habitual behavior) and thus we will act defensively (learned habitual behavior). In fact, if the partner asks us clearly why we are always defensive towards them, we will not know how to answer because we will be motivated by a limiting belief that lies deep within us.

Therefore, to change these two types of behavior, we can do the following:

1 - Admit that we have reached the point where we are reacting negatively based on our imagination and expectations rather than the truth. Open up to our partner and explain all the reasons why we behave in this way, whether they are reasons related to previous experiences or something about the present.

2 - Recognize the cause of our behavior, which is some kind of limiting belief we have about our partner.

3 - Once we have clarified our limiting belief, we can change it and not be guided by it.

4 - Whenever we start exhibiting our learned habitual behavior, we should stop and think if what we are going to do is based on the truth or our expectations.

5 - Create a positive and balanced behavior to replace the learned habitual behavior.

6 - Repeat the new positive behavior until it becomes habitual and our automatic response.

In fact, we can even prevent learned habitual behaviors if we communicate honestly with our partner. This means that if we observe our partner behaving in a certain way, which we might consider as expected habitual behavior, we should not automatically react negatively, but we should discuss with them and tell them what we have observed. If it is indeed a recurring negative behavior, let's see what we can do together. If it is not, then there is absolutely no need to create a learned habitual behavior that will damage our relationship.

Identifying these dysfunctional behaviors can sometimes be easy because they tend to be repetitive, but sometimes extremely difficult because the connections made in our minds are complex.

We can create negative-learned habitual behaviors from small and insignificant things, simply because we are guided by limiting beliefs and what we are used to and expect. So, the combination of our beliefs, habits, and expectations can be very damaging to our relationship.

In fact, learned habitual behaviors can become so deeply ingrained that they become habitual in our bodies. This means that the body learns to automatically react negatively because of strong limiting beliefs and expectations. For example, if one partner shows even the slightest sign of some expected habitual behavior, the other partner may immediately feel anxiety, pressure, anger, fear, or anything else associated with their own learned habitual behavior, and so react even more quickly based on their learned habitual behavior. This can be damaging to the relationship, and it is important to understand the relationship between our body and our inner world so that we do not reach extreme states of suppression because of our imagination. We discuss this subject in more detail in Volume Two.

So, identify the learned habitual behaviors that you have built up because you simply expect certain behaviors from your partner. Identify the limiting beliefs that are affecting you and talk to your partner about them. Work a lot on the Unlimited Aware Self Model and explore your expectations in life by working on the Existential Aware Self Model. All of this will help you to address and change your learned habitual behaviors.

Time for introspection

- Have you created any negative learned habitual behaviors? If so, what are they? How exactly do you behave? Why were they created?
- Have you identified any negative learned habitual behaviors in your partner? If so, what are they? How exactly do they behave? Why do you think they were created?
- What do you need to do to change your negative learned habitual behaviors?
- What do you need to do to help your partner change their negative learned habitual behaviors?
- Answer the ten questions from the beginning of the chapter again, this time specifically about expected and learned habitual behaviors.

2.5 — Dependency, avoidance of connection, and the past

So far, we have seen how important it is for our relationship to be the number one priority in our life, we have looked at behaviors related to criticism and conscious or unconscious manipulation, and we have understood that we can create negative behaviors because of the expectations we have.

Now let's talk a little about the past and how it can negatively influence our behavior towards our partner today. Unconsciously influenced by our past and our childhood, we can exhibit the following negative behaviors:

1) Some of the most common past behaviors that affect our present are the behaviors we imitate from our parents

Have you ever said to your partner, "You're acting like your father" or "You're just like your mother"? This is very likely because we biologically acquire many of our parents' characteristics (appearance, facial expressions, body language), but we also learn to behave and imitate the way they did when we were children (way of thinking, way of communicating, values, beliefs, principles, attitudes, etc.). For this reason, we present to our partner many negative behaviors that we have seen from our parents:

> a) This means that we can treat our partner the way our parents treated us when we were children. For example, our parents may have belittled us when we spoke to them, and so we may belittle our partner today.

> b) Or we can treat our partner the way our parents treated each other. That is, our parents may have often been aggressive and abusive in their communication, and so we may be aggressive and abusive in our communication with our partner today.

It is therefore important to identify the negative behaviors that we have imitated from our parents, or generally from the people who raised us and played a major role in our upbringing so that we do not repeat the same mistakes.

Think about negative behaviors that your parents had, for example, criticism, manipulation, and aggression, and observe yourself. Ask yourself if and when you behave in these dysfunctional ways. Also think about whether you behave in this way automatically because you were taught to react in such a way from a young age, or whether you behave negatively consciously. Then talk to your partner to see how they perceive and understand these behaviors, and agree together on the most appropriate way to commit to behaving from now on.

At the same time, if you notice negative behavior in your partner that is reminiscent of their parents' behavior, understand that this is natural and that it happens to you too. So, find a polite way to express your observation and discuss it with your partner to find a loving and non-judgmental solution.

For example, you might say, "I have noticed that you often yell at me for no particular reason, and in fact, I have noticed the same behavior in your parents. Have you been unconsciously imitating them and now showing the same behavior towards me? Do you want to talk about it and see what we can do to improve this behavior together?" instead of saying, "Why are you yelling? You keep acting like your father and I can't keep having this..."

The first, kind, and understanding approach has a better chance of having a positive effect on your partner and ending in a constructive discussion with positive results. Conversely, if we use the second and aggressive way, our partner is likely to become defensive (Reactive Unaware Self) and we will end up in an argument with an escalation of negative behavior. So, it is important to be careful and mature in how we express ourselves to our partner when we want to communicate a negative aspect of them or a negative behavior.

2) In addition to the behaviors that we imitated from our parents as children and continue to do so, we can also see the opposite in a romantic relationship

That is, our partner may remind us of some negative behaviors of our parents. This happens because we are unconsciously attracted to our parents' characteristics that we also see in our partner and find it as a way to resolve unresolved issues from the past and to grow and develop spiritually.

So as children, we may have argued with our parents, as it is natural to happen in any family, but we did not really resolve the various issues we experienced. We may not have said what we wanted to say in the way we wanted to say it, or at all, or we may have held back and suppressed our emotions. So, we continue to "carry" unresolved issues with our parents and express them to our partner.

For example, we may be discussing some issues with our partner, and suddenly, they get angry, yell, and behave in a completely unexplainable way. This happens because they are not arguing with us but with their parents. They unconsciously see some traits of their parents in us, and they react emotionally as they would, or wish, to their parents. This is a way of dealing with old issues that have not been resolved. This is why you may often get into conflict with your partner and be surprised at how you ended up arguing when you were talking so calmly at the beginning.

In addition to mentally arguing with our parents about old issues, we can do the same with issues with our siblings or even former partners. That is, we may be arguing with our partner now, but we may be expressing unresolved issues we had with our siblings, old partners, or significant others in the past. Our reasons for arguing with our partner now have little or nothing to do with them.

In any case, if our partner is unconsciously trying to resolve past issues, it is necessary to show understanding because they are not doing it purposefully, but unconsciously. The first step, of course, is to acknowledge that the conflict is caused by past issues and is not related to a current situation. To clarify this, we can discuss our past and our childhood with our partner and learn more about each other. In this way, we can identify the emotions and old conflicts that we have had and have not dealt with effectively. Then, once we have clarified a particular behavior, we can discuss whether it benefits our relationship or holds us back. We see together as a couple what is the best way forward and do not take it out on each other over issues that happened in the past and even with other people. We help each other to forgive people from the past, not to hold grudges or anything else that oppresses us, and to free ourselves spiritually from anything that keeps us trapped in the past.

This is the way to live fully in the present and to move forward in our life and relationship. Here we understand even better that the relationship purpose with our partner is love and progress (in essence, Togetherness-Fulfillment), as we said in the Existential

Aware Self Model in Chapter One. In love, we help one another overcome past problems, forgive the past, and be grateful for our life and romantic relationship, all we have, and all the life lessons we've learned.

The beauty is that, together, we can resolve past issues without having to involve people from the past. This is because the change and release of held emotions is purely internal, and we don't need to talk to people from our past to move forward in our life (we explain this in the next chapter talking about forgiveness).

3) Insecurity leads to dependency or avoidance of connection

Now that we have explored the imitation of negative behaviors from our parents and the attempt to resolve past issues in our current relationship, let's go even deeper. As we explained in Chapter One, as children we are dependent on our parents, and it is necessary to meet some of the basic needs for warmth, acceptance, and validation from our parents and caregivers. However, these needs are very difficult to meet adequately because our guardians are not machines that can serve us perfectly twenty-four hours a day. The child's mind cannot understand this and so it creates insecurity which later leads to weakness or a pretense of strength.

So, when we grow up, deep down we have a certain level of insecurity, depending on how much our needs have been met or not. We will express this in all our social relationships, but even more in our life partner, who is the person with whom we will have the deepest connection. As we have said, insecurity can be expressed either in weakness, and so we will be led to dependency, or in a pretense of strength, and so we will be led to avoidance of connection.

a) Dependency

If we are led to dependency, it will be because insecurity is linked to our fear of being alone.

That is, we will be afraid of being rejected by other people in life, especially our partner. This fear stems from the perception we had as children that our parents rejected us and were not there for us. Maybe our parents did reject us, for example by giving us up for adoption, or perhaps they didn't reject us, and just made some mistakes because they weren't perfect, as no one is. Either way, as children, we see each case as a rejection. So, we will do everything in our power to make sure that other people don't reject us again today. Because we need to be validated, we will not express our truth, be authentic, speak our minds easily, or make decisions for ourselves. Instead, we will do what others want, constantly ask others for life advice, not know what we want in ourselves, and do anything to please and satisfy others.

So, we end up living an anxious life, dependent on other people. The relationships we have are superficial because the reason for their formation is to satisfy our inferior needs, such as validation, which were not met when we were children (Reactive Unaware Self Model). So, in our relationship with our partner, we are likely to behave in all the above ways and be "addicted" to our partner. We will be dependent on them for everything we do and will not be able to function autonomously.

b) Avoidance of Connection

On the other hand, if we are led to avoidance of connection, it is because our insecurity is linked to our shame and fear of appearing weak to other people.

That is because we feel that our parents rejected us and treated us badly, we are ashamed to admit it and create gigantic defenses to protect ourselves from similar behavior in the future. Thus, we don't connect easily with other people. The defenses are created either because we were badly abused by our parents or other people in the past, or because the parents were manipulative and wanted to control us, even to a minimal degree.

So, we are ashamed of what happened to us, and we don't want it to happen again. We avoid connecting with our partner, we keep secrets, we don't open up, and we show others that we are independent and strong and that we don't need anyone, even though this is not true. We also blame other people and don't take responsibility because we act from a place of arrogance and shame. Not only that, but we don't trust people easily, and we are always busy with something (like our work), so we don't face the truth about ourselves.

This leads to meaningless social relationships because we allow little opportunity for connection or bonding, and dispute too easily with others to maintain this false image of dominance. We often end up alone because no one wants to be around us due to our oppressive and selfish behavior. So, in our relationship with our partner, we are likely to behave in the above ways and be driven by arrogance. We will not open up at all, and we will not present our truth because we fear connection.

As you can see, both dependency and avoidance of connection are dysfunctional behaviors and will prevent us from moving forward in our relationship if we don't deal with them in a healthy way. However, they can teach us a lot about ourselves, and we need to approach them with understanding. The difficulty is when we, or our partner, are in denial and do not admit that we are behaving in any of these ways. Until we accept the truth, there is nothing we can do to change our behavior. This is why patience and respect are needed. We need to give our partner the time they deserve and be there for them all the time, just as they have to be there for us.

So, identify which of the two behaviors you and your partner exhibit. You may find that you exhibit only one of these strongly, or that you exhibit both, but at different intensities and depending on the situation. You may exhibit exclusively dependency or exclusively avoidance of connection. You may also express your insecurity differently to different people. For example, you might not want to bond with your partner because you know the romantic relationship is the most intimate form of connection and thus you are afraid to open up and connect on a deep level since it makes you vulnerable. So, you want to appear independent, and that is why you often argue with them. On the other hand, in other social interactions, such as with friends or parents, you may appear dependent because, again, you have a need for acceptance and want to meet it in some way without being closely connected to them.

Having clarified whether you exhibit dependency or avoidance of connection, find out how intense it is, i.e., whether you express this behavior extremely or to a much lesser degree. Accept that you act from a place of insecurity in either case because that is the source of the issue. Find where your insecurity comes from. Then you will be able to truly change these behaviors and free yourself from past ties that are negatively affecting your present and future.

Therefore, we can see that our past and our childhood play a big part in our current relationship with our partner and how healthy it will be. This helps us understand even more how important it is that our relationship with our partner is the number one priority. This way we will be healthy role models, as a couple, for our children so that they do not exhibit excessive behaviors because of unmet needs for acceptance.

It is essential to be aware of our past and our relationship with it today. This is how we can recognize the limiting beliefs and attitudes that we still hold and deal with them. By acknowledging the mistakes, weaknesses, unresolved issues, and insecurities that we have built up within ourselves because of the past, forgiving all the people associated with our insecurities, and being firmly united with our partner, we can stop being controlled by the past and live in peace and balance in the present.

> ## Time for introspection

- What is your relationship with your past? Do you know how your past influences your relationship with your partner? Do you behave like your parents? Do you behave like your partner's parents?
- Do you show dependency or avoidance of connection in your relationship with your partner? Why do you show these behaviors?
- What do you need to do to change these behaviors?
- Does your partner show dependency or avoidance of connection in your relationship? Why do they show these behaviors?
- What do you need to do to help your partner change these behaviors?
- Answer the ten questions from the beginning of this chapter again, this time specifically about dependency, avoidance of connection, and your relationship with your past.

2.6 — Emotionally charged behaviors

Every behavior always has a small or large connection with our emotions. However, there are times when we operate entirely on our emotional level (Balanced Aware Self Model) and lose control of ourselves by doing things that we regret when we calm down.

When we operate exclusively with our emotions, we risk damaging our relationship because we judge each situation one-sidedly and react immaturely without thinking and with no awareness. In this part of the chapter, we develop the ways in which we react emotionally by examining very basic and common emotions such as sadness, anger, fear, and anxiety. Let's look at how they are commonly expressed.

Emotional behavior as a form of defense

Our emotions often act defensively. We may get upset at our partner not because they did something wrong, but because we think that not admitting our mistakes shows strength. We might say to our partner in anger, "It's not my fault and I didn't behave the way you say I did. Don't you dare blame me again." Anger works defensively in this case by denying our fault and abdicating responsibility. The same is true of other emotions. For example, in an argument with our partner, our distress can work defensively so that our partner will feel remorseful and stop the argument. Fear can lead us to procrastinate as a form of defense against everything we need to do in our lives and everything that challenges us to improve. So, it's important to know when we're using our emotions to defend ourselves, to get out of situations, and to appear strong because all of this doesn't help our relationship; it hurts it.

Emotional behavior as a reflection of our past

Other times, our emotions come from the past, as we explained in dependency and avoidance of connection. For example, we may get easily angry with our partner because we have a lot of held and suppressed emotions from our childhood that need to be addressed and soothed. We may even be afraid to pursue our goals because we have built up a limiting belief that we are not worthy. It is therefore significant to understand where our emotions come from and whether they are related to the past or our present situation so that we do not take them out on our partner unnecessarily and create tension over old issues. Whether the emotion stems from the past, the present, or a concern about the future, it is beneficial to discuss it with our partner and find the cause and solution together.

Emotional behavior due to lack of self-control

As we explained in the Balanced Aware Self model in Chapter One, when we focus on certain thoughts, we reinforce our corresponding emotions, and as we feed these emotions, they begin to take over. So, if we get angry and focus on our anger, we are giving it fertile ground to grow, and then it can control us.

For example, we can get a little angry with our partner for a trivial reason, like a disagreement about where we are going to have fun that night. This type of anger can be triggered for many reasons, such as selfishly wanting to get what we want, or feeling that our partner is being unfair to us because they don't agree with what we want. If, because of a lack of self-control, we allow our anger to grow and focus on it, we will increase it and create irrational scenarios in our minds. For example, we may believe that our partner never takes our "wishes" into account, when in fact they have just expressed their opinion. So, our now heightened anger will lead us to argue with our partner over nothing. We may speak insultingly, shout, mock, judge, and blame our partner because we are simply not controlling our anger; not because we are based on facts.

But anger, like any other emotion that we see as negative and ugly, is a teacher. It comes to help us, not to control and destroy us. Those emotions that we consider negative (anger, sadness, fear, frustration, etc.) are a sign that we need to practice self-control. It is an opportunity to improve and shows us that it is time to correct some of our mistakes and be assertive, but with maturity and control of our actions.

Often our "negative" emotions towards our partner may be justified, and it is healthy to feel them, but not to an excessive and uncontrollable degree. For example, our partner may have told us a lie, and we may have felt angry or upset. This is normal, but if we start swearing (anger) or isolating ourselves (sadness), we are not expressing our emotions in a mature way. It is vital to always be in control of what we say and do, and not to let our emotions control our actions.

Understanding our emotions is a way to improve ourselves
Seeing our emotions as a way to improve ourselves changes our perspective and we can move forward. For example, anxiety can be a sign that we care about something, a push to improve, and a challenge. This means that we may be anxious on a first date, and how we view anxiety can lead to success or failure on our date. If we perceive ourselves to be anxious because we are insecure, we are likely to behave insecurely on our date. Howev-

er, if we believe that we are anxious because we are genuinely interested in the person we are meeting and want a positive outcome, then it can lead to much better behavior. So, if we give our power to fear and allow it to affect us negatively in our daily lives, then the results in our lives will not be what we want. It's about finding and using stress in a true and quality way. Where stress is not beneficial to you, then change it and get the power back.

Something similar can happen with sadness. We can get sad because our partner has spoken to us abruptly, and so we feed our sadness, we get frustrated, and we don't speak to them. If we focus on our sadness, we make things worse. However, if we see sadness as a sign that we care about our relationship, then it is possible to ask our partner to discuss it as two mature people and find a solution to what is bothering us. That is, distress can be a way for us to understand that to feel and be truly peaceful within ourselves, we need to be strong, connected, and loving with our partner. This is how we achieve what we want.

Emotional behaviors where we take it out on our partner when it is not their fault

Often our emotions towards our partner are not justified at all. For example, we may be angry with someone else and take it out on our partner. In other words, we are emotionally charged with other people, but because of various social reasons or limiting beliefs, we do not express our emotions to those people but lash out at our partner, to the person with whom we feel most comfortable.

For instance, we may be angry with a colleague or family member, but we do not feel comfortable expressing ourselves authentically to them. We are afraid of being fired in the first case, or we don't want to appear hostile in the second. So, we hold our temper and take it out on our partner because we take them for granted, as a comfort zone where we can express ourselves as we like without consequences. But this is unfair and unhealthy because we are damaging the relationship with the most significant person in our life. We are afraid to express ourselves to people with whom we have a real disagreement (remember the ten questions at the beginning of the chapter). So, in such cases, it's good to ask ourselves: "Why was it difficult for me to take it out on the people I was furious with, and why did I take it out on my partner who was not to blame?".

Appropriate management of emotions for the benefit of our relationship

In order not to damage our relationship through immature, emotionally charged behavior, it requires not only self-control but also understanding from both partners. For example, when one partner gets angry, it is essential for the couple not to engage in verbal communication. It is better for the angry partner to calm down first and then talk about it. This applies to any emotional situation.

When we operate from our emotional level, we don't think clearly, and we react automatically. We cannot talk to our partner in a mature and balanced way. So, when our partner is emotionally charged, it is good to give them space and time to calm down and talk to us when they are ready.

Other times —in terms of fear, anxiety, or distress— we can help our partner with a hug, a kiss, lying down together, helping them to focus on their truth rather than their emotions. Also, we can easily turn intense emotions such as fear and anger, which don't serve us, into excitement and passion, and channel them into energy, love, and creativity. We can have passionate sex, exercise together, and do anything that can turn emotions of stress into something beautiful or productive. This way, we won't suppress our emotions or allow them to damage our relationship, but we will express them healthily. So, find out what works for you and what works best when you're emotionally charged so that you don't get caught up in your emotions and take them out on your partner unnecessarily.

We can see that when our emotions are amplified, they lead us into negative behaviors. It is crucial not to allow any of our emotions to turn into a habit and end up acting emotionally for no obvious reason. It is not healthy to act and judge our lives according to how we feel. Emotions are constantly changing and are not a permanent situation. This is why we need to develop healthy self-control, as described in the Evolved Aware Self Model in Chapter One.

Whenever we are emotionally charged, it is good to take a few breaths and not speak right away. Let's think about why we feel this way, and whether there is any reason to get into conflict with our partner just because we are feeling an emotion too strongly. This way, we give ourselves the opportunity to act in a healthy way, or at least not so intensely.

Moreover, whenever we are emotionally charged, it is useful to make our partner aware so that they understand that we will be more irritable. It is good to ask our partner for help and to give us space and time to calm down. Thus, instead of being at the mercy of our emotions and behaving in a way that we will later regret, we can balance them by practicing self-control as well as with our partner's understanding and help.

Time for introspection

- How often do you react emotionally and lose control of your emotions?
- What are the main emotions that control you?
- Every time you feel like lashing out, what could you do to prevent the outburst and act in a healthy way? Discuss with your partner to find balanced ways to help each other, depending on each other's emotional weaknesses and needs, until you reach a point where you have total control over your emotions.
- Answer the ten questions from the beginning of this chapter again, this time specifically about your emotionally charged behaviors.

2.7 – Communication difficulties

Have you ever been in a situation where you say something to your partner, and they understand something entirely different? Do you find it difficult to get your point across to your partner? Do you end up arguing? Often, we get into arguments with our partner simply because of misunderstandings. This happens because we have not developed our communication skills sufficiently, and we need to work on this a lot. Here we will mainly talk about authenticity and honesty and their importance in effective and quality communication with our partner.

When we argue with our partner, the cause may be a difficulty in communication rather than an emotion or a past issue. Our communication may be dysfunctional for a very simple reason. That reason is that we have not been completely clear with our partner since the beginning of the relationship. It is very important for both partners to be truthful and authentic with each other from the beginning of the relationship. This will help our relationship to develop much faster, but it is also a way of seeing if our partner is not just a random partner, but our Fulfilled Reflecting Self (see pp. 83-84).

We can see if our partner is our Fulfilled Reflecting Self if they accept us as we are and do not want to "change" us. Because if they don't accept us as people who make mistakes and have certain preferences, and perhaps different from their own, then they are not our life partner. So, you understand the importance of being authentic with each other from the beginning of the relationship.

Another reason why it is essential to be honest and clear with our partner is that if we present a fake persona at the beginning, we will eventually be exposed. Over time, or through living together, we will see aspects of the other that we didn't know about, and we may reject them because they are not the person we thought they were. Of course, we will always have a lot to learn about our partner, just as we do about ourselves, but there is a big difference between putting on a false face and taking time to get to know each other.

As we explained at the beginning of this book, we are such complex beings that we cannot know exactly every experience, every memory, and every stimulus that our partner has had. We can, however, have a genuine interest and love for the truth and authenticity of our partner.

So, when communicating with our partner, to avoid misunderstandings, it is essential that we never expect our partner to read our minds and know exactly what we want without us telling them first. This means that we can be clear about what we want and what we don't want and not expect our partner to guess our needs. Even in a very close relationship or even in a relationship of Togetherness-Fulfillment, which we will develop in the last chapter, it is still crucial to express ourselves clearly to our partner and not think that they have to understand everything on their own.

In conclusion, even if you and your spouse have worked hard on your relationship and know each other thoroughly, meaningfully, and sincerely, you cannot know everything going on in their minds.

So don't take anything for granted, no matter how close and loving you and your partner are. Discuss what you each want and don't want, and work together on all the models from Chapter One. This will help you be clear with each other in every conversation, and you will get to know each other even better without jumping to any conclusions. Don't hide anything and be completely naked mentally, emotionally, and spiritually.

So, think about the last conversation you had with your partner, and you did not communicate effectively. Think about why. Were you not being clear?

Communicating effectively by actively listening to your partner

Often, what we think to say is different from what we end up saying, which confuses our partner, who may even understand what we have said very differently.

It is important to formulate what we want as best as we can. When our partner is talking, we should listen carefully and try not to jump to conclusions but understand what they are trying to say. If we jump to conclusions and do not ask our partner to confirm what we have understood, then we may be thinking entirely different things. So, we may end up arguing because we had a different picture in our minds and created a misunderstanding. In the misunderstanding, some emotions will be triggered, as we have analyzed before. We may end up throwing the responsibility at each other, saying "But that's what you told me yesterday", while the other person says "No, I didn't tell you that", and then the criticism, some arrogant tone, or the need to defend ourselves arise and make things worse.

So, the key is to listen effectively to your partner and articulate your thoughts as best you can. This means expressing your truth and actively listening with interest to what your partner is saying without trying to prove that you are right. It is a pity to get into arguments because you are not honest, and you are afraid to show your authenticity. Therefore, be clear and truthful, and this alone can prevent and solve many issues. Lying and hiding the truth will get you nowhere. But with honesty and complete spiritual nakedness, you can work wonders.

Time for introspection

- Do you communicate effectively with your partner? If so, what do you do to communicate effectively? If not, what do you do that makes communication unsuccessful?
- Do you always tell your partner the truth? If yes, why? If not, why?
- Do you tell your partner clearly what you want, or do you wait for them to draw conclusions about what you want?
- How often do misunderstandings occur in your communication? What is the reason for this?
- What do you need to do to improve your communication with your partner?
- Answer the ten questions from the beginning of the chapter again, this time specifically about dysfunctional communication.

2.8 — Compromise and stagnation

Have you ever compromised in a romantic relationship? Have you ever accepted being with someone simply because you got used to them and didn't want to be alone? Have you ever accepted being treated badly and disrespected in your relationship? Unfortunately, the answer to these questions is yes for many people. Compromise is a huge obstacle to any form of development and progress. Many people tend to compromise in relationships because of various "musts", their limiting beliefs, insecurity, and fear of loneliness. In fact, some end up in marriages for many years without loving each other, simply out of habit, a "must" or a "need". Here, we are going to discuss the issue of compromise and how destructive it can be to our life and relationship.

Compromise is never a good thing
Many people are driven by fear in their lives. They are afraid of being alone; they are afraid of losing their job; they are afraid to follow their dreams; they are afraid to work to achieve their goals. So, without realizing it, they settle for a loveless relationship, a job they despise, a routine they feel trapped in, and a life that dulls their brain and makes them uncreative and unproductive, but out of fear, they do nothing to change the situation. They are afraid of losing what they have, so they don't take risks in life. Thus, they believe that compromise is the only way to live. That is, they have a life of hardship, with few temporary pleasures. They wait for the weekend to come and have temporary fun so that they can forget the miserable life they have. But they do nothing to deal with the difficulties, and so they go on living with them and multiplying them. They don't engage in new things that will help them to live a beautiful life of fulfillment. They remain stagnant and purposeless.

These people want to escape from life, themselves, and their relationship. Some are addicted to sex as a way of escapism, others to alcohol, others to porn, others to gambling, others to cigarettes (which have become many people's "best friend"), others to the fake world of social media because virtual reality is easier for them than real life, and others to meaningless friendships to feel good at least a few moments. Many couples even want their partner to spend long hours away from home because they want to spend as little time together as possible. They are happy that they have no common interests and that their relationship or marriage is nothing more than a conversation at night before going to bed. This is because they cannot stand each other as their relationship is one of compromise, not love.

But why do we say this? Because there is a possibility that many people believe that compromise is beneficial to a romantic relationship. However, compromise means that one partner will always be dissatisfied and unfulfilled because they will settle for less, suppress their needs, set aside their values, and lower their standards (Existential Aware Self Model). This is not helpful in a relationship. The solution is to understand our partner deeply and work together to find the best way forward. Not through compromise, but through love and profound understanding. So, if you find yourself compromising often in life, and see your life as a prison from which you want to escape, know that there is no way you can live in love and Togetherness-Fulfillment. Even if only one of you in your relationship lives this way, you will not be able to move forward together easily. The point, then, is not to chase after transient pleasure, but to live with lasting satisfaction in your relationship. That is, to make your life and relationship so beautiful that you have no need to flee from anything; to live with peace of mind, which is what people who have compromised in life are desperately seeking.

If you are in a relationship of compromise, ask yourself why you are in it. Ask yourself if you really love your partner, or if you have compromised and are afraid of separation. Depending on the answers, you will make decisions accordingly.

- Have you accepted being with someone who is not your Fulfilled Reflecting Self out of insecurity?
- If you are in a relationship of compromise, why are you staying?
- If the reason for your relationship is not love, then what is the point of being together?

- If you don't help each other grow, what's the point of being together?
- If you don't enjoy every moment of your relationship, whether it's good or bad, then what's the point of being together?
- If you don't want, with every single cell of your being, to spend every split second together, then what's the point of being together?

How to free yourself from compromise and be guided by love

If, based on the answers you gave to the above questions, you see that your partner is your Fulfilled Reflecting Self and you love each other, but that your life is full of difficulties and compromises in other areas, such as work or other social relationships, then you simply need to discuss and decide together what you need to change.

First, it is essential to define the purpose of your existence together, as we explained in the Existential Aware Self Model in Chapter One. This means clarifying your life purpose, your relationship purpose, your legacy, and your vision. Once you have done this, you have already partially escaped compromise, because you have taken the first step towards living a unique life with your partner. You will find that compromise is limiting because you now know where you stand. But it still takes commitment and action to change your life for the better. And it is important that you are on the same path with the same values (Unlimited Aware Self Model) as your partner. For, if two people do not evolve together on a common path, the relationship will eventually fall apart. We cannot evolve if one of us is progressing and the other is stagnating. So, it is vital that the priorities and goals in your relationship are shared.

This is where change comes in, and its enemies are compromise and stagnation. If we don't change, we don't move forward in life. It's as simple as that. Change is inevitable, and it is therefore vital that we change by choice for the better and not for the worse. To change the situations, we don't want in our life and relationship, as well as our negative behaviors, we need to change our perceptions, and our limiting beliefs and understand our values and priorities. This means we have to change our mindset of compromise. In essence, we will not have lasting change unless we focus on our values and who we are. So, as a couple, you should work from a place of change instead of one of compromise, where things stay the same.

It is also essential to understand two important truths about change:

The first truth

We can only change one person in our life. That person is us. We can help our Fulfilled Reflecting Self to change, but we cannot change them, just as we cannot change any other person.

The second truth

Change is not a process that takes a long time. In fact, change is a state that we have either reached or not yet reached. That is, there is no "I am changing" or "I will change", but rather "I have changed" or "I have not changed". So, we have two options: to either change the negative behavior altogether or stick to "I will change" or "I wish to change" and never make any progress.

Change is only one part of improvement. Improvement, unlike change, is a continuous process involving many permanent changes. This means that we never stop improving because we always have room for improvement, and during our improvement, we can make many permanent changes, such as changes in our behavior, mindset, etc.

It is up to you whether you continue to compromise in your life or whether you choose to walk with your partner on the path of continuous improvement, changing everything that is not serving you.

We have 365 days in a year. This means that every one of those days is an opportunity to become a better person and to strengthen our relationship with our partner. So, there are no excuses, only 365 opportunities for improvement.

Time for introspection

- Do you compromise in your life and relationship? If not, very well. Continue your evolution. If you do, then identify the areas where you compromise.
- Ask yourself why you compromise and why you do not change. What is holding you back? Fear, limiting beliefs, other people, rules? Find the reason you are stuck, decide to change, and take action.
- Ask yourself if you deserve to live with compromise and stagnation.
- Is your partner your Fulfilled Reflecting Self, or someone with whom you compromise?
- What do you need to do to put an end to compromise and stagnation for good?

We assure you that if you answer these questions honestly, you can get the power to do what you want and spread your wings. Don't settle for people you do not love and situations that do not support your evolution any longer. *Live life to the fullest and dare to make your goals a reality.* The only person who can trap you in compromise, stagnation, and failure is yourself. You have all the tools you need to create a peaceful life and a fulfilling relationship. So, don't wait any longer and live the life you deserve with your Fulfilled Reflecting Self now.

2.9 — The enslaving seriousness trap and the enslaving perfect relationship trap

As we finish this chapter, we should discuss two frequent traps we can fall into with our partner when starting or improving our relationship. These traps are the enslaving seriousness trap and the enslaving perfect relationship trap. So, let's look at what happens in each of these situations:

1) The enslaving seriousness trap

Some of us, when we start on the path of self-improvement and strengthening our relationship with our partner, can suddenly become serious and strict with ourselves and our partner. This happens because we are learning about discipline and self-control, stagnation and the importance of change, and the essence of life. In fact, we may even stop following the old and restrictive "musts" we used to have and follow new "musts". These "musts" can be: we must not waste our time, we must not have meaningless relationships, we must not think negatively, and many other things. Of course, these are all healthy and beneficial for us and our partner, but not if they become strict and unbreakable rules that suffocate us. When we put strict rules in our life and relationship, we do not live in true freedom and peace.

So instead of following various "musts", it is healthy to clarify our values, "wants", "needs" and "non-negotiable nos", as we discussed in the first chapter, and live by them.

This way, we act with discipline and based on what helps us to progress, and we give ourselves true freedom.

What is the point of progress if we don't live in freedom, peace, and love, and enjoy every moment with our partner?

What is the point of following rules like soldiers and not enjoying our life and relationship? To progress with our partner, we need discipline, rigor, and change because we want to and not because we must. In other words, to want to change and be disciplined so that we as a couple can enjoy life together and live life the way we like it. This is the delicate and beautiful balance between rigor and carefree living.

Even we, as authors, may appear in the book as strict, passionate, and serious because that is how we progress in life: with passion, rigor, and discipline. But the purpose of rigor and discipline is to get to a point where we enjoy every aspect of our life and relationship. That's why in your relationship it is important to laugh, relax, have fun, be carefree, and not take some things so seriously. There are times when we need to be serious and disciplined, but there are also times when we need to relax and have fun. If our relationship is not a joyful journey of love, then we have to ask ourselves what is blocking us and taking away the joy.

So, if you fall into this trap and notice it, talk to your partner, and redefine your priorities. For example, have you been so focused on your work that you have forgotten to relax and laugh with your partner? Or maybe you spend most of your day stressed out and don't take the time to have fun with your partner?

Ask yourself these questions together and find a healthier way to adjust your routine. Instead of constantly stressing about the steps you "must" take to improve and achieve your goals, give yourself and your partner time to relax and be carefree.

2) The enslaving perfect relationship trap

Many couples have a picture in their heads of what a relationship should be like. In fact, they create the image that a relationship can be perfect. They are the opposite of people who compromise and live a "dead" relationship. However, as we have already explained, there is no perfection in life. *None of us will ever be perfect because our very existence is progressive.* This means that no matter how much we improve, we will always have room for more growth. The same applies to our relationship with our partner. No matter how much we unite, there will always be room for improvement between us. Even when we reach the level of Togetherness-Fulfillment, which is the ultimate unity of two people, as we explain in the last chapter, we will still need to improve every day. This is the beauty of life and romantic relationships. The constant progress and development.

So, if you find yourself in any of the negative behaviors or situations we have described in this chapter, do not judge yourself or your partner. Do not judge your relationship. There is no relationship without such behaviors. In fact, every successful and healthy relationship has gone through many difficult times, much pain, and many negative behaviors and situations because these behaviors and situations are ways of self-improvement. They are lessons in getting to know ourselves and our partner better. Every relationship will always have difficulties and challenges because, through them, we grow and become stronger so that we can live in peace and fulfillment.

Therefore, there is no such thing as a perfect relationship. There is a healthy and spiritual relationship with fulfillment where partners make mistakes and instead of blaming themselves and each other, they take responsibility and correct their mistakes.

We suggest that you adopt the principle of continuous improvement as a way of life that has only positive aspects.

If we choose to live by continuous improvement, we can more easily achieve balance because we will not condemn ourselves for our mistakes, nor will we avoid taking responsibility for them. We will be in alignment with the truth of ourselves and constantly evolve to treat our partner with love and respect.

Time for introspection

- How strict, disciplined, and serious are you in your relationship with your partner? Do you express the above in a healthy way, or have you gone too far?
- How much do you enjoy your relationship with your partner and every moment together? Can you easily live in the present moment, or is something else always on your mind?
- Are you constantly strengthening your relationship with your partner? If so, what exactly do you do? If not, why?
- What do you need to do to balance discipline and rigor with carelessness and enjoyment in your relationship with your partner?

- Do you feel pressure to be "perfect" in your relationship with your partner? If so, why? What does that offer you? If not, why?
- Are you free in your life and relationship with your partner? Are you at peace?
- What do you need to do to escape the shackles of false perfection and live in a way that combines progress with relaxation?

2.10 — Summary and the Negative Behavior Improvement Model

Based on this chapter, we can conclude that there are generally *two main types of negative behavior in a relationship.*

In the **first type**, we do not admit our mistakes and negative behavior. We criticize our partner, we mock them, we are driven to arrogance, and we want to manipulate and control them.

In the **second type**, we allow ourselves to become victims to be exploited. We give up our power and succumb to every negative behavior of our partner.

But there is also **a balanced state** where we are driven neither to arrogance nor to submissiveness. The balanced and healthy behavior and situation between a couple is one of honest self-evaluation where both partners admit their mistakes, take responsibility, understand their partner, and commit to moving forward together by helping each other.

Now that you have studied all the Self-Awareness Cultivating Models and dealt with the key negative behaviors and situations in a relationship, you can work with your partner to cultivate balance in your relationship.

The Negative Behavior Improvement Model

To help you even more, we have created a model for improving negative behavior which we have used many times when we exhibited dysfunctional behavior. This model will help you to move from a stage of immature responses to a stage of maturity, understanding, and respect. The model is broad, meaning that it does not address every single negative behavior, as each couple has different difficulties.

Criticism, blame, ridicule, mockery, belittling, manipulation, possessiveness, control, demands, arrogance, submissiveness, expectations, emotionally charged behaviors, outbursts, past influences, dependency, denial, irresponsibility, communication difficulties, compromise, stagnation, excuses, and lies occur with varying frequency and intensity in each couple.

One couple may display all the above behaviors and situations to a small extent, another may exhibit some but to a big extent, and another may have exhibited some in the past and drastically reduced them. It is good for you to adapt the model to your particular needs and areas for improvement.

So, let's look at it:

a) The first stage is one in which the partners have not worked on themselves and their behavior. Therefore, there is usually the following dysfunctional situation:

1 - There is an external stimulus (e.g., difficulties at work), an emotional charge, an expectation, or a disagreement with the partner.

2 - One partner accuses the other because they are emotionally immature, or for one of the reasons we have discussed in this chapter.

3 - The accused partner becomes defensive and starts accusing their partner too.

4 - Tension increases and self-control is lost. The situation turns into chaos in each partner's mind. Everyone tries to prove that they are right.

5 - They compromise after a while because they can't agree (one says one thing, the other says another) and don't discuss the issue again when they calm down. So, it remains unresolved with no positive outcome.

This whole situation starts out of self-ignorance and lack of understanding and can include many of the negative behaviors we have explored in this chapter. This situation occurs in couples who have not developed their romantic relationship awareness at all. It can also exist in conscious couples who want to treat each other in a healthy way, but don't yet know how to do so.

b) Once one of the partners has worked on themselves and shown understanding and patience, the situation can improve a little and the couple can move on to the second stage, where the following can happen:

1 - There is an external stimulus (e.g., difficulties at work), an emotional charge, an expectation, or a disagreement with the partner.

2 - One partner accuses the other because they are emotionally immature, or for one of the reasons we have discussed in this chapter.

3 - The other partner is understanding and not defensive. They might say, "I understand that you have a difficulty, but it is not fair or healthy to take it out on me. Would you like to discuss it calmly and work it out together?".

4 - The partner is again unable to calm down and continues to lash out, despite their partner's positive attitude.

5 - The understanding partner politely says that they will only discuss it when they are both calm. So, when the partner calms down, they discuss. If both partners are at a level of maturity, they can find the cause and solution of the issue. If not, they remain in the same state of ignorance without having learned a healthy way of managing the dynamics between them.

Here we see how much better the situation gets just because one partner is more mature and balanced. Things may not be resolved, but they're not getting worse, and that's a positive development. It is now the responsibility of the partner who has not matured to change for the problematic situation to be resolved.

c) What is crucial in a romantic relationship is therefore the third stage, the healthy one:

1 - There is an external stimulus (e.g., difficulties at work), an emotional charge, an expectation, or a disagreement with the partner.

2 - One partner accuses the other because they are emotionally immature, or for one of the reasons we have discussed in this chapter.

3 - The other partner is understanding and not defensive. They might say, "I understand that you have a difficulty, but it is not fair or healthy to take it out on me. Would you like to discuss it calmly and work it out together?".

4 - The partner, seeing their partner's understanding, calms down a little and remembers who they are and their values. They understand that their behavior is not healthy, admit their mistake, and apologize, now with clarity of mind.

5 - There is a meaningful and constructive discussion between the couple, and they find a solution together. They clarify the cause of the argument, the lesson learned, and what they are committed to doing to prevent this particular negative behavior from happening again. They become more united as a couple.

6 - If, for some reason, there is another outburst, it is likely to be much less intense and the couple will handle it in the same balanced way, learning another lesson from which they will improve and become even more united.

You can now see how, in time and with a lot of couple work, we can improve our negative behaviors. Of course, we are all imperfect human beings who may at some point become emotionally charged and make a mistake. However, we can assure you that over time, if you don't give up, the number of arguments will decrease dramatically, and you will be able to find a solution without thinking twice. This is because healthy and mature behaviors will become your habit. So, generally, you will react in a healthy way automatically.

Notice when and why you take it out on each other. At each outburst, show at least some understanding and suggest that you talk calmly to find the real cause of the argument and then the appropriate way to deal with it. Identify what other behaviors arise from the tension (e.g., communication difficulty, belittling, etc.) and work on them accordingly. It always takes a bit of understanding and maturity from both of you. This is the first essential step. When you reach this level, you will be able to develop your relationship further and stop any negative behaviors for good. As understanding becomes your habit, you will prevent many negative behaviors before they become serious.

If you make your relationship the number one priority in your life and truly love each other, you will succeed.

To wrap up the chapter, here we remind you the ten questions we need to ask ourselves and our partner whenever we or they behave in an unhealthy way:

1 - If my partner treated me like this, would I like it?

2 - Would I treat a stranger or someone who is not closely related to me in the same negative way as my partner?

3 - If I love my partner, why do I treat them like this?

4 - Do I take my partner for granted and as a person with whom I feel so familiar that I end up taking it out on them because I "can't" do it to others?

5 - Is there a better and more dignified way to behave towards my partner?

6 - Am I the one who should behave better?

7 - Does my negative behavior stem from the truth of myself (as explained in the Unlimited Aware Self Model in Chapter One) or from defensive instincts and immaturity?

8 - Since my negative behavior is not in line with who I am (responsible, mature, strong, compassionate, etc.) then why do I choose to behave in this harmful way?

9 - I don't like my partner to treat me negatively, and I wouldn't dare treat people I know or strangers in such an extreme way, so why should I do it to my partner, who is the most important person in my life?

10 - What do I need to change to improve each negative behavior?

With this in mind, and with daily introspection and application, you can do wonders for your relationship.

3

Building trust, walking on the path
of continuous improvement

So far, we have explored the basic ways in which we operate as human beings, via the Self-Awareness Cultivating Models of Chapter One, and this way you can understand yourself and your partner much better. We have also looked at the main negative behaviors and situations that a couple can present, and now you can more easily identify which ones you present and change them. In this chapter, we talk about trust and how an aware couple cultivates it as a key foundation of the relationship.

Trust is a prerequisite so that each partner can be completely spiritually naked without fear of criticism. Building trust requires self-awareness, awareness, responsibility, forgiveness, gratitude, equality, faith, and admiration. We are going to explore the above further and see how a couple can flourish and progress. This chapter discusses the continuous improvement in our romantic relationship, looking at the different ways in which we create and maintain unshakable trust, and looking at improvement from different perspectives which are equally important.

3.1 — The Eight Steps to Romantic Relationship Awareness

It takes time for a couple to build trust, except in some cases where trust is gained rapidly, as was the case with us. However, trust is usually cultivated over time, and an essential element in building it quickly and effectively is awareness. If the partners in a relationship have not developed their awareness, even to a small degree, it will be difficult for them to trust each other. That is because they will not really know themselves and therefore will not be able to understand their partner. For this reason, the first chapter of this book deals mainly with self-awareness and understanding the way we operate as human beings.

Romantic Relationship Awareness

But what is awareness in our romantic relationship? After a profound understanding of the first chapter, you may already be clear about what awareness is. However, it is important to develop the subject of awareness further, as it is one of the main components of a successful relationship.

Romantic relationship awareness is knowing our partner and our relationship on a deep level. This means that after we have individually developed the basic elements of our self-awareness (who I am, what my values are, where I am in life, what I want in life, etc.), we re-evaluate them with our partner and create a strong connection and unity between these elements. This way, we gain essential knowledge of each other and have a common and clear path in life. More simply, romantic relationship awareness is knowing our partner as well as we know ourselves and applying the positive things we know to our relationship without dwelling on theoretical knowledge.

Of course, awareness in our relationship does not necessarily require the already developed self-awareness of each partner, as some may believe, although this is a very positive thing to happen. Many people are not deeply aware of themselves when they start a relationship with their partner. This can be damaging to the relationship, but it does not mean that the relationship is doomed. Partners, if motivated by true love, can come to mutual awareness by helping each other to develop self-awareness within the relationship. That is, if partners face difficulties in their communication and behavior, but at the same time love each other, they may be confused. Love can lead them to learn more about themselves and thus develop their self-awareness (true knowledge of themselves) and then develop their romantic relationship awareness (true knowledge of their partner and the relationship situation). In short, their relationship will be the trigger for them to begin the journey of truly knowing themselves.

So, it is not necessary to develop self-awareness before the relationship. Whatever stage of developed or undeveloped self-awareness and romantic relationship awareness one is at, it is essential that each partner continues to develop and learn, and does not rest on what they know. This is the importance of self-awareness and romantic relationship awareness. So don't worry about where you are now and if you don't know yourself and your partner well yet. With individual and couple work, you can do it, and you deserve it. Willingness and action to improve, driven by love for your partner, is more than enough to help you develop awareness in your relationship and unite.

Here, we are going to explore eight simple steps towards awareness, consisting mainly of the key elements of the Self-Awareness Cultivating Models we have created in Chapter One, but also in combination with elements from Chapter Two. This path to awareness, through the eight simple steps, is an easier path than the path through the Self-Awareness Cultivating Models. Any couple can follow this path if they are having difficulty with practicing these models. That is, instead of working on each Self-Awareness Cultivating Model, which takes a lot of time, you will follow eight simple steps to romantic relationship awareness and then work more on the models in Chapter One. It is important that you complete these steps together, as a couple, not individually, so that you use your time wisely and march towards the same path together. The aim here is to build strong trust with each other. So, let's look at the Eight Steps to Romantic Relationship Awareness.

The Eight Steps to Romantic Relationship Awareness

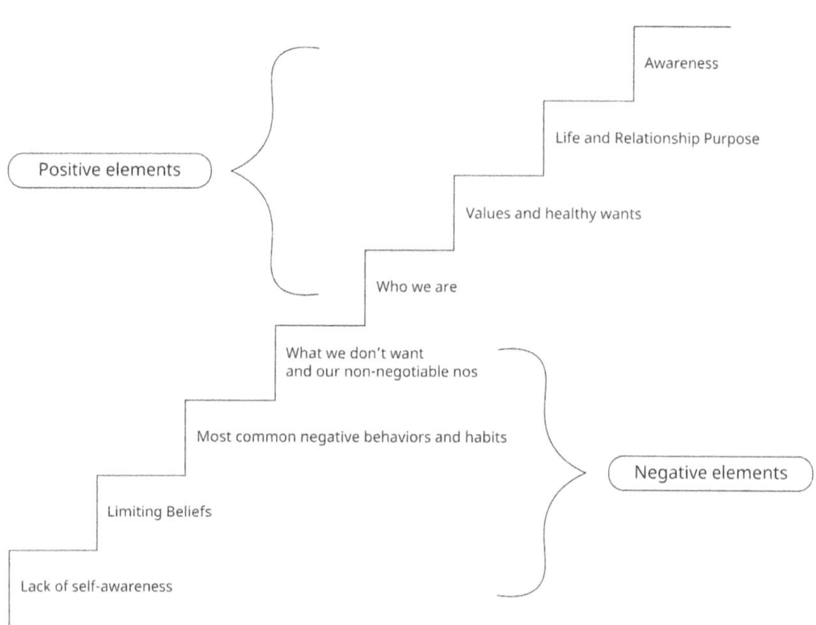

As we can see in the model above, we have created eight steps that lead to awareness within a romantic relationship. These steps illustrate the path a couple can take to become aware of themselves and their partner. This way, partners will explore and clarify the very basic elements of their existence, which will help the evolution of their relationship.

1. Lack of self-awareness

The first level is confusion, where we don't know ourselves. When we are at this level it means that we go through life with what we have learned from parents, teachers, peers, and whatever education we have had. We follow the opinions and beliefs of other people and society without having explored what we really want within ourselves. We have not explored the meaning of our existence and we do not know ourselves deeply, only superficially. Furthermore, we do not know the reasons for our decisions and why we do what we do. The knowledge we have in life is limited and often restrictive. We are in complete darkness, and so we do not know how to manage our relationship in a healthy way because we do not know how to manage ourselves.

Most of us have been through this stage. The question is how long you stay there, how much you want to get out of it, and whether you will leave at some point and not stay there for the rest of your life. So, it is useful to ask yourself the following questions:

- How long have you been in this state of ignorance? Do you want to get out? If not, why? If you do, what's stopping you?

- How willing are you to do whatever it takes to get out of this stage?

2. Limiting Beliefs

If you are in the ignorance stage, it is useful as a couple to first identify your limiting beliefs, as these are the ones that block you in life. This is the second level and the first step towards awareness for those who find it difficult to work on the Self-Awareness Cultivating Models from Chapter One. For example, a limiting belief that can damage a relationship is that women should only be involved in household chores and not pursue a career. This can lead to a relationship with compromise or even an oppressive relationship.

Identifying and changing any kind of limiting beliefs about ourselves, other people, and life is an excellent step to freeing ourselves from the shackles of society and other people's "wants". Thus, we begin to discover ourselves and what we want in life as a couple.

3. Most common negative behaviors and habits

Once we have changed the prejudices and beliefs that hold us back, we can identify our most common negative behaviors and bad habits. By identifying our negative behaviors, we can find the opposite positive ones and reinforce them. So, as we address our negative behaviors and habits, we will increasingly make room for our positive and helpful behaviors to build new habits that help our relationship. For example, we can identify criticism as a habitual behavior and address it by developing our understanding and ability to listen meaningfully to our partner without arrogance.

4. What we don't want and "non-negotiable nos"

All of this can help us to move on to the fourth level, where, as a couple, we become clear about what we don't want in life, as well as our "non-negotiable nos". Be careful though, focusing on what we don't want in life is not beneficial at all and can lead to a lot of anger, sadness, and frustration. However, it is very helpful to be clear within ourselves about what we don't want and where we want to say "no" in life. This alone helps us to be clearer in our relationship with each other. It also helps us to deal more easily with other people and unhelpful situations where we want to say "no". For example, as a couple, we may not want to go to our colleague's party because we don't have many things in common with them and want to spend quality time just the two of us. On the other hand, a "non-negotiable no" might be that, as a couple, we will not allow another person to come between us under any circumstances.

So, these four levels are about our basic negative elements, things that limit us and that we need to say no to in order to improve, and how we can use them to develop our awareness and strengthen our relationship. Already at this stage, having clarified all the above, trust is strengthened.

5. Who we are
Once we have worked as a couple on our main negative elements, we can more easily develop our positive elements, because we have given ourselves and our relationship a lot of room to grow, having thrown away a lot of "rubbish". So, the next level is clarifying who we really are.

It is useful for a couple to use the following positive qualities as a basis for who they are, such as:

- responsibility,
- humility,
- determination,
- honesty,
- patience,
- and kindness.

By working on these qualities, we are led to appropriate behaviors that help our relationship. Who doesn't want an honest relationship where their partner is responsible, decisive, humble, and patient?

6. Values and healthy wants
Having clarified the very basic positive qualities that we both want to express in our relationship daily, we can then clarify our values and healthy "wants". Key values that are useful for a couple to prioritize are, of course, love, health, progress, and fulfillment. Some healthy "wants" might be quality couple time and help with household chores. Up to now, we have reached a point where we know ourselves and our partner quite well, and we are focusing on what is of great value to us rather than what we don't want and don't need.

7. Life and Relationship Purpose

We can find our life and relationship purpose without having to deal with the other elements of the purpose of our existence, which is our legacy and our vision. Now it is more important to lay the healthy foundations in our relationship so that we can then move on. Clarifying our life and relationship purpose are essential key steps in developing our awareness.

8. Awareness

Having worked on all the above, we come to the final step, which is awareness. This means that we now know many elements, both positive and negative, both for ourselves and our partner, and we have mapped out our common life path. All that remains is to develop our awareness, to learn more about ourselves, our partner, and our relationship, and to apply this to our daily life because awareness is a never-ending process of improvement.

Therefore, if you have not yet worked on the Self-Awareness Cultivating Models in Chapter One, or if you are finding it difficult to apply each model to yourself and your daily life, we suggest that you follow these Eight Steps to Romantic Relationship Awareness. By finding your limiting beliefs and prejudices, your bad habits and what you don't want in life, you will gain more clarity. Once you have clarified and corrected the main negative elements of yourself, you can move on to finding your main positive elements: your qualities, what you want, your values and life and relationship purpose, and move forward together as a couple on that basis.

Companionate Romantic Solitude

The more you work on your awareness together, the more connected you will be and the more you will build a solid foundation of trust in your relationship. The second volume of the book also provides you with more practical and easy-to-follow steps.

The development of our awareness is important because it begins with the development of our self-awareness. The more we know ourselves and understand our faults and weaknesses, the more we become empathetic to other people and, of course, even more, empathetic to our life partner, with whom we can unite on every level of our being. We understand that our partner has weaknesses, and we become more compassionate, we express our love more, we forgive more easily, and we learn to focus on the beauties of our life and relationship. This way, we grow in understanding and when our partner makes a mistake, we are there to help them, not to judge them. This is how trust grows.

By following the Eight Steps to Romantic Relationship Awareness as a couple, we begin to understand that our partner has learned to communicate and to behave in a certain way since childhood, and carries with them years of beliefs that are deeply rooted in them.

So, if one partner is used to tension, and anger and the other is used to peace, tranquility, and stability, then both will come into conflict and feel alienated. But by working through the Eight Steps to Romantic Relationship Awareness, we learn to appreciate our partner's diversity and find a way to balance our very different behaviors and even become aware of what our partner needs to behave in a healthy way. This helps us to avoid behaviors that our partner does not like and that damage our relationship. Thus, we create a healthy environment of love, understanding and continual improvement that is also stable and secure.

This healthy environment in our relationship is also what helps us to evolve comfortably and without pressure. Because we have developed our awareness to a very high level, we know that time with our partner is precious. That's why we want to spend as much time together as possible and prioritize our relationship. So, we consciously choose to be alone, but not in the usual sense of the word. We choose to be *alone together* and devote ourselves to our relationship, giving much less importance to other social relationships. This does not mean that there are no other social interactions in our life; but because we have no emotional voids to fill, we have few quality relationships apart from the relationship with our Fulfilled Reflecting Self. We call this beauty of life Companionate Romantic Solitude. In our Companionate Romantic Solitude, in silence and away from the bustle of society, we get to know ourselves and our partner even better. This is a wonderful experience that comes as we develop our awareness as a couple and build trust with each other.

The 3 zones in a romantic relationship

Companionate Romantic Solitude is so beautiful that if you manage to reach this level in your relationship, you will not think of accepting anything less than this peaceful unity. When we are in this state of healthy reflection and tranquility with our partner, we enter a zone of rapid development and at the same time peace and real security.

This is how we see the 3 zones in a romantic relationship:
- the zone of comfort and stagnation,
- the zone of progress and risk,
- and the zone of romantic relationship awareness.

The zone of comfort and stagnation is the state in which we do not improve, compromise with our partner and place very little value on our life and relationship. This means that we have not developed a healthy relationship with our partner, we do not address our negative behaviors, we do nothing to improve, and so we continue the same negative behaviors.

On the other hand, *the zone of progress and risk* is where we take risks in life and improve by facing our fears. For example, we are in constant creativity and productivity with our partner by doing our best to grow in knowledge and awareness. Obviously, the zone of comfort and stagnation offers us nothing, but the zone of progress and risk helps us. However, it is exhausting to be in the zone of progress and risk all the time because we do not give ourselves the time to just be and be at peace.

That is why it is healthy for a couple to be in *the zone of romantic relationship awareness*. This is the state where we know ourselves and our partner very well, we don't need other people and we are safe, but within that security, we know well when it is useful to be energetic and productive and when it is useful to just enjoy each other without doing anything. That is, we live in a balance that includes both our dynamic improvement and a peaceful state in which there is no reason to be busy with anything.

The zone of romantic relationship awareness is the state in which we have reached where we want to be with our partner and are therefore completely satisfied with our life and relationship. This doesn't mean that we don't need to improve or that we know everything, but that we experience peace and fulfillment. So, we will work on moving forward in life, but with steady and calm steps, without stress and pressure. In the zone of romantic relationship awareness, we are motivated by our truth, our values and our pure "wants". *To reach the zone of romantic relationship awareness, we must first go through the Eight Steps to Romantic Relationship Awareness and enjoy our Companionate Romantic Solitude. This is when we experience peace with our life partner.*

So, strengthen the trust in your relationship by working on the Eight Steps to Romantic Relationship Awareness if the Self-Awareness Cultivating Models seem like too much work. With love and consistency, you will be able to experience the beauty and uniqueness of Companionate Romantic Solitude and live in the zone of romantic relationship awareness. Progress must be a process of balance, not fear, and it is to this understanding that the development of our awareness leads us.

Once you have successfully completed the Eight Steps to Romantic Relationship Awareness, we encourage you not to neglect the Self-Awareness Cultivating Models and to work on each of them as a couple, as they will help you to grow even more. This will make it easier and faster for you to experience Togetherness-Fulfillment in your life (to be explored in the next chapter).

However, before we go any further, it is important to say that the whole process of the Eight Steps to Romantic Relationship Awareness, Companionate Romantic Solitude, and the zone of romantic relationship awareness must be a mutual "want" of the couple. Usually, it is not beneficial to start the process of developing your awareness if you know that your current relationship is not the relationship of your life. Of course, you can learn a lot about yourself and romantic relationships in general by following the Eight Steps to Romantic Relationship Awareness with a person who is not your Fulfilled Reflecting Self, but it still won't lead you to a vibrant and true relationship.

We have said that the goal is to develop trust, so it is critical that you work on the path of awareness only with your Fulfilled Reflecting Self. Otherwise, you are not likely to be open and completely honest in your relationship as you work towards awareness because you will not feel comfortable with someone who is not your Fulfilled Reflecting Self. Thus, you will create a blockage to trust. But what is needed to build trust is for you to feel and be free and completely comfortable with your partner. It is therefore essential that you are fully aware of the person you are with and the seriousness of your relationship.

Time for introspection

- Do you develop awareness in your relationship? If so, how do you do it? If not, why don't you?
- Are you willing to follow the Eight Steps to Romantic Relationship Awareness with your partner? If so, why? If not, why?
- Do you experience Companionate Romantic Solitude with your partner? If so, how exactly do you experience it? If not, why don't you experience it?
- Are you in the zone of romantic relationship awareness with your partner? If so, why? What exactly do you experience in this zone? If not, why? What prevents you from living life in the zone of romantic relationship awareness?
- How can you help yourself to develop self-awareness? How can you help your partner develop self-awareness?
- What do you need to do to further develop awareness in your relationship with your partner?

3.2 — The Stages Towards Couple Responsibility

Now that you understand more about awareness in a romantic relationship and how important it is to be aware of your partner's inner world, it is time to talk about responsibility. Throughout this book, we have mentioned responsibility many times because it is an essential and fundamental element that helps to develop trust in a relationship. In fact, responsibility is a quality trait of all people, as we explained in the Unlimited Aware Self Model, but few people express it practically in their daily lives. This is because many people receive a mediocre to poor upbringing as children and therefore do not become mature and responsible adults.

It is therefore crucial that we take responsibility for our lives and for ourselves, for without this, we will not be able to grow and, above all, create a successful relationship with our Fulfilled Reflecting Self. We will describe the stages of responsibility we believe is necessary for all of us to go through as we age to have a spiritually mature romantic relationship with our life partner.

The Stages Towards Couple Responsibility

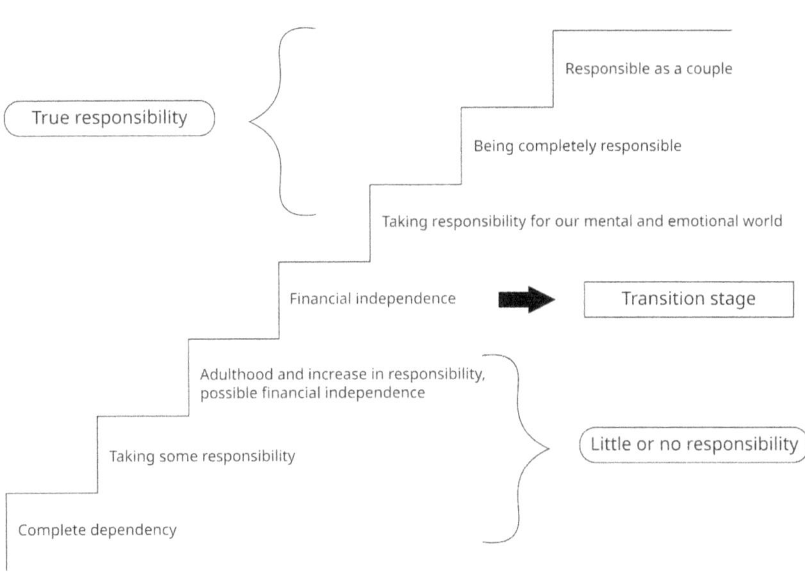

As we can see in the model above, there are seven stages towards responsibility. The first three, are the ones where we take little or no responsibility for our lives. The fourth stage is the stage of transition, and the last three are the stages of true responsibility. We have created these based on our experience and views and, of course, it does not mean that they are definitive.

1. Complete Dependency

The first stage begins at birth and lasts until the age of 12. In this stage, we are completely dependent on our parents and other people. Our lives and survival are in the hands of other people, and we are not responsible for ourselves. Our food, water, clothing, home, money, and education are the responsibility of others. At this stage, when our school life begins, we begin to acquire a small sense of responsibility.

2. Taking some responsibility

The second stage lasts from the age of 12 to the age of 18. In this stage, other people are still responsible for us, but we start to grow up and take more responsibility for everything we do. We now judge life more in terms of our peers than our parents. Peer relationships become more interesting, and we even start to have romantic relationships. We also have more responsibility for our education as it becomes more demanding.

3. Adulthood and increase in responsibility

The third stage starts from adulthood and goes up to financial independence and living without our parents. This is different for each person and absolutely necessary for the development of responsibility. Some people become independent at a very early age, having received a good upbringing, while others remain attached to their parents and do not grow up spiritually, only physically and in age.

4. Financial Independence – Transition Stage

The fourth stage is the stage of transition where we move from superficial responsibility to substantial responsibility. It starts with financial independence and goes up to the moment when we decide to take full responsibility for ourselves and stop blaming other people. This stage is crucial, but unfortunately, many people stop there and never go any further. Yes, they have managed to become financially independent and live on their own or with their partner or even have children, but they are still not taking actual responsibility for themselves.

5. Taking responsibility for our mental and emotional world

But what does it mean to take responsibility for ourselves? Taking responsibility for ourselves begins the moment we understand that we are fully responsible for our thoughts, emotions, actions, and results in life. This is the fifth stage where true responsibility begins, and we explore it more below.

6. Being completely responsible

The sixth stage is where having exercised our responsibility and cultivating our self-awareness daily, we take full responsibility for everything we do without difficulty and are now strong, mature, and responsible people.

7. Responsible as a couple

The final stage is when we are responsible people in the context of our relationship with our partner. Both partners continue to be responsible people who don't complain like little children when they don't get what they want or when they have difficulties. We both take our fair share of responsibility and make good use of the dynamics between us in a mature way. So, when one of us makes a mistake, we admit it and commit to fixing it. At the same time, the other partner shows understanding. In our communication with each other, we do not try to solve the partner's issues as if they are incapable of doing it alone, but we always choose to find solutions together as two equal and mature people. This way, we help each other effectively and maturely, and we both take the initiative. This is the stage of true strength within a romantic relationship of pure connection, spiritual unity, and no dependencies.

Getting older doesn't mean you're mature

As we have said, unfortunately, some people remain stuck in the transition stage, and indeed many do not even reach this stage and remain children in adult bodies. They are attached to their parents and find it difficult to take responsibility for their lives. So, they cannot progress and grow up spiritually. This naturally creates difficulties in their relationship with their partner. They find it difficult to have a healthy, strong, and mature relationship with their partner because they are not at the spiritual level of maturity that a romantic relationship requires. That is, they are stuck in a childhood stage of dependency on their parents and probably don't even realize it. They believe that they do not need to be cut off from their parents and that life is experienced at an immature level of dependency because they believe this is normal. However, this is detrimental to their relationship with their partner as they are not meant to have a relationship with or marry a spiritually immature person but a spiritually mature and responsible adult.

In fact, if a partner is spiritually immature and dependent on their parents in any way (emotionally, financially, etc.), they may often allow them to interfere with their romantic relationship and cause harm. People who are in a codependent and possessive relationship with their parents and do not put their relationship with their partner first are usually motivated mainly by emotions, inferior needs for validation and insecurity. Therefore, they cannot be mature individuals. These people often end up living their whole lives in the zone of comfort and stagnation, as we explained in the analysis of awareness earlier in this chapter. However, no human being deserves this situation.

For this reason, it is crucial that we detach from our parents and other people and not be dependent on them emotionally, mentally, spiritually, financially, or in any other way. That is, to stop being as we were in our childhood, to take life into our hands and spread our wings. To understand that just because we didn't have certain needs for acceptance, validation, and approval met, and didn't get as much praise as we wanted from our parents as children, or didn't learn to take initiative, there is no reason to continue to live that way, seeking validation either from parents or other people.

Now is the time to take control of our lives and create the beautiful and meaningful relationship we are meant to have with our partner. The more we free ourselves from our emotional dependency on parents and other people in general, and the more we take responsibility for our actions, the more mature people we become.

Therefore, to move forward in life, we need to take full responsibility for ourselves and stop defining our lives based on the past, our childhood, our parents' "failures" or "successes", and other people's "wants" and "musts". The goal is to be spiritual adults, not children in adult bodies. That is, to be truly mature people and not supposedly mature just because we age.

So, you see, being a spiritual adult and a truly mature person has absolutely nothing to do with age. On the contrary, it has everything to do with whether and how much responsibility one takes for oneself and one's life, whether one is a completely independent person, and whether one is on the path of continuous self-improvement, which requires constant development of self-awareness.

A fifty-year-old who lives without knowing who they are, their values, and "non-negotiable nos" and remains imprisoned by their limiting beliefs without taking total responsibility for themselves is less mature and responsible than a twenty-year-old who has been on the path of self-improvement and self-awareness for the last two years, doing whatever it takes to clarify who they are, their values, and "non-negotiable nos". So, the second person is more mature than the first, even though they are younger and have less years of experience in life. The person who is fifty years old has fifty years of ignorance, while the person who is twenty years old has two years of spiritual search, evolution, and true responsibility.

Who would you rather spend your life with?

Someone who lives in ignorance and is emotionally dependent on their parents, or someone who is continuously developing self-awareness and taking responsibility for their actions? Would you trust a person who doesn't know themselves and is spiritually immature or a person who is cultivating themselves and learning from their mistakes?

Becoming a spiritually mature person

But how do we become truly responsible and mature people and grow up spiritually and not just in age? How do we express responsibility and maturity in the context of our romantic relationship? Spiritual maturity begins when we start to take responsibility for our inner world as well as our actions and, of course, when we stop being dependent on other people.

In the Balanced Aware Self Model in Chapter One, we discussed that we all exist in a continual state where our ideas lead to choices and actions and positive or bad life outcomes.

Let us briefly recall how our mental, emotional, and spiritual levels are connected

Although we don't always control exactly which thoughts come into our minds, we do control which ones we focus on because of our free will. Our logic can help us choose the thoughts we focus on. Those will lead to certain emotions, and thus we will have certain intentions which will lead us to adopting certain attitudes, based on the boundaries we set for ourselves. We can be confused by listening to conflicting messages from our logical thoughts and logic and our emotions. So, our intuition and our Unlimited Aware Self can help us make the best decisions. Whether we choose our mental, emotional, or spiritual level, we will make certain decisions and choices. Depending on our decisions and choices, we will behave and act relevantly. Our actions and attitudes will lead us to corresponding results in our life and romantic relationship.

So, we have total responsibility for the following: our inner world, the thoughts we focus on, the emotions we feel, the choices, actions, and behaviors we make, and therefore the results we experience. No one else is responsible for the above; we are.

Not our partner, nor our neighbor, nor our parents, nor our friends, nor the weather, nor the government, nor the economy, nor the universe. We are solely responsible for everything that happens within us and for every single action we take. We cannot control other people's thoughts and behavior, nor many of the situations that happen to us. But we do have total control over how we behave towards other people and how we deal with every situation we experience.

No one can "make" us feel anything

No one else, not even our Fulfilled Reflecting Self, can "make" us feel anything internally. There is no such thing as "making" someone feel joy, sadness, anger, or any other emotion. The truth is that only *we* are responsible for whether we feel joy, sadness, anger, etc. We alone have total control over our emotions. Of course, our partner or other people and external situations play a role in our emotional state, but they are not responsible for what and how we feel.

A couple, in which each partner takes sole responsibility for their emotions and is a mature and responsible adult, has already prevented too many negative situations and behaviors. This is because they do not blame each other for their emotions, but recognize that it is their responsibility and choice where to focus and whether to feel good or bad.

For example, if one partner speaks insultingly to their partner, they are responsible for their immature behavior and bad language, but not for how their partner feels and responds to that behavior. If their partner is a strong and mature person who is confident in their truth, they will not be offended or feel bad because they know that how they will feel is their choice. But if they tend to be weak and immature, they are likely to be offended, upset, or angry and will retaliate. So, whatever happens inside of us is only *our* responsibility and is related to how strong and mature we are. This is the way a mature and responsible person, a spiritual adult and not a physical adult with the mind of a small child, operates.

Therefore, as mature people, it is important to understand that other people and external situations do not influence us, nor do they ever control us. In fact, even our emotions do not affect or control us unless we allow them to. Our emotional state depends on how much or no control we give to other people and external situations. We can be in complete control of our inner world if we want to.

Apply this truth to the relationship with your partner and to the rest of your life. You will find that you will not blame any person or situation, nor will you take excessive responsibility for things that are not your fault. So, you will take responsibility for your own actions and apologize for what you have done, and your partner will take responsibility for their actions and apologize for anything negative that they do. This is a relationship of strength and evolution, where two mature adults are responsible and dedicated to their evolution. When both partners behave in such a mature and responsible way, they naturally trust each other.

Let's look at the characteristics of a couple where both partners are spiritually mature and responsible people:

1) Each partner is independent of their parents and other people.

2) Each partner is a healthy human being with no need for validation.

3) Each partner takes full responsibility for their thoughts, emotions, decisions, behaviors, actions, and results and does not blame their partner.

4) Each partner admits their mistakes and is not afraid to apologize.

5) Each partner recognizes that they are only responsible for themselves. They help their partner with love and strength, and not because they believe that their partner cannot take responsibility for themselves.

6) No partner tries to solve their partner's issues for themselves. Partners face every difficulty together and as equals.

7) Each partner lives in the present, not in the past or the future. They make decisions based on the present moment and not on their childhood or fantasies of the future.

8) Each partner walks the path of continuous self-improvement and awareness.

Now you have clarified the Stages Towards Couple Responsibility, the blocks that many people may have in their development, and the characteristics of a healthy relationship with responsibility and maturity. So, it's time to develop your responsibility even further. When you see that your partner is a responsible person, you will begin to trust them more. Of course, your partner needs to see the same in you to trust you.

Responsibility, as we said in the first chapter, is an integral part of everyone's essence, but we need to cultivate it and then maintain it by expressing it every day. The more we behave responsibly, maturely, respectfully, kindly, understandingly, honestly, and lovingly towards our partner, the faster this behavior will become a habit and a way of life. We will never be perfect, and at some point, we may behave irresponsibly, but we have the potential to improve all the time. Responsibility can truly free us from many worries, difficulties, obstacles, limitations, and weaknesses if we are willing to take responsibility for ourselves and not hide behind our finger.

Taking control of your life as a couple

At some point in our life, we, as a couple, decided that no other person or external situation would determine our life, our emotions, our decisions, and the course of our relationship and marriage. We decided to live on our own terms and within our own boundaries and to do what we wanted to do, taking full responsibility for ourselves, and setting high goals. We knew that even if we didn't achieve our goals, we would enjoy the journey and the lessons we learned together at our own risk. This, of course, rewards us in wonderful ways every day, and we have no regrets whatsoever. So don't be afraid to live responsibly and take life into your own hands to grow your relationship.

Work on the Stages Towards Couple Responsibility together, and you will change your relationship for the better. You will find that as you work on your responsibility as a couple, you will grow in awareness and vice versa. As you work on the Eight Steps to

Romantic Relationship Awareness, you will also grow in responsibility. In short, the more responsible you become, the more you will grow in awareness because to become responsible you must know yourself better and progress. The more you develop your self-awareness and romantic relationship awareness, the more responsible you will become because you will know yourself and your partner in depth. The more responsible you become, the more you will trust each other.

Time for introspection

- In which stage of responsibility are you? Why are you at this stage?
- Are you still spiritually immature or not? Are you stuck in the transition stage or are you taking charge of your life?
- Do you blame other people, or do you take full responsibility for yourself?
- Are you truly responsible and mature in your relationship? If so, how do you show it? If not, why aren't you?
- Do you take responsibility for your thoughts, emotions, decisions, actions, and results in life? If so, how do you do this? If not, why don't you?
- What do you need to do to become more responsible and mature spiritually?
- How can you help your partner to become a more responsible and mature person?

3.3 — Forgiveness and Gratitude

So far, we have explored the path of awareness and the importance of responsibility. As aware, mature, and responsible people, it is certain that we will be forgiving and grateful in our life and relationship. We accept the imperfect nature of ourselves and our partner and focus on the present.

Forgiveness and gratitude are essential elements of a successful and balanced relationship, and therefore a couple must forgive and be grateful with purity and honesty. Forgiveness and gratitude go hand in hand and grow in parallel. They blossom when we are in the zone of romantic relationship awareness with our partner. When both partners in a relationship forgive and express gratitude, it means that there is already trust. So, let's look at some key elements of forgiveness and gratitude.

3.3.1 — Forgiveness

Forgiveness is so important in life, yet some people overlook it or do not understand its meaning and value. Forgiveness leads us to peace of mind and soul. It frees us from held and suppressed emotions of anger, sadness, and anything else that may be a burden to us. It frees us from things that are causing excessive harm to ourselves and therefore to our relationship with our partner.

Forgiveness is not so much about the person we forgive, but about ourselves.

It is about being in peace within us and not allowing our emotions, other people, and external situations to overwhelm us, as we explained above in responsibility. So, we see that forgiveness is closely related to responsibility. We take responsibility for our emotions, forgive any person for their actions, and move on.

The same thing happens when we forgive ourselves. We forgive ourselves for whatever we have done and stop living in the past. We continue to live in the present moment and plan for the future. This is not selfish at all. On the contrary, it is true inner freedom. It is the mature choice of a person who loves themselves and not judges themselves. Of course, forgiving ourselves also requires a commitment not to repeat what we forgive ourselves for. So, we can forgive ourselves for all the negative and ugly things we have done, but we need to commit ourselves to positive change.

For example, we may have spoken badly to our partner in a tense situation and now feel bad about it. Instead of judging ourselves for our mistake, we choose to ease the pain of distress and forgive ourselves. At the same time, we make a commitment never to speak to our partner this way again.

When we forgive other people, forgiveness is again related to our peace and health, but it changes in tone depending on the person we are forgiving. For example, when we forgive our partner, who is the most important person in our life, we forgive them sincerely for what they have done so that we can be in a state of inner health both individually and as a couple. Forgiveness in our relationship with our partner is about understanding, compassion, unconditional acceptance, and love.

Together, we are an unbreakable fist.

Commitment to positive change is necessary, as it is when we forgive ourselves. We understand that we make mistakes in our relationship, but instead of becoming our mistakes, we push away the burden of any negative behavior and move forward with forgiveness.

The same is true when we forgive the people with whom we want to continue our relationship. We forgive them and have a conversation with them so that neither of us repeats our mistakes.

But when forgiveness involves people with whom we do not want to have further contact, we forgive them and remove them from our lives. That is, we forgive them for whatever they have done so that we can maintain our peace of mind, but this does not mean that we have to continue this relationship. We don't have to trust them and bring them back into our lives.

If they are not on the same path in life as we are, then they have no place in our daily lives and our inner world. For this reason, forgiveness is more about us and our peace of mind than about the people we forgive. In this case, we do not expect people we forgive to change. We are not interested in them changing because that is their responsibility. We are interested in ourselves being at peace. We forgive them within ourselves and move on, wishing them the best.

So, we can forgive some people by having a conversation with them, but we can also forgive them without telling them. That is, we can forgive them internally and not cling to the past. This can be done, for example, with an ex-partner with whom our relationship did not end well. We don't have to forgive them in person, we just have to forgive them in our hearts and move on with our lives, learning from our mistakes. We are not interested in that person being in our life, we are interested in being in balance and health within ourselves. At the same time, we wish them all the best.

The same thing happens when, as a couple, we decide together that we no longer wish to have contact with certain people. If we just push them away and don't forgive them, we carry a lot of emotional baggage and it can spill over into our relationship with each other. But if we forgive them, then they really do leave our lives because we have removed all the emotional baggage from us.

Therefore, forgiveness has the following forms:
1 — Forgiving ourselves
This is the most important form of forgiveness because if we do not forgive ourselves, we will find it difficult to forgive other people, including our partner. This can lead to a cycle of self-condemnation. The motivation for forgiving ourselves is always love.

2 — Forgiving our partner
This is an equally essential form of forgiveness that is absolutely necessary for the health of our relationship. If we do not forgive our partner, we will not be able to move forward in our relationship and will be stuck in the past. The likely result is the continuation of negative behavior that we do not forgive because we are constantly focusing

on it and keeping the burden inside. The motivation for forgiving our partner is always love.

3 — Forgiving other people we want in our life
This is important for our peace of mind, but also for maintaining formal or more meaningful relationships in our lives. The motivation for forgiving other people we want in our lives is for our peace of mind, but also to connect with these people.

4 — Forgiving people with whom we don't want to have contact anymore
This is crucial for our inner peace. If we stop having relationships with people that we despise but do not forgive them internally, we are likely to continue to be tormented within ourselves. The motivation for forgiving people we don't want in our lives is our peace and tranquility.

Do you mean it when you say, "I'm sorry"?
So, from the above, we can see the true nature of forgiveness and its immense value for peace in our life and relationship with our partner.

But before we move on to gratitude, it is important to clarify that *forgiveness is essential to be pure, sincere, and motivated by love and peace*. This is true not only when we forgive our partner or another person, but also when we apologize. There are instances where people, whether in the context of a romantic relationship and marriage or any other social relationship, apologize for their mistakes without meaning to. "Sorry", here, is empty and fake. It does not come from love and a genuine admission of error with a commitment to change but is superficial and sometimes even manipulative. These people apologize so they can take advantage of the other person's distress or pity. "Sorry" is used here either purely superficially, or as a means of manipulation so that the person apologizing can repeat the negative behavior sneakily. In either case, there is no real desire to change.

So, if you find that someone is apologizing to you without meaning to, ask yourself if you need that person in your life. Forgive them for what they have done but ask yourself if it is worth accepting their negative behavior. For example, in a romantic relationship, if one partner is constantly disrespectful and apologizes but continues to be disrespectful and doesn't change, what is the point of this relationship? It is very possible that this person doesn't want to actually improve, and their partner just accepts this destructive behavior. It is more likely that there is no love in this relationship. Be careful about which apologies are real and which are fake, which people deserve to be in your life and which not. Forgiveness, however, is beneficial to always be an integral part of our mental and emotional peace of mind.

Time for introspection

- How do you see forgiveness? Is forgiveness for you something superficial, manipulative, or meaningful? What value does forgiveness have in your life and relationship with your partner?
- Do you forgive yourself? If not, why? Do you forgive your partner? If not, why? Do you forgive other people? If not, why?
- How exactly do you experience forgiveness within yourself? How do you express forgiveness to other people, and especially to your partner?
- Are you sincere every time you apologize to your partner? Do you apologize out of love or formality? Do you make a real commitment to change for the better or not? If you don't apologize sincerely, do you think your partner will trust you? Is your partner worth trusting you if your various "apologies" are fake or superficial?
- Is "sorry" a simple word or an experience for you?
- What do you need to do to forgive sincerely?

3.3.2 — Gratitude

When we realize the truth and power of forgiveness, we begin to be more grateful in life. We are grateful for the lessons we have learned that have helped us to become more mature and stronger people and to let go of people who have been obstacles in our lives. We forgive our past and are grateful for our present. Likewise, we become more aware of what is of real value to us. Everything starts to become clear.

But gratitude is not just about forgiveness. It is an enormous force of life itself. *Gratitude, like forgiveness, is a state of being.* It is an extension of ourselves, and it helps us to keep our feet firmly on the ground when we face difficulties.

No matter how difficult the situation is, gratitude reminds us that we have much in life, but most importantly, it reminds us of who we really are. In every difficulty or challenge, it is the light that shows us that we are strong, responsible, and determined to overcome anything and caring to help other people. It shows us that we are healthy and alive, and that is more than enough. It shows us that titles, wealth, and fame don't matter; what matters is the relationship and precious time with our life partner. It shows us that there is no need to complain.

So, we focus on the truth of ourselves, the gift of life, the wonderful gift of our relationship with our partner and what we have. Gratitude is a way of viewing life that is full of love, strength, happiness, and growth.

Occasionally, we take for granted many things in our lives. We take for granted our food and shelter; we take for granted our health; we take for granted our money; we take for granted that we can see, hear, smell, feel and taste; we take for granted that our partner will continue to be with us, no matter how badly we behave. So, we ignore all of that, which is what actually matters, and focus on what we don't have yet. The result is that we live in a state of nagging and anxiety, damaging our relationship with ourselves and our relationship with our partner, which we have neglected. We disconnect from ourselves and forget our partner because we take them for granted.

For example, we neglect our health, our diet, our exercise, and our self-care because we take it for granted that we will always be healthy. We neglect our partner, don't spend quality time together, or even have emotional outbursts at them because we take them for granted in our daily life. But nothing in life is a given.

We need to stop chasing everything we don't have and think we want so much, and focus on the essence.

To focus on the beauty of our life and relationship; to focus on ourselves and our life partner; to focus on every moment with our partner, every kiss, every hug, every touch, every look, every smile, every laugh and to enjoy the present moment.

To say "thank you" to our partner for everything that may seem small and taken for granted, but is not; to be devoted in our relationship with and to cherish every second we spend with our partner.

What is more preferred? Living a life of anxiety, complaints and the constant pursuit of material possessions and titles because of our insecurity, or living with fulfillment and love in the arms of our partner and being grateful for our life?

Unfortunately, some people do not realize the power of gratitude and take everything in their lives for granted. At some point, however, they may lose something or someone in their life and then realize their tragic mistake of not appreciating everything they have. They fall apart because they have wasted so much time chasing what they don't have instead of lovingly experiencing what they have now.

It is a shame, then, that you have to lose everything to begin to appreciate. Don't get to that point. Start appreciating now. You certainly have a lot to be grateful for in your life. Start by thanking your partner from the bottom of your heart for being together, for being alive, and for being able to see, hear, and feel each other. Focus on the now and each moment. Say a thousand thanks every day and take nothing for granted. Take your partner in your arms and experience love in every cell of your being. Don't waste a single minute. Unite now. Appreciate now. Love now.

So, ask yourself, how much more beautiful your life will be if you focus on what you really value, if you focus on your health, if you focus on your relationship with your partner, and if you stop chasing the future and focus on the present moment?

Gratitude helps us achieve our goals and build trust

Of course, gratitude does not stop us from setting goals and planning for the future. Instead, it helps us to understand what is important to us now so that we can move through life without stress and pressure. We will continue to set and achieve our goals, without it being the purpose of our life. We know that our life and relationship with our partner are beautiful just the way they are, so we don't stress about achieving every goal we set. Whether we succeed or fail will be the same because we are grateful and do not define our life by our successes or failures. This way of living is an expression of freedom in which trust is developed.

Do you trust people who complain or grateful people?

Do you trust people who take life for granted, or people who appreciate every moment?

In your relationship with your partner, do you think you are building trust by complaining about what you don't have or by thanking your partner for experiencing life together?

Reflect on these questions and ask yourself whether it would be beneficial to change your perspective on life if you are at a stage where you are complaining and taking your partner for granted.

If you want to evolve in your relationship with your partner and build a strong foundation of trust, it is important to bring forgiveness and gratitude into your daily life with complete honesty. Trust in our romantic relationship is built when our apologies are genuine and followed by corresponding acts of change. It is built when we forgive out of genuine love; when we sincerely thank our partner; when we are grateful. Below, we are going to explore other ways in which we build trust in our relationship with our partner, and how through trust we grow rapidly together.

Time for introspection

- How grateful are you to be healthy, to have a home, food, and water? How grateful are you for your relationship with your partner? How grateful are you to be alive?

- How do you express gratitude in your relationship with your partner?
- Do you say "thank you" sincerely? If so, how exactly do you experience this "thank you" within yourself? If not, why?
- What do you need to do to be more grateful in your life and relationship with your partner? How can you help your partner to be more grateful in life? How will you express these changes in your daily life?

3.4 — Continuous self-improvement and Companionate Flourishing

So far, we have laid a solid foundation for building trust in our relationship with our partner through self-improvement based on:

1) development of self-awareness and romantic relationship awareness,

2) responsibility and maturity,

3) and forgiveness and gratitude.

These are the foundations upon which we grow, both individually and as a couple. It is on this foundation that trust is developed in our relationship. However, trust also requires the presence of equality, faith, and admiration in the relationship. So, let's explore all these.

3.4.1 – Equality, Faith, and Admiration

Equality is expressed in our relationship with our partner when we both recognize that we have equal value in our life and relationship. Neither is superior or inferior. No one is submissive and no one is in charge. There is no need to manipulate and control our partner because we are equal. We make decisions together, seeing what is best for our relationship. We don't blindly follow the opinion of one or the other, but through discussion, we find the best option, which may be the opinion of one partner, the opinion of the other partner, and occasionally a third option that has emerged through discussion. This is true equality in the relationship with our partner.

This kind of equality can also exist in other social relationships. In the relationship with our partner, however, it can be combined with a strong faith in our partner and our relationship, where, yes, we are equal, but we also do not stop admiring our partner with all our being. We do not consider our partner to be superior, but at the same time, we are aware of their enormous potential. In this way, equality is not only a matter of mutual respect but also combined with admiration and faith in our development.

To better understand the relationship between equality, faith, and admiration, let us look at the forms that a romantic relationship can take, depending on the place of equality in the relationship:
1 - Devaluation of our partner and glorification of ourselves.
2 - Glorification of our partner and devaluation of ourselves.
3 - Equality.
4 - Equality, faith, and admiration.

In the *first case*, one partner underestimates the other and considers them to be inferior. They think that their views and perspectives are the only ones worth having. So, there is not even basic respect in the relationship.

In the *second case*, one partner considers their partner to be superior. They devalue themselves and become dependent on their partner.

In the *third case*, both partners believe that they are equal and therefore neither undervalue the other nor consider the other superior. This is a healthy situation in a romantic relationship, necessary for trust to exist.

But there is also the *fourth case*, in which the partners know that they are equal, but admire each other wholeheartedly. Not only are they equal in the relationship, but at the same time, they "deify" each other. Be careful, though, they do not deify the partner as in the second case, nor does the word deify have any religious connotations. What we are emphasizing here is that each partner admires the other intensely and lovingly. Whether the partner fails or succeeds in what they are doing, the partner's admiration is the same and even increases. So, in this case, there is great faith in the partner and the relationship. Not religious faith, but faith that comes from love.

In simple terms, we can say that our partner is our "God", just as we are "God" to them. This means that we are equal, but at the same time, our partner is significant to us because they are our life partner, and they are of immense value to us. We see our partner as the wonderful, unique, and incomparable being that they are. So "deification" here has the connotation of intense and healthy admiration of the partner in the context of equality.

A relationship of equality, faith, and admiration is only achieved with our Fulfilled Reflecting Self

In a relationship where equality, faith, and admiration are in balance (the fourth case), the connection between the partners is unbreakable. That is, it is the relationship with our Fulfilled Reflecting Self in which there is constant evolution between us. Within this evolution, there is equality, admission and correction of mistakes, but also great faith in the potential of ourselves, our partner, and our relationship.

In contrast, a relationship of simple equality (the third case) can be one in which both partners are happy with themselves, and have a good time together, and the relationship goes as far as that. They do not judge each other, but they do not develop or evolve. For example, a relationship of simple equality can be a marriage where the partners have been together for years and respect each other, but the flame between them has been extinguished. There is equality but no evolution. In short, a relationship of simple equality can even be a simple relationship with a friend or a colleague, where you respect each other as equals. All is well and good, but there is no flame for evolution.

On the other hand, a relationship of equality, faith, and admiration can only exist with our Fulfilled Reflecting Self, where our connection goes beyond the superficial level and reaches very deep levels of unity, as we will explain in the next chapter on Togetherness-Fulfillment. This is why we use the words "deification" and "God" to emphasize the importance, the immense power, and the tremendous strength and faith in connecting with our Fulfilled Reflecting Self. The unity and fire for evolution in this case is difficult to describe in words and is only truly understood when experienced by a couple.

So, these are the four cases of equality in the context of our romantic relationship. Obviously, the first two are harmful and the last two are beneficial. As you can see, although being equal in our relationship with our partner is necessary, it is not enough. That is, a good and balanced relationship cannot exist if the partners are not equal, but it will not develop if there is not strong faith in our partner.

Therefore, the fourth case is the one that will benefit our relationship and should come naturally, without any effort. For if we have to try to see our partner as our equal, to admire them, and to believe in them with every cell of our being, then they are probably not our Fulfilled Reflecting Self. If that partner is our Fulfilled Reflecting Self, then from the beginning of the relationship we feel that we are equals, and we admire them. This sense of equality, faith, and admiration initially builds trust, as we see that neither of us underestimates the other, nor considers the other superior, and at the same time, there is a strong admiration and desire to grow. As the initial impressions of equality, faith, and admiration are confirmed, trust is strengthened and consolidated.

The relationship in which we are equal to our partner and believe deeply in them is the relationship in which we devote ourselves every day. Here we combine:

    1) the development of self-awareness and romantic relationship awareness,

    2) responsibility and maturity,

    3) forgiveness and gratitude,

    4) and equality, faith, and admiration that we have explored so far.

This means that we are aware of the greatness and value of our relationship, we take responsibility for every action and behavior, we forgive ourselves and our partner for every mistake, we are grateful to be together, we recognize that we are equal, we admire each other, and we believe in our relationship. So, *not only we are our best selves every day, but we actually surpass ourselves all the time*. We continue to improve through constant individual and relationship evaluation. Thus, there is no doubt in each other's minds because we have established life trust. That is, we trust each other with our life.

This trust is built when we show understanding in our communication with our partner, always listening carefully to what they are saying. When our partner is talking, we are quiet and listen without distraction. We do not talk to them because we just want to say what we think, but because we want to understand them better, to see things from their perspective. Because our partner and our relationship are what is most important in our life, we don't allow outside factors and our opinions to interfere with our communication and meaningful connection. So, the reason we communicate is for connection, understanding, and love.

Time for introspection

- In which case of equality do you fall into in terms of your relationship with your partner? Are you equal to your partner or is one of you considered superior or inferior?
- Do you admire your partner? If so, why? If not, why? Do you believe in your partner and your relationship with all your heart? If yes, why? If not, why?
- When you communicate with your partner, do you listen carefully, or do you get lost in your thoughts? When you communicate with your partner, do you try to impose your views, or do you try to understand each other?
- Do you trust your partner? Do you trust your partner with your life? If so, why? If not, why?

3.4.2 — Personal and Relationship Improvement

So, we have reached the point where you know all the basic and necessary elements that you need to cultivate within yourself to build trust and develop the relationship with your partner. The path of personal and relationship improvement can be compared to the growth and development of a tree. We have therefore created two models of improvement to help us better understand and structure our personal and relationship development.

a) We call the first model "The Self-improvement Tree Model". This model is about our individual development.

The Self-improvement Tree Model

Ability to experience unconditional love

Responsibility

Understanding

Non-judgmental

Forgiveness

Honesty

Active listening

Gratitude

Continuous development of self-awareness

More positive elements to develop

More negative elements to improve

Positive elements to develop

Negative elements to improve

Will for self-improvement and taking action to improve

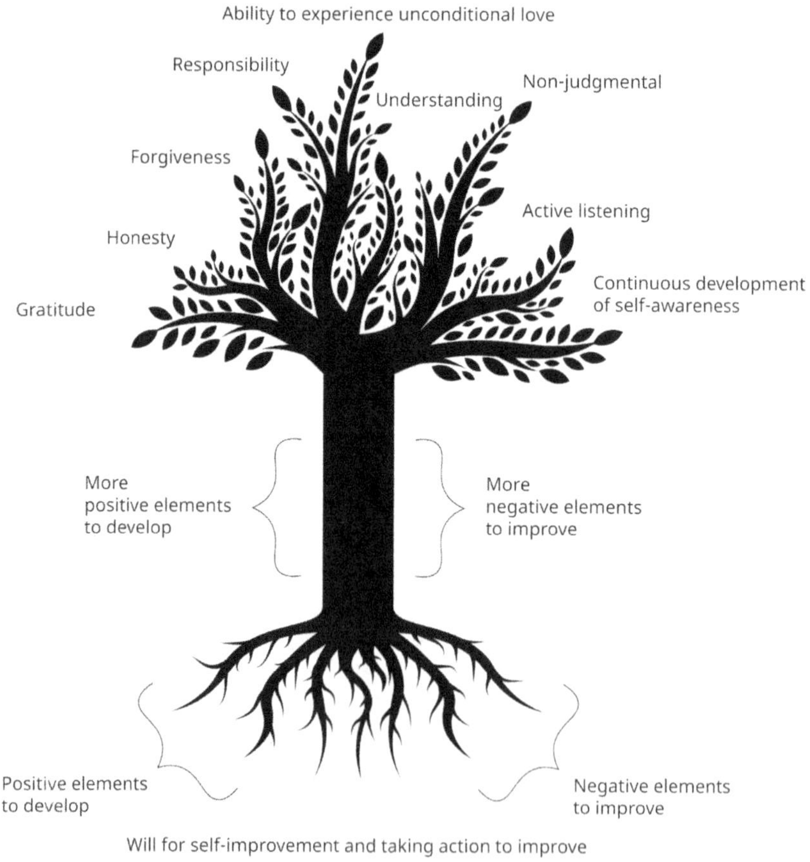

As we can see in the figure above, we have the soil, the roots, the trunk, and the branches of the tree.

1. The soil represents the will for self-improvement and taking action to grow.
2. The roots of the tree represent the positive elements that we need to develop and the negative elements that we need to correct. These are different for each person, depending on where they are in life. They are qualities, positive behaviors as well as limiting beliefs and negative behaviors and habits. In the next volume of the book, we help you to discover them easily with powerful exercises.
3. As we discover and develop our positive elements and as we discover and improve our negative elements, we reach the trunk of the tree, where we have grown spiritually to a satisfactory level. That is, we have developed our self-awareness to a highly satisfying level. We realize that we have even more positive elements in us, but also more negative elements that need to be improved. We understand that our self-improvement and self-awareness are two journeys that never end. Every day we have the opportunity to know ourselves better and to progress.
4. Through self-awareness and constant self-improvement, we flourish. That is, we reach the branches of the tree where we are now responsible, honest, grateful, forgiving and apologizing, non-judgmental, understanding, listening carefully to other people, constantly developing our self-awareness, and able to experience unconditional love in our lives.

This is the process of continuous self-improvement that we all need to follow in life if we are to create a healthy relationship with our Fulfilled Reflecting Self.

b) So, after each partner has cultivated their Self Improvement Tree, we move on to the second model, which we call "The Tree of Relationship Blossoming Model".

The Tree of Relationship Blossoming Model

1. As we can see in the figure below, the branches of each partner's tree become the roots and the foundation for the tree of their relationship to grow. The roots of the relationship tree include responsibility, honesty, gratitude, forgiveness, non-judgment, understanding, listening carefully to our partner, and self-awareness. The soil in which the roots of the tree grow is the un-

conditional love that the partners are willing to experience.

2. So, the first part of the trunk, where trust and equality are found, is developed in the ways we have explained in this chapter.

3. Then the trunk of the tree grows all the way up and, as a couple, we walk the path of continuous improvement. Through our relationship, we identify additional positive elements to develop, new knowledge and skills to acquire, and negative elements to correct.

4. This way, we grow our branches and blossom together, fully united, aware, now experiencing unconditional love, the purpose of our existence, and Togetherness-Fulfillment.

So, this is the path of the relationship blossoming. Ask yourself where you are in terms of self-improvement and your relationship development.

Time for introspection

- Have you blossomed individually so that you can establish strong roots in your relationship tree? If so, where do you need further improvement? If not, what do you need to do to blossom?
- If you have already developed trust in your relationship, what do you need to do to grow even more with your partner? Once you have answered this question, ask yourself how you will achieve what you want as a couple.

Answer these questions and you will see that even more questions will arise, and you will be able to honestly evaluate your relationship with your partner and do what is necessary to improve it.

3.5 — Summary and the Requirements
for an Unshakable Romantic Relationship

We have noted that self-improvement and relationship improvement is a never-ending journey, involving many elements and many paths, but all leading to the unconditional love and Togetherness-Fulfillment that we will explore next. Whether you work on developing awareness, responsibility, gratitude, and forgiveness, or equality, faith, and admiration in your relationship, you will notice great improvement. The point is to develop all of these, not just one.

This chapter has shown you many paths to self-improvement and relationship improvement so that you can choose the one that suits you best, but then also follow the ones that you find most difficult. There is not only one right way and only one right perspective. As you grow in one area (e.g., romantic relationship awareness) you will discover that you need to improve in another (e.g., gratitude) and you will find even more ways to improve. One thing leads to another as long as you want to make progress in practice and don't settle for stagnation.

So, based on the first three chapters of the book, let's look at the basic requirements for a couple to be inseparable, unshakable, and unstoppable:

1. The romantic relationship should be your number one priority in life.

2. Be clear about your life and relationship purpose.

3. Be completely honest, clear, and authentic with each other.

4. Listen carefully to each other.

5. Develop self-awareness and romantic relationship awareness.

6. Responsibility and spiritual maturity.

7. Forgiveness and gratitude.

8. Equality, faith, and admiration.

9. Trust.

10. Continuous self-improvement and relationship improvement.

With the above in mind, let's move on to the last chapter, where we will talk about unconditional love and Togetherness-Fulfillment.

4

Togetherness-Fulfillment and Love

We have come to the final chapter, and we would like to say congratulations for being here and continuing this journey of improvement for the purpose of love. It is not an easy path, for it takes courage, strength, and determination, and you have proven to yourself that you have all of these and more.

We hope that we have helped you to get to know yourself and your partner deeply and that you are ready to dive deeper into the ocean of your existence, life, and romantic relationship.

Now that we are diving deep, it is time to explore love and the greatness of Togetherness-Fulfillment. In this chapter, we explore:

1. the nature of love,
2. infatuation and how it differs from love,
3. unconditional acceptance of our partner,
4. individual fulfillment,
5. Togetherness-Fulfillment, which is the ultimate unity with our partner,
6. and the elements of a relationship of unconditional love and Togetherness-Fulfillment that it is beneficial to work on.

This chapter is likely to shake, challenge, and inspire you to work with healthy passion to strengthen your relationship with your Fulfilled Reflecting Self. You will read challenging truths about love and the meaningful and total unity with the Fulfilled Reflecting Self that will powerfully shake many limiting beliefs you may have about love. We are people who speak authentically, for it is only through raw truth and action that we can all truly evolve. Challenges are the greatest opportunities to activate the forces that motivate us in life and help us make lasting positive changes in our life and relationship. It is through challenges and questioning what we believe to be true that we find the truth of our existence. So, keep your horizons open to understand the richness of this chapter.

Also, in this chapter, you will further understand the importance of working deeply with what we have explored in the previous chapters so that you can fully unite with your partner and experience Togetherness-Fulfillment. Finally, by the end of this chapter, you will have clarified what a relationship of Togetherness-Fulfillment looks like and how you can achieve this unique and high level of unity and love. Let's begin...

4.1 — Love and Infatuation

A relationship of Togetherness-Fulfillment is a relationship with infatuation and love. Without love and infatuation, we cannot achieve Togetherness-Fulfillment. So, it is important to understand what love and infatuation are, what their meaning is, and how we experience love and infatuation so that we can then understand and experience Togetherness-Fulfillment. We will explain why infatuation, being in love, and love are not the same.

4.1.1 — Infatuation, Desire, and Passion

Let's start with infatuation, which, if not everyone, at least many people want so badly to feel. Infatuation is so beautiful that it often drives us mad. As beautiful and wonderful as infatuation is, though, it is crucial to understand that it is not the same as love, and that is why we are going to explain it first.

Infatuation is an essential and necessary starting element of a healthy relationship, but it is not all there is, as some people may think. It is just an emotion. It is the feeling of intense attraction between two people who also want to have sexual intercourse.

Infatuation can be expressed in two main ways: desire and passion

When infatuation is expressed as *desire*, we desire a person and want to have physical and emotional contact with them. Here, attraction is healthy, but frequently it does not lead to positive results because we do not yet know the other person deeply and truly. That is, we are only judging based on our emotions and not based on the truth of that person. We have not taken the time to really get to know each other, and we are simply attracted to each other.

When infatuation is expressed as *passion*, it comes out stronger because we not only want to be with a person, but we are passionate about them. We are "crazy" about the other person. With intense passion, we usually do not think logically and act mainly emotionally, losing control of ourselves and sometimes doing irrational things that we would not do if we were only feeling desire. For example, at the beginning of a romantic relationship, when we feel infatuation and passion intensely, we may forget and neglect everything else in our lives, such as everyday obligations. This, of course, negatively impacts our life. This is why we mentioned above that you should work on strengthening your relationship with *healthy* passion, because passion can sometimes be irrational.

So, desire is often a strong attraction between two people, and passion is an even stronger attraction that can sometimes be completely irrational. Desire and passion are elements and expressions of the emotion of infatuation.

Infatuation is just an emotion

But why is infatuation not as great as many people think it is? The answer lies in the fact that *infatuation is an emotion and nothing more*. As we have explained in previous chapters, all our emotions come and go. They are not permanent states. Infatuation is no different. There are times when we feel infatuation, times when we don't feel this way, and times when infatuation is not very intense. This is natural and there is no such thing as an ideal situation where many people believe that every day of their lives they will fly like butterflies in the sky, experiencing the ultimate infatuation, being passionate every minute. Just as we feel some moments of joy, some moments of sadness, some moments of anger, and so on, we may feel some moments of infatuation, some moments of desire, and some moments of passion. Our emotions are constantly changing within us. The challenge is to be able to balance them and not lose control of them, for example in moments of anger or passion.

Being in love vs. the emotion of infatuation

So now we can explore the situation where we are in love with a person, which is different from infatuation and from love itself (to be explored later). As we have said, infatuation is just an emotion.

Being in love is the state where we experience the emotion of infatuation in different ways, at different frequencies, and with different intensities, depending on the level of our awareness. Being in love with our partner is a state that can last either a few months, a few years, or our whole life if there is true unconditional love at the same time. So how we perceive infatuation will play a big role in whether we stay in love with our partner forever, or stop being in love because we don't actually love unconditionally each other.

So, there are two different situations in which we can be in love:
a) Being in love for a short time
The first situation is when we are in love for only a few months or a few years. In this case, we are mainly physically attracted to a person, either in the form of desire or in the form of irrational passion, as described above. For example, a couple who have been married for many years may have been very much in love in the first few months of their relationship and felt infatuation every day, but now they never feel any infatuation at all. At the beginning of the relationship, they may have wanted to have frequent physical contact, have fun, take risks, and experiment, and now they have no appetite for any of this. This is an all-too-common phenomenon.

There are two explanations for why infatuation "fades" after a long time, and we stop being in love with a person:

The *first explanation* is that the partners no longer take care of their bodies and are no longer as attracted to each other as they were at the beginning of the relationship when they took better care of themselves. Since infatuation is mainly about physical and sexual attraction, its expression is not very intense when partners do not have an attractive body in the eyes of their partner. As they are not sexually attracted, they stop being in love.

The *second explanation* is that infatuation is intense only in the early phases of a relationship, such as a few months or years, and subsequently it fades if there is no unconditional love. The ideal image we have built up of our partner because of the initial infatuation now begins to fade. As a result, we identify all the negative elements and faults in our partner, leading to arguments and frustration. This way, we stop being in love.

This is because, after a long time in a relationship, we begin to know who our partner really is. At the beginning of the relationship, within a few months or even a few years, we do not know in depth who our partner is. Getting to know a person deeply takes many years and a lot of couple work, as well as living and working together, which we will discuss later. It is not something that happens in a short time.

So, at the beginning of the relationship, we feel infatuation, desire, passion, and excitement, but we don't know who our partner really is. When, after a few months or years, we get to know them a little better, we are disappointed because they don't live up to our expectations. In short, the early stage of our relationship is one of fantasy and unrealistic expectations. Each partner is influenced by their strong emotions, inferior needs for validation, and the image created by society of what a romantic relationship "should" be like, and so they build up expectations. When these expectations are not met because the truth is revealed and infatuation is weakened, we are confronted with reality. As a result, many couples break up after a few months or a few years. They give up because they cannot bear to really put in the work with their partner and because the relationship has only been one of temporary infatuation and not true unconditional love.

In *both cases*, we idealize our relationship based on fantasies and emotions. We are not in a mature and realistic state within ourselves. We judge the relationship and our partner based on what we feel currently, on external appearances and sexual attraction, rather than on the raw truth because we have not yet developed our romantic relationship awareness.

b) Being in love with our Fulfilled Reflecting Self

There is also a second state where being in love is a state of maturity and awareness in the romantic relationship, in which we know our partner as deeply as we know ourselves. This is the relationship with our Fulfilled Reflecting Self, where we remain in love even after many years, because of true unconditional love.

Here, being in love is not a situation created by temporary emotions of infatuation, desire, and passion. It's a situation that lasts our whole life, where sometimes we feel infatuation strongly and sometimes we don't; not because we don't love each other, but because infatuation is a simple emotion that comes and goes, and we have accepted this truth as a couple. This means that we continue to feel infatuation, desire, and passion for our partner, but these emotions do not control us.

We judge our relationship based on the truth, and we know that some days we will feel intense infatuation, while other days we won't. Some days we may want to have passionate sex, some days we may want to create something together, some days we may want to talk for hours and some days we may just want to relax. These are all situations of infatuation in which together, as a couple, act based on what we really want, rather than based on animalistic feelings and needs. That is, we operate with awareness, as we explained in the previous chapter. In short, we stay in love because there is true, unconditional love. In this case, then, infatuation stems from love, not from fleeting emotions or fantasies of an ideal relationship. It goes beyond the narrow boundaries of physical and emotional attraction and becomes an inner and spiritual attraction, connection, and then unity.

As you have noticed, when we talk about infatuation, we are talking about the attraction between two people, and we are not referring exclusively to the infatuation for our Fulfilled Reflecting Self. We do this because we can fall in love and experience infatuation with many people, but we can remain in love throughout our life only with our Fulfilled Reflecting Self because that is the only relationship with raw truth and awareness. In all other cases, we fall in love because of purely physical attraction, inferior needs for validation, and ignorance of our emotions. Only with our Fulfilled Reflecting Self we can stay in love after many years and feel infatuation frequently because our unity surpasses any physical and inferior need.

Time for introspection

- What is your relationship to infatuation? How do you express it in your daily life?
- Do you feel desire in your relationship? Do you feel passion? Do you act wisely, or are you controlled by your emotions?
- Are you only physically and sexually attracted to your partner, or is your attraction deeper? If it is only physical attraction, why are you in a relationship with this person? If it is a deeper attraction, how is it expressed? What exactly do you feel and experience?
- Are you in love with your partner? If so, are you in love for superficial or meaningful reasons? If not, why?
- If the flame in your relationship has been extinguished, what do you need to do to reignite it?
- Answer these questions honestly, and then continue reading to delve deeper into the topic of infatuation by examining true unconditional love.

4.1.2 — Love

We have seen the two situations in which we can be in love. But what exactly is love?

Many people believe that we can love more than one person. In fact, some claim and declare that they love the whole world and all people, without exception. Famous people say they love their "followers" and "supporters", meaning thousands or even millions of individuals whom they do not know at all. Is that what love is? Is love a hollow word that we just blurt out to everyone? Is it a simple emotion that comes and goes like any other emotion? Is it something we can experience with all people, even complete strangers?

As a couple, we have been experiencing unconditional love with all of our being for many, many years, and have been, are, and will continue to be totally motivated by love. Love is why we have overcome every difficulty and problem and achieved goals together that many people thought impossible. We know with absolute certainty that love is not empty, meaningless, or just another word for any human being. It is not just an emotion; it is not a need for acceptance and validation out of insecurity; it is not something formal and superficial; it is not a social obligation.

Love is so vast and great that it can hardly be properly explained by a single definition. So, we came up with many definitions that reflect our truth and did our best to explain this wonderful phenomenon of existence that is an experience and an integral part of ourselves.

Love, as we know and experience it, is this:

1. The greatest force of life. An enormous power of unity and fulfillment. The force that connects us first with ourselves and then even more with our life partner.

2. The motivation for our every healthy action. The reason we help, support, and care for ourselves and others.

3. A strong dedication and commitment to the care of our life partner.

4. The ultimate unity (spiritual, mental, emotional, physical, and sexual) between two conscious people (with our Fulfilled Reflecting Self).

5. The ultimate expression of unconditional acceptance. Accepting ourselves and our life partner exactly as we are and helping our partner without ever expecting anything in return.

6. A state of inner peace and tranquility where we are completely satisfied with our life and romantic relationship.

7. A state and a path of progress and evolution on all levels, between two completely united people (with our Fulfilled Reflecting Self).

8. The ultimate expression of total health (spiritual, mental, emotional, physical, and sexual).

9. An experience of self-awareness and romantic relationship awareness, with an abundance of balanced and healthy emotions.

10. The most important and powerful way of self-improvement, relationship improvement, and permanent positive change.

11. The ultimate expression of who we really are deep inside. Our truth. We are the embodiment of love.

12. A unique experience that can only be shared and fully experienced with our Fulfilled Reflecting Self.

13. A conscious and clear choice to support our partner through actions and not just words, which requires constant individual and couple work. A way of living with understanding and respect.

14. The sense that as a couple, we are one and the same, experiencing life as one. We are one spirit, one mind, one soul, and one body.

15. The most fiery, powerful, and energetic expression of infatuation, desire, and passion. That is, an attraction more powerful than any infatuation, desire, or passion, for it is the force that unites us with our Fulfilled Reflecting Self in ways that are not easily explained.

16. The solution to every problem, every difficulty, every hardship, and every challenge. It is a remedy.

17. The ultimate expression of unconditional forgiveness of our life partner and pure gratitude for life.

18. The most fundamental and powerful value in life that leads us to Togetherness-Fulfillment. That is, what is most valuable in our life.

19. The ultimate expression of truth, honesty, and trust with our life partner. The ultimate expression of our authenticity, being completely spiritually naked and our genuine selves in front of our Fulfilled Reflecting Self —every split second— and enjoying it. This is the only path to true and total freedom.

20. The ultimate expression of believing in the best and that together with our life partner we are invincible, unbreakable, inseparable, unshakable, and unstoppable and can achieve anything.

21. The reason to get up every morning. To see, hear, taste, feel in every way, and experience our Fulfilled Reflecting Self.

22. The healthy rigor with which we challenge our life partner to improve when they behave in a way that is not in alignment with their wonderful and beautiful nature. The balance between discipline and carelessness.

23. The conscious decision to set aside the selfish part of ourselves for our life partner and our unity.

24. It's a pleasure and a game. Not a game of frivolity, but a game of maturity and awareness. That is, it is a game in which we are carefree but at the same time aware of everything we do. We don't get lost in pleasure as if that's all that matters, but we experience it while knowing the seriousness and responsibility that love requires.

25. Life and existence itself. It is deeply rooted in us and as necessary as oxygen and water. At the same time, it is the highest stage of human evolution. We cannot survive without oxygen and water. Without love, we survive physically but we are spiritually dead. This highest spiritual need for love drives us to evolve constantly.

So, this is love as we experience and understand it. As you can see, love is something multidimensional and so powerful that it touches the depths of our being. Of course, it is not limited to the definitions given above, for we all have the potential to discover even more aspects of love once we have truly experienced it. You can therefore add as many definitions to the list as you wish, depending on how you experience love.

Be careful, though, clarifications are needed here. Even though these definitions are how we, as a couple, experience love, they also contain objective reality in addition to our own experience. If we do not experience love according to these twenty-five definitions, then it is not love. Not because we say so, but because there is no love without devotion, commitment, absolute sincerity, absolute forgiveness, absolute gratitude, faith, and all the above. For example, we cannot love our partner and lie to them, not forgive them, not believe in our relationship, etc. So, it is important to clarify all these essential elements that are love and that apply to all people. Then you can experience it in even more ways, and that is wonderful.

"I love you" and "I love me"
Whatever is true about love is also true about "I love you". This means that when we say "I love you" to our partner, it cannot just be words. "I love you" is an experience, and it expresses all the above definitions of love in practice. So "I love you" expresses connection, unity, faith, devotion, commitment, respect, understanding, maturity, responsibility, strength, honesty, forgiveness, gratitude, carelessness, fulfillment, and everything else that the definitions of love express. "I love you" are actions and daily choices to improve ourselves by doing everything in our power to offer our true selves unconditionally to our life partner.

Of course, to be able to say, "I love you" with sincerity and to be able to do it practically, we must first be able to do the same for "I love me". First, we reach a point where we really love ourselves, and then we can love our life partner with our whole "being", which is pure love. So, to find the truth, think about this seriously and responsibly.

In the rest of this chapter, we are going to explain and analyze further the definitions of love and dive deep into Togetherness-Fulfillment.

Time for introspection

- Do you experience love with the definitions we have given above? Do you experience love with all these definitions? Do you experience it with only a few definitions? By which definitions exactly do you experience it? Do you not experience it at all?
- If you experience love, where do you need to improve? If you do not experience it, what do you need to do to experience it?
- Do you honestly and authentically say "I love me" to yourself? What exactly do you do to support and express these words?
- Do you sincerely and authentically say "I love you" to your partner? What do you do to support these words with actions?
- What exactly are you going to do to express love daily, more frequently, and authentically in your life and relationship with both you and your life partner?

4.1.3 — With whom can we experience true and unconditional love?

Based on the definitions above, do you believe that we can love the whole world, as many people say, or that love is so great that we can only experience it with one person?

The truth is that love in its entirety and in every sense of its nature can only be experienced with one person, and that is our Fulfilled Reflecting Self. We can have compassion and pure and intense concern for other people, such as parents, children, siblings, friends, and colleagues, but we cannot connect, let alone unite, with these people on every level of our being. So, the relationship with them is more a relationship of interest and compassion for their life, health, and happiness. But that's about it. There is a limit. Any family relationship can go as far as caring, respect, and understanding. Any friendship can go as far as support and fun. Any professional relationship can go as far as having a good collaboration. Any relationship with someone we know can go as far as providing help. These are the limits of these relationships.

Just because we help and support someone and are there for them in difficult times, it doesn't mean that we love them. Just because we feel nice emotions for someone, it doesn't mean that we love them. Just because we spend quality time with someone doesn't mean that we love them. It means that we respect them and care about them. But love is much more than respect, support, and care as we explained in the twenty-five definitions. So, people tend to confuse love with emotions, respect and support, and that confusion is why they never actually experience true love with their partner. When we understand that every other human relationship has its limits, we will be able to see the unlimited potential of the romantic relationship with our life partner.

The love we experience with our Fulfilled Reflecting Self, has no limits, no conditions, no rules, no "musts" and no compromises, whereas in other relationships these exist to a great extent.

Think of your relationships with members of your family, friends, colleagues, acquaintances, etc. Do you make compromises in these relationships? Do you hide any aspects of yourself from these people? Are you always open and honest about what you want or do not want? Are you completely authentic and raw in every moment with these people, whether they are your children, parents, friends, colleagues, or neighbors?

Chances are, the answer to the first two questions is "yes" and the answer to the last two is "no". But this is not the case in our relationship with our Fulfilled Reflecting Self, for there is true love that transcends every fear, every "must", every compromise, and every weakness. The strength, dynamics, and oneness we experience with our Fulfilled Reflecting Self is unsurpassable, utterly unique, and unrepeatable. This beautiful expression of love is only possible and true with our Fulfilled Reflecting Self for the following reasons:

1 - Time

Time is one of the most precious values we have in life. Once we give it away, we cannot get it back, regardless of what we do. So, you understand how important it is and that we need to use it with care, awareness, and maturity.

But what has time got to do with true love? It does because to devote ourselves to a person, we have to spend meaningful time together, and as we said in one of the definitions above, love is devotion. We all have twenty-four hours a day, and if we take away eight hours of work and eight hours of sleep, we have eight hours left to do whatever we really want to do. If we subtract the time spent on commitments, cooking, chores, etc., then there is very little time left to develop as human beings and unite with our Fulfilled Reflecting Self. So, the time we have left can be spent meaningfully and deeply only in our self-improvement and uniting with another person, our Fulfilled Reflecting Self. To connect with ourselves and then unite with our Fulfilled Reflecting Self, we need time and dedication. We cannot really get to know every aspect of our partner unless we spend a lot of quality time together.

So, if we waste our time in coffee shops, with transient friends, relatives, commitments, and so on, we cannot unite with our Fulfilled Reflecting Self. As you can see, we can only give meaningful time in high frequency and quantity to our Fulfilled Reflecting Self. All other people who come and go in our lives, or our relationship with them, are of less importance and especially of less substance and connection. This does not mean that we undermine other human relationships. It's just the truth that if we want to achieve Togetherness-Fulfillment and total satisfaction with our life partner, we need to spend our precious time on what really has the most significance, which is the relationship with our Fulfilled Reflecting Self.

It is only when the partners decide to have a child that the devotion goes to another person too, the child. But still, it is cru-cial to keep their romantic relationship as the number one priority. Otherwise, they might end up creating a harmful relationship of dependency with the child, and the child will not become the mature and independent person they are meant to be. This is the delicate balance of love, time, and realistic commitment within a romantic relationship.

Many couples end up in a miserable relationship of compromise because they don't make the most of their precious time with their partner. So, it's up to you what your priorities are, and whether your relationship with your Fulfilled Reflecting Self will flourish or wither away.

2 - The absolute oneness

Our Fulfilled Reflecting Self is the only person with whom we can unite on every level of our life. We cannot unite with other people spiritually, mentally, psychologically, and sexually/physically. You understand that we cannot have total unity with parents, children, relatives, friends, acquaintances, neighbors, co-workers, "followers", a one-night stand, and strangers. Only with our Fulfilled Reflecting Self can we be completely spiritually naked and know every aspect of their mind, spirit, soul, and body. Only with our Fulfilled Reflecting Self can we be inseparably united. This is the truth, not our opinion. No other human relationship has so much potential for unity and improvement as the relationship with our Fulfilled Reflecting Self.

Of course, the relationship between parents and children is also crucial and brilliant, but it does not even come close to the level of unity that we can create with our Fulfilled Reflecting Self. That's because parents cannot be completely spiritually naked and united with their children and vice versa, and they cannot be in a state of Togetherness-Fulfillment, which we will explain below. This of course also relates to time, for as we said above, to unite with our Fulfilled Reflecting Self on any level requires dedication, and quality and quantity time. It is therefore essential to have healthy relationships with other people, such as family, friends, colleagues, and acquaintances, but it is equally important to understand the limits and boundaries of these relationships to avoid meaningless or codependent interactions in life. This way, we can be devoted to the relationship with ourselves and our life partner, with whom we can unite in all areas of our existence.

3 - Being completely spiritually naked

Our Fulfilled Reflecting Self is the only person with whom we are completely authentic and honest in every moment, regardless of what is going on and what the circumstances are. It is the only relationship in which it is natural to be our pure and honest selves. In short, it's the only relationship where we are completely free to express ourselves as we wish and do whatever we want (that doesn't hurt us or our partner, of course) without being criticized. In all other relationships, no matter how authentic and honest we are as people, we always maintain some formality. Let's see some examples: We will not speak authentically and openly to colleagues or a manager at work if we have an issue with them. We talk to children in a certain way, hiding things that, we think, are inappropriate for them. Parents, relatives, and families hide some or many aspects of themselves and keep secrets because of shame. They have various "musts" and fears because they are afraid that their relatives will see their true faces and judge them. It is certain that you have noticed all these things, even to a small extent, in your relationships with your family, friends, colleagues, etc. That is why we all maintain a facade in these human relationships, whether it is small and subtle or large and impenetrable. We all choose a false image that is comfortable and defensive against potential criticism, no matter how good the relationship is or appears to be.

But in the relationship with our Fulfilled Reflecting Self, there are no secrets, no lies, no hiding the truth, and no fear. Everything shameful that we have done has been revealed and discussed between us. There is naked, clear, and pure truth. Even our most perverse thoughts —which we all have, although many don't want to admit it— have been revealed and there is no judgment between us. We can only reach such a level of unity and complete spiritual nakedness with our Fulfilled Reflecting Self (you will understand this better in the next section, where we will talk at length about complete spiritual nakedness).

4 - Mutual life at every level

Based on the above, we can see the final reason we can experience true love in every sense of the word only with our life partner. Relatives, friends, colleagues, and all the other people in our environment, lead different lives from us. That is, they live with other people, in different houses, have different families, different jobs, different "wants", different goals, and a different life purpose. When one of them leaves our life, we may be upset, but we will continue with our lives because we just shared a few moments with them and were not deeply connected or spiritually united with them.

Our Fulfilled Reflecting Self, however, is the only person with whom we cannot imagine not being together, and with whom we can literally share completely every moment of our life. If we never see other people again, no harm is done (as harsh as that may sound to some people), while our Fulfilled Reflecting Self is our life.

For example, if we move abroad, with difficult access to the country where our family and friends are, we will have no problem because as mature people, we have no need to be in the same country or city as those people. We will have as much contact as we can and mutual help and there will be no issue. A meaningful relationship will be maintained as much as possible. On the contrary, with our Fulfilled Reflecting Self, we want to spend every moment of the day together. This is because of absolute unity and a conscious choice to be together, and not because of insecurity. We will come back to this later in the explanation of Togetherness-Fulfillment.

It is important not to misinterpret love

So, you see, apart from ourselves, we can only truly, totally, and unconditionally love one person in life and that is our Fulfilled Reflecting Self, not just any romantic partner. We can fall in love with many people, as we said earlier, but we can only love and stay in love with our Fulfilled Reflecting Self for the rest of our life.

Of course, there are other kinds of love. For example, friendship love, and parental love, which is also the most important and unsurpassed task and obligation of child-raising. But essentially, love here is not love in all its senses, such as erotic/sexual and spiritual unity and nakedness.

In these cases, the word love is simply used to show care and genuine interest, not with all the definitions given above, but with some of them, such as help and support. This is because we are used to using the word "love" without really understanding its meaning.

We can have strong interest and compassion for a few people close to us or people who need help because of the values of support and contribution existing within all of us.

For example, we, as authors, wrote this book to help you and to contribute to the world because we care about people. But we're not going to lie about loving you to be likable because this is not true. We don't know you and we don't have a close relationship with you. We can, however, care about you and the general betterment of humanity, and we do so sincerely and authentically. The same is true when we help a homeless person on the street or give clothes to a church that helps people, help a charity financially, give blood to a person in need, help and support family and friends in some way, or help a colleague at work who is struggling. All these show interest, compassion, and support and are of great significance. They are elements of love, but not love in every sense of the word. As we have seen above, love is much more than just care, compassion, and support.

This is so important to understand, and we repeat it many times because if we believe that love is a fleeting emotion that we can experience with anyone, then all we are doing is devaluing and degrading love. The result is that we will never experience it because we will be driven by a limiting belief that love is just an emotion that comes and goes or a mere word without meaning or depth.

If we think we can experience love with any human being, then we don't know what love really is. This is because we have never experienced true love. Usually, people tend to think they can love many people. That's because they have never experienced true unconditional love with their Fulfilled Reflecting Self, since they have not yet met them. So, they judge love based on their limited and limiting experiences that do not include love. Because they do not truly love themselves or have not found their Fulfilled Reflecting Self, they turn to parents, children, friends, acquaintances, and strangers for validation and acceptance to feel worthy (all explained in the first two chapters). Some people even try to find love and fulfillment in possessions, fame, money, power, and careers. This attempt to satisfy their inferior needs for acceptance and validation is mistaken for love. In this way, love is misunderstood, and few people experience it. However, relationships that are built for the purpose of meeting inferior needs and because of a misunderstanding of love end up being unhealthy and totally problematic.

Because of the misinterpretation of love, the following can happen:

a) Some children remain attached to their parents and do not grow up even when they are twenty, thirty, or forty years old
They do not realize their dreams because they are trying to satisfy the fear-based "wishes" of their parents. Children are meant to leave their parents and build their own lives with their Fulfilled Reflecting Self (this is one of the reasons why a parent-child relationship cannot be as strong as a romantic one). Only when they leave, they will be able to become true spiritual adults and strong and responsible human beings. If they do not detach from their parents and confuse simple support and care for love and unity, they will never become adults and will continue to form unhealthy love relationships.

b) Many parents remain attached to their children and all they achieve is putting pressure on their relationship
In fact, some people have children to fill the void left by an unhappy marriage and to have someone to take care of them in their old age. They try to impose "love" because of their own selfish beliefs and inner voids. They want to have a false sense of power over their children, and that their children belong to them so that they can feel "good" in their misery. However, if the relationship with their partner was one of true love, this would never happen.

Love cannot be forced. Love is experienced in freedom.

c) Some people neglect the relationship with their partner because they consider temporary friendships more important than the romantic relationship

They fear the immense power that arises when a couple truly and utterly unites. They are afraid of being spiritually naked in front of their partner and choose to have a temporary good time with friends. So, they cannot unite with their partner and end up constantly breaking up or changing lovers too often.

d) People stay in abusive relationships because they have a false image of what love is in their minds

When people don't understand what love is and isn't, and are guided by insecurity, fleeting emotions, and inferior needs, they can end up seeing abuse as something that is normal and acceptable in a romantic relationship. That is what makes someone say, "I know he hurts me and hits me sometimes, but I know he loves me".

Unfortunately, all this is what the misconception of love does. It is what we are most passionate about because love is sacred, and we know this because we experience true and unconditional love in every cell of our being.

When we have a "love for everyone" perspective in life, all we end up doing is either building unhealthy relationships of oppression or meaningless and immature relationships, strange as it may seem. A misunderstanding of love leads to dependency and codependency, compromise and misery, possessiveness and manipulation, stagnation and entrapment, and an immature and weak mentality of needing other people.

To have healthy relationships both with our Fulfilled Reflecting Self and with family, friends, acquaintances, etc., it is important to understand the nature and limits of each of these relationships. The more we unite with our life partner and understand the great uniqueness and freedom of our relationship, the easier it will be to create other healthy relationships in our life that have healthy boundaries. We need to be careful of how we interpret love, for the notion that love is being subjected to such degradation, and that those who degrade it don't even understand that they do it, is tragic.

When we all understand these two truths:
1 - that love is only truly and fully experienced with our Fulfilled Reflecting Self; and
2 - that we can care for and help many people even if we don't know them personally,
imagine how much more beautiful and healthier the world could become.

Instead of wasting our time in unhealthy relationships of distorted love and need for acceptance, we would use our time and energy in the relationship of true unconditional love with our Fulfilled Reflecting Self, and in healthy relationships of pure interest and cooperation with many other people.

Therefore, when you say "I love you" to your life partner (your Fulfilled Reflecting Self), know with absolute certainty that you mean love in every single sense. Know that you and your partner are one and the same. When you say "I love you" to other people (family, friends, etc.), know that love here does not express absolute unity and has limits. Do not say this word without substance and knowledge. Use it truthfully and only to the people you really love. This is food for thought.

Time for introspection

- Do you love yourself? If so, how do you express this love? If not, why?
- Do you love your partner? If so, how do you express this love? If not, why?
- Do you experience true love? If so, how do you experience it? If not, why?
- Do you misinterpret love? Do you have meaningless and dependent relationships either with your partner or with other people, such as your family because you misinterpret love?
- What is your view of love? What is the truth about love?

- What do you have to do to love yourself? Maybe, you don't have to do anything and just love yourself as you are?
- What do you have to do to love your partner? Maybe, you don't have to do anything and just love your partner as they are?
- What do you need to do to express your love more frequently and meaningfully in your daily life and in the relationship with your Fulfilled Reflecting Self?

4.1.4 — Additional elements of love

So, let's look at some additional elements of love, which will further explain some of the definitions we gave earlier. This will help you to get a clearer understanding and to stop unconsciously misinterpreting love if you are doing so. If you are not devaluing love, we believe the following will help you just as much.

1 - Love means accepting our partner unconditionally
Accepting them with all their faults and flaws without trying to change them. But be careful here. Unconditional acceptance means accepting our partner as an imperfect person with flaws. But it is not acceptance of stagnation, compromise, unwillingness to change, irresponsibility, and self-deprecation.

So, we accept our life partner with all their flaws, and that is unconditional acceptance. However, we do not accept our life partner stagnating, undervaluing themselves, not improving, and not taking responsibility for themselves, and that is unconditional love.

That is, we do not accept our partner to devalue themselves, as we do not accept this for ourselves either. If we do this, it means that we are supporting their degradation and not loving them. Because if we love our partner, we help, encourage, inspire, push, motivate, shake, tell the truth, and challenge them to improve and progress. We embrace every negative element, but not the self-destruction and devaluation of our partner's worth, for that is not love, but indifference and compromise.

Challenging our partner to improve is, of course, difficult and can lead to conflict if there is immaturity. For this reason, we must not resort to criticism of the partner, but to help, and be brutally honest with respect. This is where the true love and strength of the couple are shown, and that is love without conditions or limits.

Again, we need to be careful of misinterpretations. Not accepting our partner to devalue themselves is not a condition. If it was a condition, it would mean that we only love them when they behave the way we want them to behave. But this is not the case. What happens is that because we really love them, we want to help them when they devalue themselves. So, we don't accept their continued self-humiliation, and we do everything possible to shake them in a healthy way. We don't threaten to break up with them if they don't change, and we don't manipulate them in any way, but we help them to develop in every way possible.

For example, in our relationship, one of us was irritable, which led to the devaluation of self-worth and getting angry at the slightest thing. This, of course, damaged our relationship. So, yes, we accepted the fact that there was an inability to deal with anger, but we did not accept that this situation would continue. Love helped us to resolve this issue with great challenge and of course with raw honesty. Had there been no love, one of us would have simply compromised, and the anger would have continued to run high. This would probably lead to separation or a miserable relationship of compromise due to emotional immaturity and lack of self-control. But love was and is the driving force behind the remedy of any negative behavior. This means that love has no limits and can deal with anything negative with sheer force.

Something else we need to understand about love is that it is always and by definition unconditional.

This means that there is no love that is not unconditional. If we really love our life partner, we love them unconditionally; otherwise, we do not really love them. For example, whether our partner talks to us nicely or badly, whether they do what we want or don't want, we love them and are there for them. We understand their mistakes, we forgive them, and together we find the solution to every difficulty. As we said before, we help each other to improve and if there is an underestimation of our value, we don't compromise, we don't become indifferent, but we shake our partner in a healthy way. This is a relationship without personal gain but with pure motives of love and progress.

Therefore, the only form of love that exists is true and unconditional love.

Anything else is not love, just meaningless words. Think about why many people consider dogs to be their best friends. It is because they believe dogs love unconditionally because they have no ego. All they ask for is food, toilet, and playtime. But this is actually a very limited and insignificant relationship, and of course, it is not about unconditional love, but an attempt to fill the inner voids of true human love.

Unconditional love does not mean that there is no selfishness and ego because we all have these. Unconditional love is when we choose to set our ego aside every day for the sake of our relationship with our partner. *This is where unconditional love is shown, in our power to overcome selfishness and every inferior element of our existence by being in complete control of ourselves.* Putting our partner's "wants" above our own, to the point where we have become so united that our "wants" are now completely mutual.

So, when we use the words "unconditional" and "true" in this book when we discuss romantic love, it is to emphasize it, not because there is some lesser kind of romantic love that is not true and unconditional. So, if you are experiencing love, then it is true and unconditional; otherwise, you have something mixed up in you.

2 - Love is not something we expect to "celebrate" one day a year when we buy our partner chocolates to show that we care

Love is an ongoing experience that grows stronger every day. If it's not an ongoing experience, it's not love. Love is seen in everyday life, in the small moments, the big moments, the good, the bad, the easy, the hard, and not on special occasions. If you really love your partner, it means that you express it in every authentic way you can, every day, and every moment.

3 - Love is not fleeting, it does not diminish, fade, or cease to exist

Love is not something we feel for a certain period and then stop feeling it. It is not something that comes and goes. There is no such thing as "I loved this person, but I don't love them anymore, and now I love someone else". You either love someone or you don't, and we can only love our Fulfilled Reflecting Self. Love is permanent, strong, infinite, and ever-growing. Love can only grow, increase, beautify, and develop. The path that love follows is only upwards. It is difficult for all of us, as imperfect human beings, to cope with the power of love because it is unsurpassed by its very nature. So, at some point, we may get angry, argue, and behave immaturely. It is love that either prevents us from making such mistakes or helps us to correct them if we do. Love, therefore, helps us to progress in every way because it is an element of our being.

4 - Love with our Fulfilled Reflecting Self overcomes every difficulty, every challenge, and every problem

Love overcomes every obstacle. It does the impossible. It accomplishes the unimaginable. Through love with our Fulfilled Reflecting Self, everything in life is possible and achievable. Love is limitless and free, and this limitlessness and freedom of love can be expressed by all of us by embodying love in our romantic relationship. Love is an integral part of who we are and our truth. We are here in life to love and be loved, and so with our Fulfilled Reflecting Self we create miracles of love that help other people to live their lives lovingly.

All the above applies to some degree to any "kind" of love other than the romantic one, as long as it is not misunderstood. And of course, it is even more powerful and intense with our Fulfilled Reflecting Self.

Time for introspection

- How does all the above reflect in your daily life? Do you experience them? Do you not experience them? Do you have faith in love or not?
- Do you wait for a day in the year to celebrate love and romance, or do you experience love every day of your life?
- Have you overcome difficulties thanks to the power of love? If so, which ones and how exactly did you do it? If not, why?
- Have you achieved the "impossible" through love with your life partner? If so, how did you do it? If not, why?
- What do you need to do to strengthen your love?

4.1.5 — How we can understand/experience love in our everyday life

Based on everything we have explored so far about love, we can summarize the main ways in which we can experience love and how it is expressed in our daily lives, so you can see if there is really love in your relationship.

1 - Unconditional acceptance of your partner with brutal honesty and without masks of hypocrisy, demands, and rules. Complete spiritual nakedness between us. For example, we don't hide anything from our partner, even if it seems embarrassing.

Do you reveal everything to your partner every day?

2 - Because there is total honesty between us, we know all the negative and "dark" elements of our life partner, and we forgive everything. We don't hold grudges or dwell on petty things. We forgive and say "thank you" for our life. For example, we forgive the mistakes our partner has made in the past and the ones they are making today, without focusing on them but on improving ourselves and the beauty of our life.

Do you say "sorry"? Do you forgive? Are you grateful every day?

3 - We help our life partner in any way we can without expecting anything in return. For example, we can do chores without expecting our partner to do anything for us. We do it out of love.

Do you help your partner every day in any way you can out of love, without expecting anything in return?

4 - Beautiful words and deeds, accompanied of course by rigor when they serve the progress of the relationship. Our words and deeds go hand in hand. This means we may say "well done" to our partner when they do something wonderful yet challenge them, with love and respect, when they do something that doesn't reflect their truth or improve our relationship.

Do you say, "Well done", "I love you", "I adore you" etc., with absolute sincerity? Do you tell your partner that you think they need to improve when they really do? Do you talk to each other about improvement?

5 - Our partner is there for us in every moment, whether it is a time of joy or a time of difficulty. We do the same for them. If one of us "falls", the other is there to help them get up. For example, we are inseparable both when we are having fun and when there are difficulties in our life, such as work issues or health problems. We don't give up on our partner when things get tough.

Do you have beautiful and special times of joy? Do you support each other when there is a difficulty or a more serious concern?

6 - We want to spend quality time together. If we would rather not spend time together, there is probably an obstacle in our relationship. If there is love, not only do we want to spend time together, but we don't want to be apart at all.

Do you want to be together all the time, or at least spend as much time together as possible?

7 - Our relationship is always our number one priority in life. No person or situation comes between us or above our relationship. For example, if we have to decide between going out with

friends or relatives and spending time together as a couple, we choose the latter without a second thought. Even more profound is the choice and support of our life partner when there are issues involving third parties. That is, the couple is not divided when another person tries to interfere in their life in any way, but the partners remain united.

Is your relationship and being together every day your number one priority?

8 - The romantic relationship is a space of freedom for the healthy expression of emotions without suppressing them. This means that each partner expresses their feelings without being criticized or making a fuss. There is always understanding. For example, if one partner is upset about something very trivial, the other will not criticize them but will understand and support them. If one partner gets angry about something, the other will help them to calm down and won't get angry with them. We are not afraid or ashamed to express our emotions authentically. There is a sense of calmness and peace in the relationship.

Do you understand your partner's emotions and help them deal with emotional outbursts in a healthy way when needed?

9 - We are fully present when talking to our life partner and are not distracted by other thoughts or external factors. When we are together, we are fully connected and united. For example, when we are talking to our partner, we focus on their words and not on our plans for tomorrow, what we ate yesterday, external noises, or the conversations of other people around us.

Do you live every moment fully connected with your partner?

10 - There is no need to spend time alone with friends and other people or to do other activities without our life partner. This is because there is no need for validation and acceptance from other people or for withdrawal from our partner. If a partner wants to spend time with other people without their partner, it means that they have some inner voids to fill. True love, however, is free from inferior needs and the person experiencing it has no emptiness because they are fulfilled and completely satisfied with their

life and relationship. This means that every healthy need is met by the relationship with the partner, which is more valuable than anything else, and the couple's life and relationship purpose surpasses any other relationship in life.

Do you want to be with your partner all the time, or do you need to be away from them for a few hours every day?

Time for introspection

So, these are some fundamental ways in which we can experience true love. Consider whether these ten elements are present in your relationship. We give you a few more questions to explore this topic in more depth, as it is one of the most important.

- Do you lie to your partner? Do you hide the truth from your partner? Do you make demands on them?
- Do you forgive your partner? Do you say "thank you" for even the simplest and most mundane things your partner does?
- Do you help your partner without expecting anything in return?
- Do you speak kindly to your partner? Do you behave kindly towards them? Do you challenge your partner to improve where necessary?
- Are you always strong and present for your partner, or do you give up when things get difficult?
- Do you want to spend quality time together, or do you prefer to be apart?
- Is your relationship your number one priority?
- Can you express yourself in your relationship freely? Are you comfortable expressing your emotions, or do you suppress them? Do you understand each other, or do you judge each other?
- Are you present when you discuss, or do you get lost in your thoughts and outside noise?
- Do you need to spend time with friends and other people without your partner, or do you want to be together all the time?

These questions will help you understand if there is true and unconditional love in your relationship and where you need to focus and improve.

<h3>4.1.6 — Differences between infatuation and love</h3>

Have you asked yourself the previous questions? Hopefully, you have, and not just read on. If you have, you have certainly benefited in many ways. Either you have realized that you are not experiencing true love, or you are and just need a lot of improvement, or that the love with your partner is strong. Either way, it is enlightening to look at these questions.

So, having considered whether you are experiencing love in your relationship, it is useful to look at some basic differences between infatuation and the state of being in love, and actual romantic love. This will help you to further understand love as an experience so we can move on to talk about Togetherness-Fulfillment.

INFATUATION	LOVE
1 - It is just an emotion and is mainly related to physical attraction. Being in love is something that lasts for our whole life, only when there is true love and only with our Fulfilled Reflecting Self.	1 - It is a permanent, ascending, and evolving state and way of life of fulfillment, unconditional acceptance, compassion, and unbreakable connection and unity at every level of our being.
2 - We think we know our partner. We are driven by fantasies and expectations of what our "ideal" relationship "should" be. So, we are easily disappointed.	2 - We know our partner truly and deeply. The truth guides us. We have high standards that we create together.
3 - We think that everything in the relationship is or should be "perfect" and get frustrated when we see our partner's flaws.	3 - We love and embrace the raw truth of our partner. We know there is no perfection. We walk together on a path of continuous development of our self-awareness and awareness and couple work and improvement.

4 - We think that the relationship should only involve "good" emotions, such as joy and excitement, and that any argument is a sign of a broken relationship. We believe that the quality of our relationship is judged by how we feel. So, if we feel nice emotions, we believe our relationship is good, but if not, then we think that our relationship is not worth it.	4 - We recognize that our emotions come and go and that we are driven by fulfillment. So, we know that it is normal to feel emotions apart from the "good" ones and that some moments of tension can be constructive for our relationship. Our fleeting emotions do not guide us. We are guided by our unity on every level of our existence.
5 - We expect our partner to give to us and think that a relationship is like a transaction. When we give to our partner, we do so because we want to get something in return. It is about meeting inferior needs for validation because we are not steady on who we are. We feel the need to "take something" from our partner because we have inner voids to fill. We do certain acts and expect our partner to do the same. We say some words and expect our partner to say the same. We feel some emotions and expect our partner to feel the same. If they don't behave, speak, and feel in a similar to us way, we believe that they don't "give" us love, as we think love is a commodity to exchange. We don't understand what it means to be united.	5 - We know that our relationship is not a form of transaction. It is not about giving and receiving. We don't have the mentality "I do this for you; therefore, I am owed this". We know that love is not about meeting our needs or meeting anyone else's needs. Our relationship is not based on any kind of transaction but on being our pure and honest selves every single moment in an environment of freedom, support, fulfillment, and unity. Giving our time and devotion to our life partner is essential for our unity, but it doesn't mean that we exchange something. It means that we become one and the same. It is a state of being of unity where we are devoted to our relationship and each other, without expecting anything.

These are the basic differences between infatuation and love, and we believe that by now you will have clarified many things within yourself about the nature of love and its value.

So, we have talked about infatuation, desire, and passion. We explained the fact that we can be in love temporarily (with any person) or permanently (with our Fulfilled Reflecting Self). We explored love through many definitions. We have come to the conclusion that we experience love completely and, on every level, only with our Fulfilled Reflecting Self. Furthermore, we discussed important elements of love, how we experience love in our everyday life, and the main differences between infatuation and love. In this way, we are ready to explore individual fulfillment and Togetherness-Fulfillment.

- Do you understand the difference between infatuation and love? How do you distinguish and differentiate between them? Are the two connected or are they completely separate?
- How do you experience infatuation with your partner? How do you experience love with your partner?

4.2 — Individual fulfillment as a path to Togetherness-Fulfillment

It is now time to explore individual fulfillment and Togetherness-Fulfillment. Here we go even deeper, and you will see that love can be developed even further than we have explored above.

To understand Togetherness-Fulfillment, it is crucial to first understand what individual fulfillment is. So, it is beneficial to start with the Individual Fulfillment Model for Togetherness-Fulfillment that we have created, which describes the stages of individual fulfillment, that we need to go through so that we can eventually experience Togetherness-Fulfillment with our Fulfilled Reflecting Self.

The Individual Fulfillment Model for Togetherness-Fulfillment

As we can see in the model above, there are five levels of fulfillment. The first four levels relate to individual fulfillment and the last level relates to Togetherness-Fulfillment with our Fulfilled Reflecting Self.

a) On the first level of individual fulfillment, we find physical health

Physical health is fundamental because if we are not healthy, we cannot deal with deeper and more substantial spiritual issues. If we are sick and weak, we can hardly develop. We will not be able to achieve what we want in life, nor will we be able to connect with our Fulfilled Reflecting Self. Our goal will be health and healing until we are healthy. In other words, it is significant and even necessary to ensure our physical health first so that we can grow further.

b) On the second level, we see our inner health

When we are physically healthy, we can work on ourselves in a more meaningful way and develop our self-awareness by improving our flaws. A healthy body is necessary, but not enough if we do not have a healthy mind, soul, and spirit.

So, inner, and spiritual health is about how balanced we are as human beings. That is, it consists of our Unlimited Aware Self, Balanced Aware Self, Evolved Aware Self, Existential Aware Self, Higher Sexual Self, and the development of these, as we explained in Chapter One. As we develop those positive elements, we learn to manage our Limited Unaware Self, Reactive Unaware Self, Lower Sexual Self, and other weak elements in a healthy way. At this stage, we develop self-control, take full responsibility for our lives, and become spiritual adults and truly mature human beings. We become more aware of our past and its influence on us, accept the present, and make plans for the future. Cultivating our spirituality and our inner health is about creating a meaningful relationship with ourselves.

You understand that this level requires a lot of inner work and is generally demanding. In fact, it includes all the work we need to do as explained in the first three chapters.

c) On the third level we see our goals, achievements, and continuous improvement

As long as we are physically healthy and cultivate our spirit, we can achieve the goals we set in life and continue on the path of continuous self-improvement.

We are satisfied with ourselves and can therefore devote our energy to further improvement in our social, professional, and financial lives. We can find a better job or start our own business, gain financial freedom, and create a circle of trusted people in our lives.

So, it is on this level that we find our achievements. But whether we achieve what we want or fail many times, we have the maturity to see failures as lessons and opportunities for growth and never judge ourselves by our successes and failures. This is essential to understand because many people think that achievements, material possessions, titles, and recognition will bring them satisfaction and fulfillment. This is not true. These are all important, but they are more superficial than essential, and they are not the be-all and end-all.

Because many people do not love themselves and have not known true love with their life partner, they look for meaning and fulfillment not only in other people with whom they end up creating needy and superficial relationships, but also in objects, clothes, cars, money, habits like smoking and drinking alcohol, seeking recognition in their professional lives to feel validated, and they end up devoting themselves to their careers and succeed in simply being unhappy and oppressed. For this reason, it is significant to focus on our achievements and career development after we have got to know ourselves very well and are unshakable in our truth. In other words, it is crucial that we act based on who we are and not on based on what we do and what we have achieved, as we explained in the Unlimited Aware Self Model in Chapter One. This is the way we can start walking on a path of continuous improvement, where we set meaningful goals in various life areas, but we also improve spiritually.

d) On the fourth level we find individual fulfillment and helping other people

Having developed and achieved all the above, we are now in individual fulfillment. In individual fulfillment we are healthy, we know ourselves, we achieve our goals, we learn from our mistakes, and so we are complete and satisfied with our lives.

Here, of course, it is important to clarify a few things about fulfillment. As human beings, we are *whole* from birth. That is, we are not half or empty when we are born, and we become whole in the process. *We are whole from birth, but not fulfilled. Being whole* means that we are unique by nature and different from any other human being, without needing anyone or anything to "complete" us. We don't need to do anything to achieve this, we are simply unique by nature from the moment we are an embryo.

Being fulfilled is a state that we only experience when we get to know ourselves deeply. This is because we have innate values and needs and because as we grow up, we create principles and beliefs and naturally want to evolve. This means that we naturally want to achieve, grow, and maintain our fulfillment by clarifying who we are, what we value the most, what we need, and understanding all the ways in which we operate and by living based on our principles and spiritual selves. As you can see, we can only realize all this when we are old and mature enough. They cannot be grasped by a young child, and therefore a young child cannot achieve individual fulfillment. But every child is whole and unique just by existing.

In short, to be whole is a state in which we are born. Being fulfilled requires inner work and maturity.

For this reason, individual fulfillment is truly experienced when we are spiritual adults and have developed and continue to develop the first three levels of this model.

Of course, these three levels can be developed simultaneously. That is, we can maintain our physical health while developing our self-awareness and inner health, and at the same time achieve our goals. For example, we can exercise, eat well, sleep well, work on ourselves, and progress professionally at the same time. So, we don't have to follow these steps to the letter, although it certainly makes the process easier. The important thing is to work on all of them and to keep developing ourselves. Only in this way will we be able to achieve and maintain individual fulfillment.

So individual fulfillment, in terms of all the above, is the state where we know absolutely where we are now, where we have come from, where we have been in the past, and where we are going in the future, and we are absolutely satisfied with that whilst being open to change our plans for the future if the development of our awareness uncovers a more appropriate path.

We are at an ever-increasing level of self-awareness, and we understand that we have to improve every day. This means that we understand that we have much more to discover and learn. We know our truth and live in inner and outer peace, free from the lower elements of ourselves. This means that the lower elements of ourselves still exist, of course, but they no longer control us. We accept and love ourselves wholeheartedly while committing ourselves to the continuous improvement of our negative elements.

Self-love is the greatest expression of individual fulfillment.

Helping others also plays a key role in our individual fulfillment. When we help other people, we experience fulfillment within ourselves. We can truly help others in a meaningful and effective way, without losing ourselves and without marginalizing who we are, our values, and everything that is important to us, only if we develop the first three levels of the Individual Fulfillment Model for Togetherness-Fulfillment. So, when we take care of our bodies and minds, achieve our goals, grow in life, and help other people, we are at the level of individual fulfillment.

If you work through everything we have explored so far in this book and apply it to your life, you can experience individual fulfillment and reach a level of peace that is truly beautiful. Once you manage to experience individual fulfillment, you will never want to accept anything less, and it will become one of the most significant standards in your life (Existential Aware Self Model).

We can be individually fulfilled, but that is not the highest state of being we can experience.

It is significant to add here that to be individually fulfilled, we do not need another human being to "complete" us because none of us is empty and does not need to be "filled". We all have the potential to be individually fulfilled and satisfied with ourselves, but this does not mean that we are meant to live alone and not unite with our partner.

So, can individual fulfillment relate to our relationship with our life partner? How can we be fulfilled with our partner? Is individual fulfillment enough, or can we reach higher levels of growth with our partner? Is our partner a person in our life with whom we simply spend some time together, and share a home and a few common interests? Is our partner the person with whom we accidentally had children and were forced to marry? Or is it more than that? Not only is it more than that, but it's also a lot more than what you can imagine, and that's where Togetherness-Fulfillment comes in.

e) The final level, then, is that of Togetherness-Fulfillment, which is the ultimate unity with our partner

This level includes all the individual evolution of both partners, being individually fulfilled, and the deeper connection and unity between us. At this level, our Feminine and Masculine Self and our partner's Feminine and Masculine Self are balanced and united. As a couple, we are in the zone of romantic relationship awareness where there is responsibility, forgiveness, gratitude, equality, faith, admiration, and trust. We are in love and love each other in all the ways we have explored earlier.

Togetherness-Fulfillment is the highest level we can reach as human beings because it is the highest and deepest form of unity that exists. No matter how individually satisfied we are with ourselves, our lives, our achievements, and other social relationships, individual fulfillment is not enough. Yes, we can be individually fulfilled and satisfied in life, but we are meant to go higher.

There is always something within us that urges us to evolve. That something is Togetherness-Fulfillment and true unconditional love, and it is what we are all ultimately looking for.

Togetherness-Fulfillment and true unconditional love can only be experienced with our Fulfilled Reflecting Self. No person, no material good, no possession, and no achievement are as beautiful, as meaningful, and as great in life as experiencing Togetherness-Fulfillment with our Fulfilled Reflecting Self. This is because whatever we achieve in life, we always want to experience it with our Fulfilled Reflecting Self, and indeed to unite our fulfillment with theirs.

Togetherness-Fulfillment is our innate urge/inclination to find, evolve with, and unite with our Fulfilled Reflecting Self.

Time for introspection

- Which of these five levels are you on? Why are you at that level? What do you need to do to be fulfilled?
- Do you take care of your body? Do you eat healthily? Do you exercise? Do you sleep well?
- Do you take care of your mind? Do you improve every day? Do you develop your positive qualities? Do you correct your mistakes?
- Are you satisfied with life and yourself?
- Have you achieved individual fulfillment? If so, how did you achieve it, and what are you doing to maintain it? If not, how will you achieve it?
- Do you experience individual fulfillment by helping others and being valuable to society?
- Are you satisfied with your relationship with your partner? If so, why are you? If not, why are you not?
- How do you experience fulfillment within yourself? Is it through money, material goods, achievements, holidays and travel, professional work, and social relationships, or through helping others and connecting with your Fulfilled Reflecting Self?

Answer these questions honestly and let's continue to explore Togetherness-Fulfillment and understand its immense and great value and uniqueness.

4.3 — Togetherness-Fulfillment

4.3.1 — Definition and nature of Togetherness-Fulfillment

As we said above, no human being is half and does not need to be completed by another human being or by achievements and acquisitions. We are all autonomous human beings, whole and unique from infancy, and after much inner work, we can reach the level of individual fulfillment. But this does not mean that individual fulfillment is the highest level we can reach. We are destined for greater things, and this is where unity with our Fulfilled Reflecting Self comes in.

But what does this mean? When we experience individual fulfillment and have a relationship with another person who is also experiencing individual fulfillment, does this mean that we are experiencing Togetherness-Fulfillment together? Is Togetherness-Fulfillment the relationship between two people who are individually fulfilled and are just having a good time together, just living in the same house, whether they are married or not?

Togetherness-Fulfillment is something much deeper and more substantial than that. It is not the romantic relationship between two people who are ignorant, nor is it the romantic relationship between two people who are individually fulfilled and have developed self-awareness. That is, it does not mean that because two people are individually fulfilled, they can achieve Togetherness-Fulfillment together through a romantic relationship. Togetherness-Fulfillment requires enormous individual and couple work and is only experienced with our Fulfilled Reflecting Self (You can remember the definition of the Fulfilled Reflecting Self to better understand Togetherness-Fulfillment: *The Fulfilled Reflecting Self is our one and only life partner with whom we unite as one on every level (spiritual, mental, psychological/emotional, and physical/sexual), where in our relationship we are both individually fulfilled and free from inferior needs and become each other's reflection.*).

Let's look at the definition of Togetherness-Fulfillment that we have given it:

Togetherness-Fulfillment is the highest spiritual state and evolutionary course of our existence, in which we unite with our Fulfilled Reflecting Self wholly and on every level (spiritual, mental, psychological/emotional, and physical/sexual), being completely spiritually naked in front of each other, with awareness, and experiencing true and unconditional love, with constant individual and couple work and improvement.

Now, let's explain the definition and the nature of Togetherness-Fulfillment by analyzing each phrase of the definition separately.

1. "Togetherness-Fulfillment is the highest spiritual state...".
This means that it is the highest state of being we can reach and embody in life, as it goes far beyond individual fulfillment and requires the attainment of the tremendously powerful and unique unity with our Fulfilled Reflecting Self, which is the most difficult, but also the most beautiful and meaningful endeavor of life. It is a spiritual state, not in a religious way but in a day-to-day practical way because it is primarily about our spiritual elements, who we really are, our values, our principles, and their inseparable unity with those of our Fulfilled Reflecting Self. It is a continuous experience of fulfillment and love with our Fulfilled Reflecting Self. This means that we are completely satisfied with our Fulfilled Reflecting Self and live in inner peace. As a state of being it means that we can embody and be Togetherness-Fulfillment, and Togetherness-Fulfillment as a state of being encompasses many other powerful states of being such as love, growth, awareness, and unity. So, we are love, we are growth, and we are unity, and we express this in everything we do and say in our relationship with our Fulfilled Reflecting Self.

2. "... and evolutionary course of our existence, ...".

Although Togetherness-Fulfillment is a state that becomes permanent when we reach it, it is also a continuous process of evolution in which we not only maintain the state we have already reached but also become better every day. A couple that has reached Togetherness-Fulfillment cannot stop experiencing Togetherness-Fulfillment because, quite simply, the partners have already united deeply. But this does not mean that the couple's evolution stops. When we reach the level of Togetherness-Fulfillment and Togetherness-Fulfillment becomes our new way of life, it does not mean that we now remain stagnant. Togetherness-Fulfillment is not a goal that we achieve and then move on to another goal. It is a permanent state of true unconditional love, but it is also a process of progress that requires constant work from the couple. It is a way of life.

Togetherness-Fulfillment is not only an evolutionary process for the couple but also an evolutionary course for humanity because couples who experience Togetherness-Fulfillment create healthy social relationships free from inferior needs, raise healthy children and, in this way, help in the creation of healthy societies.

3. "... in which we unite with our Fulfilled Reflecting Self wholly and on every level (spiritual, mental, psychological/emotional, and physical/sexual), ...".

Togetherness-Fulfillment is only possible with our Fulfilled Reflecting Self, for our Fulfilled Reflecting Self is the only person with whom we can unite on every level of our being and whom we can know completely and so deeply.

4. "... being completely spiritually naked in front of each other, with awareness, ...".

This phrase reinforces the previous one. Complete spiritual nakedness, raw truth, pure honesty, and the revelation of every element of our spirit, mind, soul, body, and our dark and negative elements only happens with our Fulfilled Reflecting Self.

Complete spiritual nakedness is an ongoing process of Togetherness-Fulfillment that requires great strength and comes from love. It is the most important element in a relationship of Togetherness-Fulfillment. It is about partners revealing *everything* to each other so that we can get to know each other in-depth and truly, and unite in practice.

What do we mean by "everything"?
- We mean everything that has to do with ourselves, our partner, other people we know,
- the past, the present, the future, memories, old secrets, possible lies, any concealment of the truth,
- positive, negative, neutral, strange, sad, distressing, hopeless, uncomfortable, frustrating and any other kind of experience,
- thoughts, feelings, moods, knowledge, worries, concerns, sorrows, problems, obstacles, crises, difficulties, inconveniences, discomforts, dissatisfactions,
- embarrassments, upsets, guilt, blurriness, desires, passions, pleasures,
- idiosyncrasies, whims, strengths, weaknesses, frailties, mistakes, faults, flaws, vulnerabilities,
- victories, defeats, recklessness, follies, foolishness, regrets,
- sick and violent instincts, cruelties, tensions, conflicts (internal and with other people), injustices, enmities, hostilities, vices, dislikes, aversions,
- unfulfilled desires, sexual desires, lusts, urges, fantasies, perversions, paranoia,
- stupidities, pettiness, arrogance, self-degradation, craziness, enthusiasm, quests,
- embarrassing incidents, humiliations, jealousies, insecurities, anxieties, fears, phobias, hesitations, doubts, uncertainties,
- challenges, oppressions, sufferings, and pains of all kinds, traumas,

- way of thinking, perspectives, ambitions, ideas, possibilities, dreams, goals, aims,
- and anything else you can think of, as well as every aspect of all the Self-Awareness Cultivating Models that we discussed in Chapter One.

All of this without any exception or excuse between the couple, and all of it revealed in detail and depth in every situation, regardless of the circumstances, no matter how difficult it may be or seem. As you understand, complete spiritual nakedness is magnificent and extremely rare because the strength it requires to cultivate complete spiritual nakedness in a couple is extremely rare.

Experiencing Togetherness-Fulfillment means that we are aware of who we are, our purpose, our positive and negative aspects, and we apply our knowledge to improve daily. We don't just stay in theory. Of course, awareness and its continued development are the result of complete spiritual nakedness, through which as a couple we unite as one on every level of our existence.

5. "... and experiencing true and unconditional love, ...".
Love is practical, daily, continuous, growing, evolving, unconditional, and everlasting, and it manifests in all the ways we have explored in the section about love. We could say that Togetherness-Fulfillment is indeed the greatest and strongest expression of true and unconditional love in a romantic relationship, according to one of the twenty-five definitions of love we introduced earlier: *"The ultimate unity (spiritual, mental, emotional, physical, and sexual) between two conscious people (with our Fulfilled Reflecting Self)"*. As a couple experiencing Togetherness-Fulfillment, we do not misinterpret love but fully understand it, honor it, and experience it purely and completely, without illusions or dependency. Love expands as partners keep being completely spiritually naked in front of each other.

6. *"... with constant individual and couple work and improvement.".*

This phrase reinforces the second phrase of the definition, *"... and evolutionary course of our existence...".* The individual and couple work never ends when the couple experiences Togetherness-Fulfillment, and this is something we emphasize all the time because it is crucial. Anything that is revealed and discussed between the partners during complete spiritual nakedness is not just left at the level of discussion, but the partners are constantly taking action to progress and evolve together, developing all the positive elements and improving all the negative ones together.

So, based on the above, in Togetherness-Fulfillment we are completely united with our life partner out of love. This means that as partners we do not have any spiritual or psychological/emotional voids because we have absolutely no need for acceptance and validation, and we have overcome, dealt with, and forgiven any issues we may have had with other people in the past, either as children or as adults.

We also have nothing to prove to anyone because we are grounded in our truth, unity, and fulfillment. So, the purpose of our relationship is love and progress, not to satisfy inferior needs for validation. We are both fulfilled, strong, and responsible human beings, constantly developing our self-awareness, who consciously and out of unconditional and boundless love choose to connect, unite our lives, and walk together in every area of life.

That is why we consciously want to be together and improve our relationship and unity with each other even more than we have improved on our own. We are both absolutely certain of who we are, and as conscious human beings we know that we are not dependent on each other, nor can we increase or decrease the quality of each other (see p. 102 Chapter Two on behaviors). We can, however, be fully united without dependency, but with love, and evolve together. This is how we unite our strength in maturity, committed to helping and supporting each other with absolute purity.

As a couple that experiences Togetherness-Fulfillment, we realize and know that the unity of love is the greatest strength in life. Alone, we can achieve many things; but with our life partner, we can do wonders that seem impossible for one person alone. As we said in Chapter One, people progress when they work together. The cooperation, connection, and unity with our life partner is the greatest form of connection that can exist in human relationships, and that is what we achieve when we experience Togetherness-Fulfillment. We are not only a spectacular team; we are one and the same. With our Fulfilled Reflecting Self, we are even stronger, more intelligent, and more capable. Together, we can achieve the impossible.

In Togetherness-Fulfillment, both partners are fulfilled individually, and so we unite as a couple on an even greater level. This means that we don't just have a good time together and get along. Our unity is even deeper.

We unite with our Fulfilled Reflecting Self as one, on every level of our existence:

1 - We unite on a spiritual level

We unite spiritually, at the level of who we are and the truth of ourselves. We become each other's true reflection. Spiritual unity is not only about the unity of qualities and positive states of being we can embody, but also about our values, principles, helpful beliefs, life and relationship purpose, legacy, and vision for the future. All of these are the same in both partners.

2 - We unite on a mental level and think in the same healthy and progressive way

We fully understand our partner's way of thinking and therefore their way of behaving. We set common goals together and aim to achieve them.

3 - We unite on a psychological/emotional level

We feel each other in-depth and essence, fully understanding our partner's emotions as if they were entirely our own. We understand our partner's every need and exactly what they need from us.

4 - Our Feminine and Masculine Selves are united

We unite the feminine and masculine elements of each of us in such a way that we can only experience them with our Fulfilled Reflecting Self. We explore this further below.

5 - We unite on a physical and sexual level and become one and the same

Our sexual unity is not only physical, like the sexual interaction someone can have with any random person, but it is at the same time spiritual, mental, and emotional, for we are united on every level of our existence.

This is not something general, vague, and theoretical. It is something completely practical.

This is most evident in the *raw and complete spiritual nakedness*, where with brutal honesty, and authenticity we come to know and accept every aspect of our life partner.

We know the truth about each other to the point where we become the realistic reflection of each other.

This means that we know, accept, and love every element of our partner's essence, thoughts, emotions, body, mind and every other aspect and truth of our partner's existence as if it were our own. In other words, we accept and love even the negative elements and thus, as two fulfilled human beings, we become practically one and the same in absolute love in every moment of life, having changed our negative behaviors for the better. As a united couple, we have the same values, standards, "non-negotiable nos", "wants", needs, principles, goals, and a common purpose of existence without of course each of us losing our uniqueness.

Therefore, Togetherness-Fulfillment in our relationship goes far beyond romantic relationship awareness, which is the actual knowledge of our partner, as we explored in the previous chapter. *In Togetherness-Fulfillment, we not only know our partner well; we are our partner.* We are one mind, one spirit, one soul and one body. This means that spiritually, mentally, and emotionally, we are one. We share the same mind, soul, and spirit. We have different bodies, but we unite physically in a spiritual way. But Togetherness-Fulfillment does not end here. We continue to improve as one with our life partner, learning more and more about ourselves and each other through this ultimate unity that grows stronger every day, every minute, and every second. So, we know that we have only one important "job" in life: to help each other be healthy, free, content, and fulfilled. This is the true peace of life, Togetherness-Fulfillment, away from the pursuit of superficial success, material wealth and fame.

In short, Togetherness-Fulfillment is not just something we feel, like our fleeting emotions, but something we experience.

But what does it mean to *"experience"*? It means that we both *think* with love, *act* with love, and *feel* beautiful emotions of joy, infatuation, and excitement; that we choose every day to be our best for our relationship and our partner, and that we commit ourselves to constantly improving in every way; that we are completely united with each other, devoted to each other. This means that Togetherness-Fulfillment as an experience involves everything: positive states of being, thoughts, actions, emotions, choices, commitment to improvement, connection, unity, faith, and complete spiritual nakedness (which is the quality that makes Togetherness-Fulfillment unique). It is how we live. So, it is good in your life and relationship to try to experience situations and not to chase after fleeting feelings, because love and Togetherness-Fulfillment are powerful and lasting experiences.

Time for introspection

- Now that we have explained Togetherness-Fulfillment to you, do you think you are experiencing it? If so, how, and why? What exactly do you think, feel, do, and experience with your Fulfilled Reflecting Self? If you are not experiencing it, why are you not experiencing it? Do you think you can experience it?

- Do you become completely naked spiritually, mentally, and emotionally in front of your life partner? Do you know each other's inner world, be it spiritual, mental, or emotional? If so, how? What benefits do you see in your relationship and life? If not, why don't you become completely spiritually naked in front of your life partner? How can you be completely spiritually naked in front of each other?
- What do you need to do to reach this high level of unity with your Fulfilled Reflecting Self?

4.3.2 — The importance of time in Togetherness-Fulfillment

As a couple experiencing Togetherness-Fulfillment, we choose to live every aspect of our life together. We live together, work together, create together, have fun together, spend our spare time together, do our daily tasks together, travel together, and do everything in life together because that's what we want to. So, both our work and our commitments, which for many people are constraints, become free and quality time because we are together. We don't live ten hours a day in a different environment and then get together at home to exchange a few words. We experience everything together. So, every difficulty or challenge seems like a piece of cake and becomes something enjoyable that we do together to improve ourselves.

In Togetherness-Fulfillment, our time is precious and priceless, and we want every moment to be lived with love. Therefore, we never waste our time. We experience every moment together. We realize that anything is possible in life when we are on a shared path of undying love with our life partner.

In Togetherness-Fulfillment, not even the sky is the limit.

There are no limits, only unlimited potential, and when we experience this, we are now completely satisfied with our life. In individual fulfillment, we are simply satisfied, but looking for something more, whereas in Togetherness-Fulfillment we are completely satisfied and have no need for anything else.

At this point, it is significant to discuss the time you spend together as a couple because it is closely related to the development and achievement of Togetherness-Fulfillment. If you don't live and work with your Fulfilled Reflecting Self, then something is missing from your relationship. This is because you live two entirely different lives, and only socialize a few moments together, probably for fun or entertainment in your spare time.

You may love each other, which only you know, but that doesn't change the fact that you live different lives and can't develop your relationship meaningfully. Even if you live together but don't work together, you spend a great deal of your lives apart, and so you have different experiences, associate with different people and deal with different situations. This pushes you to grow apart. That is, you walk in a different direction. So, you will not be able to take advantage of all the ways in which you can unite.

Working together helps you unite even more as a couple

So, it's important to live together, of course, but also to work together. Working together brings you closer, not only because you spend more time with your partner, but also because you have to deal with the challenges of your work together and find your level of collaboration and limits. This way you grow stronger together.

In order to want to work and spend all your time together, you have to *surpass yourself every day* by committing to continuous improvement, as we said in the previous chapter. If you both surpass yourselves every day, you will have no reason to want to be apart. You will have many reasons not to be apart because you will be more and more united. This is how you use your time constructively.

Couples who experience Togetherness-Fulfillment will inevitably want to work and do everything together. A couple experiencing Togetherness-Fulfillment will also have excellent cooperation. So, if you prefer to work alone and don't collaborate very well with your partner, then you need to re-examine and re-evaluate your relationship, because there is a chance that it is just a typical relationship of compromise and not one of love.

Of course, your relationship may not be great yet, but that doesn't mean that you don't love each other or that you are disconnected. It means that you have a lot of room for improvement, and that goes for all of us. The longer you work together, the more you will improve since you will face the same pressure, stress, and issues at work and deal with it together rather than taking it out on each other. That means you will learn how to deal together with difficult situations that involve other people when you are out of your comfort and the safety of your home. You'll get to know your partner even deeper. You will learn many lessons and become better people as your relationship develops. This will make your work a pleasure rather than an oppression.

It is possible to work together if you want to

Even if you are now in a situation where it is not easy for you to work together, it is good to start moving in the direction of working together. You may have to sacrifice some time at first to learn the necessary skills of a new career or continue to work apart for a period, to build a life in which you can do everything together, share the same experiences, unite on every level of your being, and experience true fulfillment and love daily.

Of course, there are many parameters that can make this difficult, such as children, and two very different careers, and we know that in many scenarios, working together as a couple may seem unrealistic and impossible to some people. But couples who really want to move in the direction of working together can indeed achieve this and build such a life. There are no excuses, only challenges to improve.

Enjoy each other every day, every moment, whatever you do. Work together, have fun together, exercise together, relax together, create together, learn together, grow together, and live life together, not apart.

Of course, it is the quality time that counts the most, but the quantity of time is also crucial. Because if you have one hour of quality time a day, ten hours apart, and three hours of typical time, you won't be able to be united easily. But if you turn the three hours of typical time into quality time and the ten hours apart into time together (whether it's quality time or not), then you understand how much more you can unite and enjoy each other. In essence, what we all need is quantitative time, which is also extremely qualitative.

So, if you're not already working together, make the most of the rest of your time together qualitatively. For example, learn each other's work, create something together, work on a project together, start a business together... It may seem difficult to create a common career path, but you can certainly do something together on the side of your main jobs and experience working together in your own way. There are many solutions if you really want to experience life together and not just connect your two different lives in the evenings and weekends.

Togetherness-Fulfillment is created when we do everything together with our Fulfilled Reflecting Self because only then can we be fully and completely one on every level of our being. That is when our time together is both qualitative and quantitative. So, living every moment fully with our life partner is a one-way street if we want to experience Togetherness-Fulfillment.

Time for introspection

- How much time do you spend together with your partner? How much quality time do you spend together? Do you do everything together or not? If yes, why? If not, why?
- How much do you value your time with your partner?
- Do you want to spend only a few hours with your partner or all the time? If you only want to spend a few hours together, why? Don't you love each other?
- If you want to be together all the time, what's stopping you? What do you have to do to make it happen?

4.3.3 — Marriage and Togetherness-Fulfillment

As we have said before, Togetherness-Fulfillment is the state of total unity with our partner on every level of our existence, and therefore also the spiritual connection and unity between us. Connection and unity of who we are, values, principles, and purpose of our existence. So, it is very likely that a couple experiencing Togetherness-Fulfillment will also come to marriage. But what is marriage?

Many people believe that once they get married their whole life changes and some even say that this is when the hardships and difficulties of life begin. They believe that marriage is such a serious event that needs to be celebrated, but at the same time that a person is no longer "free" after marriage. However, these limiting beliefs are mostly about people who have typical superficial relationships and simply go through a marriage of compromise driven by their fleeting emotions rather than love. In other words, they are about people who see life from a meaningless perspective.

The couple's unity should be spiritual, not about signatures on a piece of paper

The truth is that marriage is nothing more than two signatures on paper. The point is to be spiritually connected and united with our partner, not to think that our relationship changes because we sign some papers. When we are spiritually united with our Fulfilled Reflecting Self, we are truly free. This is the opposite of what many people believe. Commitment and devotion to our Fulfilled Reflecting Self is true freedom. In contrast, loneliness, failure to unite with our partner, wanting to spend time apart from them, and constantly changing romantic partners is the opposite of freedom.

If we are not spiritually married before signing, we should not sign because we will end up in divorce or a marriage of compromise we will regret, and our children will suffer for it.

The examples of people who have ended up divorced or with a partner who is not their Fulfilled Reflecting Self are countless. In fact, there are many cases in which such people have children and do tremendous damage to them. We are sure you know many people who are or have been in similar situations.

If we do not experience spiritual marriage from the beginning of the relationship, then the relationship will most likely not have a positive future. *This is the simplicity and beauty of marriage: a spiritual unity.* It is not the dressing up, the party, and the gathering of all the random people from our and others' social circles to "celebrate" this event and the possible life of compromise to come.

Moreover, marriage is not about the vows we take, especially when we have no idea of the meaning of those vows. Saying a few words at that time, such as "we will always be together in good times and bad", has no meaning if a spiritual unity does not precede it.

Nor is there any point in sharing the "joy" of our marriage with anyone because there is no joy to celebrate. Be careful though, we do not mean that marriage cannot be a joyful event; marriage can be pleasurable, but it's not that important because the key is to create a spiritual bond long before marriage.

As explained earlier, love is not something that is celebrated only one day. It is celebrated and experienced practically by the couple every single day. So, there is absolutely no need for a special occasion and celebration. There is nothing new. There are no new emotions created that we didn't have before because we're getting married. Nothing in our relationship has changed. We have been spiritually married for a long time and nothing has changed in our life. Life after marriage is healthy to evolve as it evolved before marriage. This is experiencing Togetherness-Fulfillment in a romantic relationship and in a spiritual marriage. The partners were completely united before marriage and remain completely united after marriage.

Marriage is a conscious choice made by the couple and even something that has more to do with social and formal purposes. It is not a big event or something random. In short, a couple doesn't need to get married to prove to themselves or others that they love each other.

The essence, then, is to be found in love and not in the misinterpretation of love, fleeting emotions, ignorance, and formal celebrations. How can marriage be meaningful and spiritual if partners think they love each other just because they feel infatuation occasionally and focus on superficial things?

If the marriage is not spiritual and not based on true love and Togetherness-Fulfillment, then it is unlikely to last. That is why people who have been married for twenty and thirty years end up getting divorced. Because they have never been spiritually married. All they did was dress up one day, invite everyone they knew or even didn't know to their wedding, and sign up for a life of compromise.

This sounds harsh, but unfortunately, it is the truth, and that is why the decision to get married requires great care, responsibility, and self-awareness. Of course, if the couple wants to celebrate the wedding with friends and family, there is nothing wrong with that and indeed it can be a beautiful and meaningful thing, but it is vital that the spiritual unity comes first and that the partners know deep inside them that they are experiencing love, not just falsely believing they are.

We say all this with rigor so that we, as humanity, can finally escape from the superficial, the shallow, and the meaningless so we can experience true love with essence. It is important to have a realistic and meaningful view of marriage, one that is based on spiritual unity and Togetherness-Fulfillment, not on superficial celebrations, fancy dresses and satisfying inferior needs for validation. When marriage is spiritual, the relationship will last forever and flourish through Togetherness-Fulfillment.

Time for introspection

- What do you believe about marriage? What is the truth and essence of marriage?
- Do you prefer a formal, superficial, and shallow marriage or a marriage with a solid foundation of unconditional love, awareness, trust, and Togetherness-Fulfillment?

- If you are married, is your marriage a formal one of compromise or is it a marriage of love?
- If you are not married, would you marry for love or do you not even know why?
- What is important to you, love and spiritual unity or festivities, celebrations, and fleeting emotions?

Consider all this to evaluate your view of marriage and to find out what changes you need to make in your thinking and life in order to experience the depth of life and not live superficially.

4.3.4 — Togetherness-Fulfillment as a way to improve every other social relationship

As humans, we naturally want to interact with other people, and socialization is significant to each of us. So, we are not meant to live alone in a cave without any human contact, no matter how happy we are with ourselves. But this does not mean that we are meant to maintain superficial human relationships and waste our time with just anyone, especially with people who are on a different path from us. We are meant to live with our Fulfilled Reflecting Self, experiencing Togetherness-Fulfillment.

When we experience Togetherness-Fulfillment with our Fulfilled Reflecting Self, we cease to need other people in our life, as we explained about love earlier. This is not because we lose our sociability, or because we are shy, or because we despise other people, or because we get locked into a bubble with our partner, or because we don't like other people or anything else you can think of. It simply happens because our Fulfilled Reflecting Self becomes our life. They become our parent and our best and truest friend and our brother or sister and our co-worker and our partner and our family. They become everything to us, and we become everything to them.

We don't need validation from anyone, and we don't need to have social relationships with many people to feel valuable. All that has been eliminated in us. Before we reached Togetherness-Fulfillment, the relationships we had with other people were mostly relationships to meet needs for connection, acceptance, validation, or approval.

For example, a child needs its parents to meet its need for acceptance, and this is natural and necessary in childhood. A parent may need to keep their child dependent on them even into adulthood for them to feel that they have a purpose in life, and this is not healthy. Some friends hang out together to meet validation needs because their parents did not meet them when they were children. When we experience Togetherness-Fulfillment, all that is in the past.

The relationships we have with other people as a couple are few and qualitative, always with a focus on help, support and meaningful connection and enjoyment. We don't have social relationships because we have to, but because we want to. Because we want to help these people (parents, friends, relatives, etc.) and spend quality time with them together as a couple. We value these people, appreciate them, and enjoy spending quality time with them. So, these relationships are meaningful, progressive and of great importance because they stem from awareness and kindness, not from unmet needs for validation.

We understand that the relationships that matter, apart from the relationship we have with ourselves and our life partner, are the meaningful friendships that are created out of connection and not insecurity; the family relationships that we cherish, not because we are only biologically related, but because we are truly connected in some way; the relationships with colleagues and other people that are based on support.

We are selective and rigorous in our social relationships because we recognize our value and do not want to waste our time with people who do not walk on a similar path with us. This helps our development as a couple, but also the development of other people around us, as we all put our energy into quality human relationships, rather than relationships to satisfy inferior needs.

We no longer have needs for validation, acceptance, approval, or the need to prove our worth to anyone because we know who we are, we know our self-worth, we are individually fulfilled, and we are united fully and on every level of our existence with our Fulfilled Reflecting Self. So, we don't behave in a negative, needy way to other people in our lives, like trying to seem significant in other people's eyes. We don't live by other people's standards, expectations, and beliefs. We don't follow the rules that we have been taught by our parents, teachers, peers, and society about how we should live life, and what is good for us and what is not. We free ourselves from our upbringing and the beliefs we created as we grew up, and we start thinking on our own. Every time we make a decision, we ask ourselves if this decision comes from what we have been taught by others or comes from who we really are. We make our own path that is aligned with who we are, what is truly valuable to us, and Togetherness-Fulfillment not with other people's expectations, what others consider as significant, or to please others. This way the relationships we keep with other people, such as friends and family are more meaningful, enjoyable, honest, genuine, authentic, and caring, free from inferior needs. We radiate the pure light we are, we are our truth, and whether other people talk negatively about us, ignore us, or praise us with the highest praises, it has no impact on us because we know our truth, and whether other people see that or not, it is not something that we care about. This way, people around us don't have to deal with an immature and needy part of us because this part no longer has control and power. So, they can just connect with the purest parts of ourselves. Love, growth, and awareness are now our leading forces in life. This is the power of Togetherness-Fulfillment: the complete freedom from inferior needs and the absolute unity with our Fulfilled Reflecting Self. This way we build healthy social relationships that lead to the betterment of society.

Therefore, you can see that Togetherness-Fulfillment is not only crucial for our relationship with our life partner but also helps us to create meaningful social relationships with other people and to be aware of the reasons why we choose to connect with them. Togetherness-Fulfillment enlightens and shows us that it is wise to use our invaluable time to be with our Fulfilled Reflecting Self, people we care about dearly and to share our purpose with the world and help humanity evolve.

Time for introspection

- Do you have unmet needs for validation? If so, why? If not, why? Do you maintain social relationships because you want these people in your life or because you need to feel accepted by them?
- Are you completely satisfied with your relationship with your partner? If so, why? If not, why?
- Every time you make a decision, does this come from what you have been taught from other people growing up or is it something that is truly aligned with who you are, and what is most valuable to you?
- What do you need to do in order not to have an inner need for other people in your life and to become strong people with your partner?

4.3.5 — Togetherness-Fulfillment and codependency

Many people, because they have never experienced anything remotely close to the high levels of Togetherness-Fulfillment and have never known true love, may confuse Togetherness-Fulfillment with codependency. Usually, when people hear a couple say that they want to be together all the time and do everything together, they are either jealous of the relationship or think that the couple is in a codependent relationship. Especially when they hear that the partners in this relationship are each other's parents, best friends, etc., they conclude that the partners are codependent.

This is because they cannot imagine that two people can be so connected, united, and loving to each other because they know only compromise, misery, and dependency of all kinds in their relationships and lives. So, they judge other loving and deeply connected people based on their limiting experiences of compromise and dependency.

Togetherness-Fulfillment has nothing to do with codependency. In codependency, partners need to be together because they are dependent on each other and are motivated by insecurity, and inferior needs for acceptance and validation, not love. So, you see, Togetherness-Fulfillment is the extreme opposite of codependency.

Codependency is a state of ignorance, weakness, and insecurity, whereas Togetherness-Fulfillment is a state of awareness, strength, unity, and love.

A codependent relationship is about the couple's survival in a world full of demands, difficulties, and challenges. To cope and survive, partners need each other's validation. However, a relationship of Togetherness-Fulfillment is not about survival, but about the couple's evolution in this world of demands, difficulties, and challenges, as the partners consciously choose to be inseparable together. *Rather than depending on each other, they stand side by side, strong and resilient as equals.* Of course, codependency is not a permanent situation and can be remedied. Any person who is motivated by fear (codependency) can find the strength within themselves and experience true love (Togetherness-Fulfillment).

So, let's look at the main differences between codependency and Togetherness-Fulfillment so that you can free yourself from codependency if it is present in your relationship:

CODEPENDENCY	TOGETHERNESS-FULFILLMENT
Sacrificing your authentic self for fear of rejection by your partner. Hiding the truth or lying.	Both partners are genuine and completely honest with each other. They are not acting out of fear, but out of love. They are constantly being completely spiritually naked in front of each other.

They do not know what their wants, needs, and values are. If they do know what they are, they sacrifice them to please their partner.	They clearly understand their own and their partner's wants, needs and values, and they make decisions together. In fact, they reach a level where they have common wants, needs, and values.
They fear conflict with their partner. They have constant communication problems and do not develop their communication skills.	They embrace conflict with their partner when it is healthy and aimed at improvement. They are constantly developing their communication skills and have imperfect but clear communication.
They have low self-worth, self-esteem, and self-confidence. They need their partner so they can feel they are valuable.	They have high self-worth, self-esteem, and self-confidence with a realistic and humble approach. They don't need their partner to feel they are valuable. They are worthy as individuals and choose to unite with their partner out of love.
They operate with inferior needs for approval and validation. They constantly seek their partner's approval for everything they do. If they don't get their partner's approval, they can't make decisions.	They do not operate with inferior needs for acceptance and validation, but with their values and the truth about themselves. They are decisive and strong. They make decisions easily on their own, but consciously choose to make decisions about their life as equals with their partner.
They are insecure and anxious. They have a strong need for reassurance from their partner. They need their partner because they can't be alone.	They are confident about who they are and their relationship with their partner. They have no need for reassurance. They help each other out of pure love, not out of fear or need.
They have a childish mentality and are adults only in age and not in spirit. They behave immaturely, emotionally and without self-control.	They are spiritual adults, truly mature people and responsible for themselves. They have healthy self-control and are not controlled by their fleeting emotions.
They have a relationship with their partner just to try to fill their huge inner voids. They feel "empty" and try to "feed" emotionally from their partner. Their relationship is a place to hide from their fearful existence.	They are fulfilled as individuals and consciously choose to evolve with their partner together. The relationship is a path of progress and evolution for the couple.

They accept being in a relationship with anyone because they are afraid of being alone and afraid of rejection.	They accept to be in a relationship only with their Fulfilled Reflecting Self. They have unwavering faith in their relationship and enjoy their Companionate Romantic Solitude.
They are ignorant of themselves and their partner. They have not worked internally on themselves, and so they do not know who they are. This leads to possessiveness and dependency.	They constantly develop their self-awareness and romantic relationship awareness. They improve individually and together, as a couple, every day. They know their partner as deeply as they know themselves. This leads to a spiritual unity.

You can see that codependency is a problematic state of imbalance, whereas Togetherness-Fulfillment is a state of health, balance, and unconditional love.

In the state of Togetherness-Fulfillment, the partners are together not because they cannot function individually, as in codependency, but because they choose to triumph together as one. That is, they understand that they are not just a couple, but an unstoppable force of love.

Time for introspection

- Are you in one of these situations? If so, which one? If you experience codependency, which of the above is manifested in your relationship? What do you need to do to improve?
- Are you in a relationship with your Fulfilled Reflecting Self or with just a romantic partner? If you are in a codependent relationship with just a random romantic partner, why do you choose to stay in it? If you are in a relationship with your Fulfilled Reflecting Self and yet, you experience codependency, what do you need to do to escape the state of codependency and experience Togetherness-Fulfillment?

4.3.6 — The Togetherness-Fulfillment Model

So far, you have seen many aspects of Togetherness-Fulfillment, and you can understand to what extent it is present in your relationship, or if it is present at all. Here, we will look at how you can unite with your life partner through your feminine and masculine elements.

Togetherness-Fulfillment with our life partner is therefore evident when our feminine and masculine elements are united and interact in harmony and balance with the feminine and masculine elements of our life partner.

As we explained in Chapter One, in the Feminine and Masculine Aware Self Model, we all have both feminine and masculine elements within us. These can easily clash both internally, within us, and with the corresponding elements in our partner.

For example, if one partner is angry (masculine element) and the other is irritated (again, masculine element) by their partner's anger, then they will clash. However, when partners experience Togetherness-Fulfillment, they can use the dynamics of their feminine and masculine elements in a way that helps them grow and support each other effectively. So, when one partner is angry, the other partner connects with them and does not fight them. What does this mean? It means that they will express a feminine element of themselves, such as understanding, to help their partner calm down, rather than a masculine element, such as anger, which will create more tension.

So, in a relationship where one partner's feminine or masculine elements are intense, such as intense anger (masculine) or intense sadness (feminine), it is vital that the other partner expresses opposite elements to those of their partner, so as not to cause tension and conflict. This does not mean, of course, that when identical elements are expressed between partners, there will always be conflict. It depends on what those elements are and how they are utilized by the couple.

This can be linked to the Negative Behavior Improvement Model in Chapter Two (see pp. 137-141) to understand how you might use your feminine and masculine elements to prevent unnecessary arguments with your partner. You may wish to re-read the Feminine and Masculine Aware Self Model (see pp. 74-79) to remind yourself of some essential aspects, such as the ways in which the feminine and masculine elements connect or clash, before moving on.

So, how are the dynamics of our feminine and masculine elements expressed in Togetherness-Fulfillment?

Let's look at the Togetherness-Fulfillment Model that we have created by studying ourselves and the interrelationship and conflict of the feminine and masculine elements in our relationship, and by observing people around us and trying to understand their relationships. This way, you will see how these elements are expressed.

The Togetherness-Fulfillment Model is a way that we can understand ourselves and our life partner deeply and a way to improve our behaviors, conversations, and interactions. It is connected to every other model we have created and everything else we have explored in this book and can give you another perspective of how our mental, emotional, and spiritual levels can clash or be in balance by examining our feminine and masculine elements.

We call the feminine and masculine elements forces because they are actually the driving forces that drive us to either a positive or negative direction. They motivate us in life, ignite the flame in our relationship, rekindle our desire and healthy passion, and at the same time lead us to peace. All these, if, of course, we develop our self-awareness and know how to utilize these elements and understand their dynamics, which are the way in which the feminine and masculine elements in each partner smoothly connect or clash. However, if we don't know how to use these elements, they can damage our relationship and be used as destructive forces, as in the example of anger above.

In short, the feminine and masculine forces within us can be either positive and helpful, or negative and damaging.

This depends on:

1. The nature of the forces, i.e., whether they tend to be positive or negative (e.g., insecurity is a negative feminine force, compassion is a positive feminine force, arrogance is a negative masculine force, responsibility is a positive masculine force).

2. Our awareness of them, i.e., whether we know they exist, what exactly they are (their clear definition) and what influence they have on us.

3. How we use them (in our relationship with ourselves and with our life partner). Any negative force can be used to improve ourselves, just like any positive force.

For example, insecurity is negative in nature, but if we are aware of it, then we can learn from it and deal with it or be motivated to evolve. In other words, by being aware of our insecurity, we can be inspired to change this negative state and use a positive force like responsibility to become secure in who we really are. So, our will to not be insecure anymore works like a positive motivator for change.

Let us analyze the Togetherness-Fulfillment Model to better understand these forces and their dynamics.

The Togetherness-Fulfillment Model

As we can see in the model above, every human being has either a feminine or masculine force at their *core*, symbolized by the inner circle, and the same on its *surface*, symbolized by the outer circle. But the middle circle, *the inner space*, is the exact opposite force.

So generally, you could say that a woman has feminine force in her core and surface and masculine force in her inner space. That is, she has predominantly feminine forces within her and expresses them more often to others. But she also has masculine forces, which she expresses less often.

A man, on the other hand, has masculine forces in his core and surface, and feminine forces in his inner space. That is, he has primarily masculine forces within him and expresses them more frequently to other people. However, he also has feminine forces, which he expresses less often.

However, this is not fixed as any person can have any forces as their dominant ones no matter their sex and gender or how they identify as.

In short:
- The core shows which force (feminine or masculine) is dominant deep within us.
- The surface shows which force we usually express in our relationships with other people, and is usually the same as the core force.
- The in-between circle (the inner space) shows the opposite of the predominant force within us, but it is just as strong and can also be expressed many times.

Examples of how the feminine and masculine elements can influence our behavior and determine the quality of our relationship

Of course, we have created this model to understand how the feminine and masculine forces flow within us and how they interact with the forces of our life partner. This means that these forces can constantly alternate with each other and are not absolutely fixed.

For example, a woman who has feminine force at her core e.g., sensitivity and compassion, may express more often masculine forces in her relationships with others, such as dynamism and assertiveness, and even in a negative way like arrogance, rather than feminine forces as might be expected.

This can happen for several reasons. One reason may be the insecurity and fear (feminine forces) she created as a child because of her unmet need for validation from her parents (see p. 116). Insecurity and fear make her want to appear strong and independent to other people because she is afraid of being hurt again, as she was hurt as a child. So, her core is pure positive feminine force (compassion), but instead of expressing compassion, she expresses masculine forces to others (dynamism and assertiveness), usually with a negative charge (such as arrogance). This is because if she expresses compassion (positive feminine force) or fear and insecurity (negative feminine force), she thinks she will be considered weak because of her limiting beliefs. This way, the masculine forces emerge as a defense. And of course, because of this inner imprisonment, it will be easier for the negative masculine forces to come out on the surface rather than the positive ones. This leads her to damage her relationships with other people, and especially her relationship with her partner because that is the most intimate relationship where these forces are most strongly expressed negatively.

So, you can see how these forces can alternate within us and lead us into confusion and negative behavior.

Let's look at another example. A man who has at his core masculine forces of courage and dynamism expresses to others negative feminine forces of shame and fear and so does not speak authentically and confidently, which contradicts who he is deep inside. This may be because as a child, he created negative masculine forces of anger and tension due to unmet needs. But because he was criticized for his anger and was taught that he shouldn't get angry in front of other people and that he should be the "good guy", he was driven to insecurity. As a result, he stopped expressing himself authentically to other people.

So, although deep down he is brave and strong (positive masculine forces), he does not express bravery and strength and expresses shame and fear (negative feminine forces) because he has suppressed his anger (which can be usually a negative masculine force) and this has led to insecurity (negative feminine force).

Anger in this case is suppressed and suffocated internally, leading to a passive rather than active expression of anger. The result is shame and fear. Thus, this man is unable to be his authentic, dynamic self with other people, and therefore unable to have a healthy relationship with his partner.

We see here that although we typically express the forces we have in our core and surface and only sometimes express the opposite ones we have in our inner space; this is not always the case. The feminine and masculine forces can get very mixed up and become a big mess. At the same time, we understand that this confusion and any negative expression of our feminine and masculine forces have some relation to our insecurity and our inferior needs. That's why it is important to constantly study ourselves with care so that we remain in balance. We also see how everything we have said so far in this book is connected, especially the Feminine and Masculine Aware Self Model, the Reactive Unaware Self Model, limiting beliefs, negative behaviors and situations such as past behaviors (dependency and avoidance of connection) and of course Togetherness-Fulfillment.

How understanding our feminine and masculine forces helps us cultivate Togetherness-Fulfillment

Togetherness-Fulfillment is cultivated and developed when both partners are very aware of their feminine and masculine forces and connect them in a healthy way. Thus, a woman with a feminine core, feminine surface and masculine inner space connects and unites with the opposite and identical elements of her partner who has a masculine core, masculine surface, and feminine inner space. This means that the woman's feminine core and feminine surface are connected to the man's feminine inner space, and the man's masculine core and masculine surface are connected to his partner's masculine inner space.

In this way, the similar forces of the couple (feminine with feminine and masculine with masculine), which exist in different intensities and quantities in each partner, are united. The opposite forces (feminine with masculine) of the couple are connected in the way explained above and in the Feminine and Masculine Aware Self Model, where when one partner expresses a masculine element, the other partner is often helpful to express a feminine element and vice versa.

Here you understand that each partner is fulfilled and whole as they are (see p. 220). That is, each partner has their core, surface, and inner space complete (they are fulfilled) and in an entirely unique way (they are whole). The greatness and beauty of Togetherness-Fulfillment lie in the fact that each partner is fulfilled and whole on their own and can further unite, as a couple. They can unite their unique and complete core, surface, and inner space with the counterparts of their Fulfilled Reflecting Self, who is also fulfilled and whole.

This is one of the many expressions of Togetherness-Fulfillment. The forces of each partner are combined into one enormous force. The feminine elements of one partner unite with the feminine elements of the other. The masculine elements of one partner unite with the masculine elements of the other. Their opposite elements work together in balance without conflict.

Each partner becomes the purest reflection of the other. The couple becomes one and the same.

In Togetherness-Fulfillment, the expressions "opposites attract" and "likes attract" are equally correct because the couple is connected and united both by their different elements and their identical elements. Thus, they unite both their different and identical feminine and masculine forces. They also unite their same values and principles, their common purpose of existence and many other elements of themselves which we have mainly explained in Chapter One.

How to use your feminine and masculine elements in a healthy way

So, based on all the above, a couple experiencing Togetherness-Fulfillment uses their different feminine and masculine elements in a healthy way. For example, if a woman, who has feminine forces at her core, becomes angry for some reason, expressing masculine forces of anger towards her husband, who has masculine forces at his core and surface, they are likely to clash.

However, if the husband handles the situation with maturity and self-control, he will not be expressing masculine elements, especially negative ones, even though they are predominant within him, but will be managing the masculine forces of his wife healthily, expressing the feminine forces of balance and peace that he has in his inner space. By putting his partner and their relationship first, the man will speak kindly and understandingly to his partner, hug her, kiss her, and help her to calm down.

This way, the feminine and masculine forces of each partner are connected and united in health and balance. This is a relationship of Togetherness-Fulfillment. It does not mean that the couple is perfect and will not make mistakes or have conflict at some point. It means that the partners know how to manage these forces effectively when tensions arise, always putting their love first. Thus, they overcome every difficulty and conquer everything together.

Togetherness-Fulfillment and sexual attraction

The feminine and masculine forces also play a crucial role in the sexual attraction of the couple. It is important that the forces expressed by the couple are mostly opposite in order for there to be sexual attraction. This means that if both partners are expressing masculine elements, it is very likely that they will not have a desire for sexual intercourse. The same is true if both partners express feminine elements. But if the partners express different elements, then there is desire, passion, and attraction between them.

Togetherness-Fulfillment is about love and not labels or prejudices

Of course, all the above does not only apply to heterosexual couples because Togetherness-Fulfillment is not about the connection of the two opposite sexes, but about the total connection and unity of two people who love each other with all their "being" regardless of their sex, gender, and sexual orientation.

So, no matter how a person is labelled according to their gender and sexual preference, it makes absolutely no difference, as *love and Togetherness-Fulfillment know no rules, limitations, genders, nationalities and religious, political or any other kind of beliefs and prejudices.* Love and Togetherness-Fulfillment free us from pettiness and reveal our truth and our true strength.

When we experience Togetherness-Fulfillment, it is as if we are reborn, as we uproot the rubbish of the past and begin to experience a much purer and transcendent state than we have experienced before. This state is one of self-awareness, romantic relationship awareness and love. In Togetherness-Fulfillment we embrace our nature, which is a nature of constant positive change and love, and so we evolve rapidly and with tremendous power with our Fulfilled Reflecting Self every day, being free and creative.

So, through Togetherness-Fulfillment we break the enslaving rules, and the false limitations of society, other people, and ourselves, and take the step of true and meaningful spiritual unity with our Fulfilled Reflecting Self.

You can unite with your partner in this way if you work together with passion, commitment, dedication, devotion, and love on everything we have discussed in this book.

Time for introspection

- How do you use and manage your feminine and masculine forces in your relationship?
- Are you aware of these forces in yourself? Are you aware of them in your partner? Do these forces clash or are they in har-

mony? Do you help each other when you strongly express a feminine or masculine force, or do you clash?

- What do you notice when you express feminine forces? How does your partner behave when you do this?
- What do you notice when you express masculine forces? How does your partner behave when you do this?
- What do you notice when your partner expresses feminine forces? How do you behave when they do this?
- What do you notice when your partner expresses masculine forces? How do you behave when they do this?
- What do you need to do in order to unite your own feminine and masculine forces with those of your partner so that they do not clash?

4.3.7 — The power of Togetherness-Fulfillment

We have seen the nature and greatness of Togetherness-Fulfillment. We have seen its relationship to time, marriage, its impact on the improvement of other social relationships, codependency and how to deal with it, and to unity through the feminine and masculine forces of the partners. We hope you have a good understanding of its immense power. But to understand the power of Togetherness-Fulfillment even more, if you do not already experience something similar with your partner, we will tell you about some things from our own life.

When we started our relationship, we were very young, and we loved each other from the first moment. We wanted to move in together right away because we wanted to share every moment of our life together. But there were financial difficulties and objections from our family members, as well as immaturity on our part. However, we didn't give up and did everything we could to stay together and grow.

Along the way, we had support from some family members and none from others. In fact, some "close" people in our life wanted us to starve, stay on the streets and suffer rather than stay together. So, that's what happened to some extent. There were times when we literally didn't have enough to eat, and we ended up losing about twenty kilos each. In fact, we worked hard for peanuts, often unpaid, and had been experiencing a tremendous amount of stress, that is difficult to describe, over a very long period.

But we never gave up. We never backed down. That's because we continued to keep our relationship and our love as our number one priority and refused to be separated because of anyone or anything.

So, through these difficulties and overcoming them because of our love, the idea and the truth of Togetherness-Fulfillment began to be born. By putting our love first, we were able to find a job that we cherished and improved ourselves financially. We even managed to work together, although at first, we faced difficulties and refusals because we were not allowed to work together as a couple in that particular job. So many people thought it was impossible. But again, we didn't give up and to this day, we always work together.

Through all this development we have also improved our health, regained our weight and grown in every area of our life. This has happened because we have put "together" above everything else in our life, and, of course, above other people's "egos". So since then, nothing and no one has come between us, we are steadfast in our love, and nothing can stop us. From the bottom, we climbed to the top together, and every day we grow more and go even higher.

This is the power of Togetherness-Fulfillment, and it is something you can experience or develop even further if you already have a great connection with your partner. We all deserve a life and relationship of love, Togetherness-Fulfillment, health, and peace and no one can ever take that away from us if we are strong and responsible people who always have love and our relationship with our Fulfilled Reflecting Self as our number one priority.

By developing Togetherness-Fulfillment in our relationship, we can help many people in life because we are strong and unbreakable with our Fulfilled Reflecting Self. In this way, we can offer our knowledge, experience, and gifts to the world. As a couple, we can help and inspire other people and couples to grow and create a legacy of true love and support.

When a couple experiences Togetherness-Fulfillment, they can take on the massive responsibility of having children. For only then can they raise them in the best way possible, providing them with everything they need, and helping them to become healthy and responsible adults, not dependent on their parents, but able to live their own lives. Through Togetherness-Fulfillment, partners can work wonders and achieve any goal they set. Togetherness-Fulfillment is a power through which the couple becomes a light of help and evolution to the world in every way they can be.

Time for introspection

- Have you experienced a similar power in your life? If so, what happened? What did you achieve? If not, why?
- Has your life ever been better because you chose to be with your partner and always put your love first? If so, how exactly? If not, why haven't you?
- Have you been able to get through very difficult situations with your partner because of the power of your love? If so, how exactly? If not, why haven't you?

4.4 — Differences between a typical romantic relationship and a relationship of Togetherness-Fulfillment

To further understand the nature of Togetherness-Fulfillment, here are the differences between a typical romantic relationship, where there is usually ignorance and compromise, and a relationship of Togetherness-Fulfillment, where there is awareness and love.

TYPICAL ROMANTIC RELATIONSHIP	RELATIONSHIP OF TOGETHERNESS-FULFILLMENT
The partners prioritize their needs over their partner's needs. The individual "I" takes precedence. This can be either unconscious or conscious.	There is unconditional love between the partners. This means that they help each other in every possible way and are equal in the relationship. "Together" prevails.
They are ignorant of themselves and their partner.	They know themselves and their partner in depth.
Their relationship and/or marriage is not the number one priority of the partners.	Their relationship and/or marriage is always their number one priority in life.
They have no common path in life. They connect their two different lives only by living in the same house. They are typically unaware of the direction they want to go.	They have a clear and common life path with the same purpose of existence (life purpose, relationship purpose, legacy, and vision). They are two leaders who are united as one. One is the life of the other.
There is excitement and infatuation only at the beginning of the relationship, and then it fades.	Partners stay in love because they truly love each other without conditions or limits.
Each partner usually does not love themselves, so they cannot really love their partner.	Each partner loves themselves completely, and so they love their partner with every cell of their being.
They misinterpret and confuse love with mere fleeting emotions and inferior needs.	They know that they love each other, and that love requires constant individual and couple work.
They pay little attention to their physical, mental, emotional, and spiritual health.	Physical, mental, emotional, and spiritual health is of paramount importance to the couple.

They have demands and expectations of their partner. They expect their partner to give their best to the relationship, but they don't expect it from themselves. When they offer something to their partner, they usually expect something in return. They believe romantic relationships are about giving and receiving.	They always embody their positive states of being such as Togetherness-Fulfillment which encompasses love, and unity. So, they don't need to give and take anything back because they simply *are* love and unity and express these to their partner without expecting anything in return. Together, they do what is best for their relationship. They find fulfillment in being their best selves for each other. They know that their relationship is about unity, growth, and love.
There is criticism. They are quick to blame their partner and do not always take responsibility for themselves. They are reluctant to admit their mistakes. They are typically physically adults but mentally immature children.	There is understanding. They take full responsibility for their thoughts, emotions, actions, words, and the role they play in causing conflict. They admit their mistakes and act to avoid repeating them. They are spiritual adults, mature and responsible human beings.
They lie to each other or hide the truth from each other because they cannot bear the truth. They don't fully trust each other.	They will accept nothing but raw truth and honesty, even if it "hurts". There is pure and strong-rooted trust and constant complete spiritual nakedness in their relationship.
They think they are always right and that their individual way is the right one. They believe that their beliefs are the only truth.	They understand that they are not always right and discuss with their partner to find out what is the best decision together. They are truth seekers.
They put up with their partner's negative elements and behaviors and do not help them to improve. They do not make a real effort to improve their relationship.	They accept their partner with their imperfections and flaws and work together to help each other. But they do not accept compromise, stagnation, and procrastination. They help each other to overcome these when they occur. They correct their negative behavior respectfully. They constantly evaluate their relationship and themselves to improve as much as possible.

They don't know what they want and don't want from their relationship and/or marriage. They don't know why they are in a relationship/marriage.	They are clear about what they want in their relationship and what they don't accept for any reason. They know that they are meant to be together and are constantly working to evolve together.
They become stubborn and complain too much.	They forgive and focus on the best, on all the beauty of their life and on love. They are grateful.
They are mostly stuck in the past or the future and rarely live in the present.	They live in the present, enjoying every moment together, learning from the past and making plans for the future.
They want to spend time apart because their relationship is not strong. Their conversations are usually superficial.	They never, and for no reason, think about not being together and especially not spending quality and meaningful time together. They have many meaningful and constructive conversations, and this helps their relationship to develop. They want to have time to relax together and devote themselves to each other. They want to live and work together.
The relationship often resembles a typical friendship, except that there may be sexual intercourse. They do not have a meaningful and profound relationship, but a superficial one.	The partners are completely united at every level of their existence. Their relationship is one of depth and essence. They experience life as one.
They don't always respect their partner and don't always listen actively when their partner speaks.	They are humble, respect each other and listen actively to their partner.
They remain stagnant and do not evolve in life. They want convenience and chase after fleeting pleasures.	They are passionate about learning new things together and exploring the world. They seek challenges and are committed to positive change. They have an enormous zest for life, creativity, and productivity. Their relationship is one of evolution and progress.

They live mostly in fear, insecurity, negativity, and pessimism. They accept things that they don't deserve in life. The relationship is essentially "dead".	They walk through life together and in faith. They take risks and dare to make their dreams come true. Their relationship is vibrant, fiery, and energetic. They believe that anything is possible when they are together and accept only what they deserve and nothing less.
a) Either they fight a lot because they lack self-control and have emotional outbursts at each other, b) or they rarely fight because they are completely estranged, c) or they avoid confrontation because they are afraid.	When they are in tension, the only reason is to strengthen the relationship. They speak bluntly and firmly, but with respect and love, to bring about positive change. They accept confrontation if it is done in a way that is healthy for their development.
They act primarily emotionally, without fully understanding their emotions and those of their partner.	They operate mainly based on their qualities and understand that their emotions are not permanent states. So, they work to develop Togetherness-Fulfillment as they develop their emotional awareness.
They judge themselves and their partner by what they do, how well they do it, and their social roles.	They operate from the truth of who they really are deep inside, not from enslaving labels.
Usually, one partner is considered "superior" and the other "inferior".	There is equality and admiration between partners. The partners believe in each other and their relationship with all their being.
Differences between partners are often considered a problem rather than a means of improvement.	Each partner helps the other based on their strengths. In this way, their differences become common strengths.
They want to "fix" their partner according to their expectations.	They understand that no one needs to be "fixed" and that the path of continuous improvement is their mutual conscious choice.
They try to find security and validation in other people, external situations, and material things. At the same time, they may show arrogance.	They are confident in who they are and do not need other people or external situations to feel secure. At the same time, they are humble.

They are influenced and controlled by other people, external situations, and their fleeting emotions due to internal imbalance.	They live their life spiritually and do not allow themselves to be controlled by external situations, other people, and their emotions.
They do not choose wisely the people they have in their lives (friends, acquaintances, relatives, etc.) as a couple.	They choose wisely the people they associate with as a couple, not wanting to waste their time in unhealthy social relationships. They want to have meaningful and honest social relationships.
They have instability in their relationship and avoid change.	They are conscious and stable in their relationship, yet open to any positive change.
They tend to have high expectations and low standards in their life and relationship.	They have high standards and low to zero expectations in their life.
When one partner "sinks" emotionally, the other "sinks" with them, either because they are not strong and easily affected, or because they do not help their partner in a meaningful way.	When one partner "sinks" emotionally, the other remains a solid rock to help them.
There is often competition and jealousy between the couple.	Each partner rejoices in their partner's successes and helps them to be even more successful in everything they do.
Usually, responsibilities are not shared fairly and equally between the couple.	Partners help each other with their responsibilities, so they actually have a beautiful time together even during this tedious time.
They imply things in their communication and expect their partner to imagine what is bothering them.	They speak clearly to each other without waiting for each other to draw conclusions about the other.
They are immersed in difficulties and give up easily.	They overcome every difficulty and problem together. They are together in good times and in bad.
Partners do not know how to manage the dynamics of their feminine and masculine elements/forces, and so they frequently clash.	The feminine and masculine elements/forces of each partner are expressed and united in harmony.

They do not enjoy life as a whole and live with fleeting moments of joy. They are not fulfilled individually and as a couple. They very typically feel oppressed in life and their relationship with their partner.	They are grateful to be alive and to be together. They enjoy life together and in peace because they are fulfilled individually and as a couple. They are free and balanced in their life and relationship.

These are the main differences between a typical romantic relationship and a relationship of Togetherness-Fulfillment. Of course, this does not mean that every typical relationship has all the characteristics we have mentioned, or that a relationship of Togetherness-Fulfillment is perfect. We list the characteristics that we see very regularly in many typical romantic relationships, the characteristics that are often exhibited by partners who are very close to each other, and the characteristics that we exhibit in our own relationship of Togetherness-Fulfillment. Now it's time for you to look at each of these characteristics and see which, if any, define your relationship.

In Chapter Three, we mentioned the main requirements for a healthy relationship. Based on everything we have explored about Togetherness-Fulfillment and the rest of the book, we can see the main elements of a relationship of Togetherness-Fulfillment which are the following:

1 – Our love, romantic relationship, and being together, are always our number one priority in life and every circumstance no matter what.

2 – We admire each other as an equal God of love, growth, and devotion having unshakable faith in our relationship. We are healthy, strong, fearless, and ever-evolving together.

3 – We have meaningful conversations where we listen to each other with undivided attention, understanding, respect, and commitment. Through this connection, we understand ourselves and each other better, unite, and prioritize togetherness and not our egos. We are free from inferior needs and walk together on

the same path of continuous individual and couple work and improvement.

4 – We have a common and clear purpose of our existence based on Togetherness-Fulfillment, and we live based on this immense power. We live in peace and absolute freedom together.

5 – We unite on every level of our existence in every way possible and become one and the same. We understand and work on the dynamics of our feminine and masculine elements, and together we are an unstoppable force of love.

6 – We are completely spiritually naked in front of each other every single moment. There is nothing that separates us, and we are a pure divine unity of responsibility, spiritual maturity, forgiveness, gratitude, and unshakable trust. We are the embodiment of spiritual nakedness, and thus we are inseparable, unshakable, and unstoppable together.

Time for introspection

- Based on this table, do you think your romantic relationship is a typical relationship or a relationship of Togetherness-Fulfillment?
- Do you have only characteristics of a typical relationship or also characteristics of a relationship of Togetherness-Fulfillment?
- Do you have more characteristics of a typical relationship or more characteristics of a relationship of Togetherness-Fulfillment?
- What will you do to change and improve the characteristics of the typical relationship you are experiencing?
- What will you do to further develop the characteristics of a relationship of Togetherness-Fulfillment that you already show?

4.5 — Summary

We have reached the end of this chapter, and you now have everything you need to experience Togetherness-Fulfillment with your Fulfilled Reflecting Self. We have talked about infatuation, love, individual fulfillment, and the nature of Togetherness-Fulfillment and how it is expressed in the relationship with our life partner.

In simple terms, and based on everything we have discussed in this chapter, we can say that Togetherness-Fulfillment is:

- a state of unshakable love and absolute oneness of the couple,

- a process of continuous evolution of the couple, with constant complete spiritual nakedness,

- a permanent experience of peace in life,

- the healthy and absolute unity of the feminine and masculine elements/forces of the partners,

- a way of life in which "being together" is the number one priority in every situation,

- an expanded view of the romantic relationship and marriage, based on a profound understanding of the partners, and

- a method and philosophy for helping couples become inseparable, unshakable, and unstoppable.

A relationship of Togetherness-Fulfillment is not one in which the partners are each other's "half", for this comes from insecurity and weakness. It is not a relationship where the partners are simply individually fulfilled and have managed to keep their marriage going for years by combining their separate lives in the evenings and weekends (i.e., what society considers a successful relationship and marriage, when in fact it is something superficial and shallow).

A relationship of Togetherness-Fulfillment is raw and complete spiritual nakedness in which the partners know each other deeply and work daily to improve themselves, and this complete spiritual nakedness drives them more and more to be together.

So, you can understand that you experience Togetherness-Fulfillment:

When you offer your everything in your relationship with absolute purity.

When seeing happiness in your partner's eyes is the only reason for your own happiness.

When you fall in love, again and again, every day with the smile, the look, the thoughts, the words, and the whole being of your partner.

When you know and understand them completely and deeply.

When you accept them completely as they are and do everything in your power to help them when they need it.

When you become completely spiritually naked in front of each other and reveal every dark and shameful element of yourself, without any criticism and knowing that your partner sees life through your eyes.

When their existence is the pure inspiration of life and creation for you.

When you are grateful for every second you are with them.

When you do your utmost to be together all the time and experience every moment of life together.

When you face every difficulty and problem together and never give up.

When you are completely free and peaceful together and enjoy every aspect of life.

Epilogue

The Togetherness-Fulfillment Method, as a method for creating unshakable romantic relationships, begins with each partner working on the Self-Awareness Cultivating Models of Chapter One or the Eight Steps to Romantic Relationship Awareness. It continues with identifying and resolving negative behaviors and understanding the unity of the dynamics of their feminine and masculine elements. It then moves on to developing responsibility, spiritual maturity, forgiveness, gratitude, equality, faith, admiration, and trust and concludes with unconditional love and Togetherness-Fulfillment, in which the couple is now in total satisfaction with their life and relationship, setting and achieving their goals together.

We can experience and live with Togetherness-Fulfillment either after we have become individually fulfilled and then have a relationship, or we can already be in a relationship and become individually fulfilled through it, as happened in our case where we created the Togetherness-Fulfillment Method. This depends on the life course of each person and each couple. Each case is positive if the partners are really meant for each other.

To summarize what we have explored so far, let us look at the elements that is useful to work on as a couple and outline the Togetherness-Fulfillment Method for creating unshakable romantic relationships:

- Limited Unaware Self and the beginning of the development of self-awareness
- Unlimited Aware Self
- Balanced Aware Self
- Evolved Aware Self
- Existential Aware Self
- Reactive Unaware Self
- Feminine and Masculine Aware Self
- Sexual Aware Self
- Fulfilled Reflecting Self

- Negative behaviors and causes
- Imprisoning situations and causes
- The Eight Steps to Romantic Relationship Awareness
- Companionate Romantic Solitude
- The 3 zones in a romantic relationship
- The Stages Towards Couple Responsibility
- Spiritual maturity
- Gratitude and forgiveness
- Equality
- Faith and Admiration
- Trust
- Continuous self-improvement and Companionate Flourishing
- Infatuation, desire, and passion
- Unconditional acceptance
- True unconditional love
- Individual fulfillment and Togetherness-Fulfillment

If you work together on all the above with commitment, dedication, and love, you are sure to achieve everything you want in your life and relationship. But the evolutionary journey does not end here. In the second volume of the book, we explore all the above even further. We share with you the exact steps you can take to discover, grow, and evolve yourself and your relationship through simple but very powerful and meaningful introspective and actionable exercises for your daily life. We share with you all the tools we created to help you and your partner be completely spiritually naked in front of each other, and there, you will see in practice the power of complete spiritual nakedness and Togetherness-Fulfillment.

Remember that we are here for a very short time and that we will all leave this world at some point, not knowing when that will be. So, it is our choice whether we continue to live based on our Limited Unaware Self, our negative behaviors and bad habits and waste our time getting angry, complaining, and arguing with other people, or whether we live based on the truth of ourselves, our constant improvement and love with our Fulfilled Reflecting Self. It is our choice to live the life we want, not the life other people want for us. It is our choice to live a life of essence and value. It is our choice whether we will use our time to help others and create something positive for the world. It is our choice whether we will be a shining example to those who wish to improve themselves. Choose wisely and with purity.

And every time you feel you are lost, and your negative elements take control, say the following phrase, and you will find peace inside:

Together we experience and we ARE Togetherness-Fulfillment.

This powerful phrase starts with *"Together..."* so it helps you to let go of your ego and have your romantic relationship as your number one priority. It continues with *"we experience..."* meaning it is not only about how we feel and think, but how we live. It then states, *"and we ARE..."* meaning embodiment, and it ends with *"Togetherness-Fulfillment"* which is the highest spiritual state that entails love, health, evolution, unity, and peace. Therefore, it is a massive reminder and affirmation that you truly ARE love and health and one and the same with your Fulfilled Reflecting Self, and thus you are fearless and unstoppable together. Smile as you say it, and you will experience the power of Togetherness-Fulfillment inside you.

This is a book of love and truth, designed to spread love and truth. This does not mean, of course, that everything we say in the book is an inviolable rule to be lived by. We express honestly all that we are experiencing, which has spectacularly evolving results in our life and relationship.

Everything we say about love, forgiveness, gratitude, appreciation, responsibility, fulfillment, and everything else in this book is an experience directly from our own life and romantic relationship, has helped us tremendously and has given us balance, harmony, and peace.

However, we have seen many couples of different ages and backgrounds who do not follow a similar path in life and do not enjoy their relationship. So, it is up to you to evaluate everything we say, try it out, and use what really helps you to grow as an individual and as a couple.

In conclusion, after meeting many people from many countries, with different beliefs and entirely different lifestyles, we have seen that very few, thin on the ground, are deeply connected to their partner and this is sad to us. We want to change this in any way we can and help people and couples to live a beautiful life.

We strongly believe that romantic relationships of Togetherness-Fulfillment are the foundation for a better world and the way for humanity to evolve.

This is because when we experience Togetherness-Fulfillment, we are free from any inferior need for validation and acceptance and so every other relationship in our life is meaningful and not needy. When we experience Togetherness-Fulfillment, we are free from the limiting beliefs of this world about chasing recognition, material wealth, and power. We are free from wanting to be considered important, and we are free from climbing any competitive ladder. We are free from wanting to impose our beliefs and views on others and accept people as they are. We believe that couples who experience Togetherness-Fulfillment can raise the spiritually healthiest children who will in turn create a relationship of Togetherness-Fulfillment with their partner in the future and then raise their own children in the same healthy way and so on. So, healthy couples create meaningful social relationships and raise healthy children, healthy children become healthy adults and create a healthy romantic relationship of Togetherness-Fulfillment, healthy adults create healthy social relationships and societies, and healthy societies create a healthy world. A world free of wars and violence. A world of peace and love.

Even when we reach high levels of self-awareness as individuals and know ourselves deeply, we will still discover even more aspects of ourselves through the relationship with our Fulfilled

Reflecting Self. It is this relationship that we devote our whole being to.

This way, relationships of inferior needs for validation and acceptance and relationships of lies and hypocrisy will diminish, and every other human relationship will be more beautiful, meaningful, and real.

Let's do this together because together we can achieve anything. Spread this book everywhere and help make the world a better place.

From the bottom of our hearts, we sincerely wish you, your family, and all your loved ones a healthy and fulfilling life.

We wish you to experience Togetherness-Fulfillment with your Fulfilled Reflecting Self and that, you too, spread true love and truth to the world. Live life with an everlasting passionate flame of growth and unity. Love unconditionally.

You deserve it!

Glossary

Togetherness-Fulfillment:
A term we coined to express the ultimate unity of a couple: *Togetherness-Fulfillment is the highest spiritual state and evolutionary course of our existence, in which we unite with our Fulfilled Reflecting Self wholly and on every level (spiritual, mental, psychological/emotional, and physical/sexual), being completely spiritually naked in front of each other, with awareness, and experiencing true and unconditional love, with constant individual and couple work and improvement.*

The Fulfilled Reflecting Self:
A term we coined to describe our one and only life partner: *The Fulfilled Reflecting Self is our one and only life partner with whom we unite as one on every level (spiritual, mental, psychological/emotional, and physical/sexual), where in our relationship we are both individually fulfilled and free from inferior needs and become each other's reflection.*

The Togetherness-Fulfillment Method:
A method we created based on our experiences to help couples become inseparable, unshakable, and unstoppable. It is our personal philosophy and way of life.

The Self-Awareness Cultivating Models:
A series of models we created to help us understand deeply ourselves and our life partner, and through this development of our self-awareness we can unite as one.

The Unlimited Aware Self Model:
A model we created to help us reach our unlimited potential by defining ourselves based on the positive states of being we can embody and any other positive element of our existence. It consists of the Limited Unaware Self which is the limited and enslaving way to describe ourselves and the Unlimited Aware Self which is the unlimited and loving way to describe ourselves.

The Balanced Aware Self Model:
A model we created to help us create balance in our life by cultivating balance between our mental, emotional, and spiritual levels, where our mental level is about our thoughts and logic, our emotional level is about our emotions and intentions and our spiritual level is about our intuition and our Unlimited Aware Self.

The Evolved Aware Self Model:
A model we created to help us create success in any area of our life by understanding the importance of our self-worth and how it can lead us to create a meaningful life where we achieve our goals and live with serenity.

The Existential Aware Self Model:
A model we created to help us find the purpose of our existence, live our life based on what really drives us as a couple, and have a crystal-clear path of togetherness.

The Reactive Unaware Self Model:
A model we created to help us understand how our negative elements can have a negative impact on our life and romantic relationship and how we can recognize them, observe them without judgment, and learn from them to improve ourselves and our romantic relationship.

The Feminine and Masculine Aware Self Model:
A model we created to help us recognize our feminine and masculine elements in our romantic relationship and understand how they can clash between them or be in balance. Through the peaceful dance of our feminine and masculine elements, we can unite as a couple.

The Sexual Aware Self Model:
A model we created to help us understand how we can unite healthily via our sexual relationship. We have our Lower Sexual Self which is about the negative expression of our sexual nature and our Higher Sexual Self which is about the positive expression of our sexual nature.

The Fulfilled Reflecting Self Model:
A model we created to help us unite as one with our Fulfilled Reflecting Self, and shows us how every previous model from the Self Awareness Cultivating Models leads us to unity with our Fulfilled Reflecting Self.

The expected and learned habitual behaviors:
The expected habitual behaviors are behaviors that we believe our life partner will display because we have built certain expectations that are very strong. The learned habitual behaviors are behaviors that we create as a response to the expected habitual behaviors that we believe our partner will display.

The Negative Behavior Improvement Model:
A model we created to help us adopt a mindset of seeing our negative behaviors as a way to understand ourselves and each other deeper and cultivate understanding and respect by having meaningful and constructive conversations as a couple.

The enslaving seriousness trap:
A trap we can fall into as a couple where we become too serious because we are focused on our personal and couple development, and we forget to enjoy our life and romantic relationship.

The enslaving perfect relationship trap:
A trap we can fall into as a couple where we believe that we need to be perfect and never express any of our negative elements in our romantic relationship, and this leads us to be miserable.

The Eight Steps to Romantic Relationship Awareness:
Eight steps that we created to develop our self-awareness and romantic relationship awareness, which are easier and faster to work with than the Self-Awareness Cultivating Models.

Romantic Relationship Awareness:
Being fully aware of who our life partner is, what is the state of our romantic relationship, and how we can constantly strengthen our romantic relationship.

Companionate Romantic Solitude:
A peaceful experience of ultimate trust that we have with our Fulfilled Reflecting Self, where we create as a couple a safe environment of love. In this state, we are completely satisfied with each other and fulfilled, and we don't need anyone else.

The 3 zones in a romantic relationship:
Zones we created to help us understand the different states that we can be in as a couple: The zone of comfort and stagnation where we live in compromise; the zone of progress and risk where we grow as a couple but eventually get exhausted because we are constantly in a state of doing; the zone of romantic relationship awareness where we are aware of what is best in our relationship and when it is time to relax and when it is time to be productive.

The Stages Towards Couple Responsibility:
Stages we created to describe how as individuals we can become responsible and spiritually mature adults and thus create a responsible relationship with our life partner.

Spiritual maturity:
Spiritual maturity is not related to any religious belief, but it is about taking responsibility for ourselves, owning our mistakes, walking on a path of continuous improvement, and knowing that we are completely responsible for how we think, feel, act, and behave.

The Self-improvement Tree Model:
A model we created to describe how we can walk on a path of continuous self-discovery and self-improvement so that we can build strong foundations to experience unconditional love with our life partner.

The Tree of Relationship Blossoming Model:
A model we created to describe how we can blossom in our romantic relationship with our life partner.

Complete Spiritual Nakedness:
This is a transcendent experience that is about pure honesty and raw truth, where we reveal every element of our existence to our Fulfilled Reflecting Self and unite as one.

The Individual Fulfillment Model for Togetherness-Fulfillment:
A model we created to understand the way we can be individually fulfilled so that we can then experience Togetherness-Fulfillment with our Fulfilled Reflecting Self.

The Togetherness-Fulfillment Model:
A model we created to explore how we can unite as one with our Fulfilled Reflecting Self by uniting our feminine and masculine elements.

The number 1 training program* that inspired us and we believe everyone will benefit from:
Kain Ramsay, The Academy of Modern Applied Psychology (Achology), Life Coaching Certification Training Course (Beginner to Advanced), https://achology.com/product/life-coaching-certification-training-course-online/

*We are not affiliated with the creators of this course, and we don't have personal or financial gain from this.